OCCULT
PREPARATIONS
FOR A
NEW AGE

Occult
Preparations
for a NewAge

by DANE RUDHYAR

A QUEST BOOK
Published under a grant from the Kern Foundation

THE THEOSOPHICAL PUBLISHING HOUSE
Wheaton, Ill., U.S.A.
Madras, India / London, England

First Quest Book edition 1975 published by the Theosophical Publishing House, Wheaton, Illinois, a department of The Theosophical Society in America

Library of Congress Catalog Card Number: 74-19054

ISBN: 0-8356-0460-8

PRINTED IN THE
UNITED STATES OF AMERICA

To Michael Meyer and Nancy Kleban
in warm appreciation and friendship.

D. R.

CONTENTS

PART ONE

*A Planetary Approach
to Occultism and its Source*

1 COUNTERCULTURE
Past and Present

As a society gradually builds a culture characterizing its way of life and embodying its collective beliefs and ideals, it usually discards many of those which still existing cultures hold or have held to be fundamental to their way of life. A new spiritual impulse is appropriated by discontented, oppressed, or more primitive groups of human beings, who often violently repudiate the old beliefs while adopting as their own new ideas and symbols which apparently are needed for their mental and emotional development. In the same manner, children often discover what they take to be their authentic nature by rebelling against the beliefs and cultured behavior which their parents have tried to teach as absolutes of truth, conduct, and morality. Later on, having grown up and, after various crises, having developed a broader mind and more mature feeling-responses, they may reconsider this stand and, with modifications made necessary by changes in their social and intellectual environment, accept what they had once emotionally rebelled against as naive childhood's beliefs.

Some of these beliefs may nevertheless have remained latent below the level of consciousness. In his midforties or fifties an individual often returns to previously discarded concepts and feelings which no longer seem so naive; these acquire a new glow, a new meaning. A similar process occurs in the development of an entire society; and what has been happening in the Western world suggests that our civilization is experiencing its "change of life."

A growing number of intellectuals, and even of official

representatives of the Euro-American tradition whose task it is to transmit it to the younger generations, have finally come to realize that, throughout the entire history of European culture, an uninterrupted current of ideas, beliefs, and practices considered archaic, naive, and religiously or morally heretical has existed, as it were, in counterpoint to the mainstream of official thinking and even, in some instances, of Church-approved morality. We speak today of our "counterculture"; but the numerous secret societies which have persisted or changed from one into the other since the days of the early Councils that hammered an orthodoxy out of the mass of conflicting remains of ancient cults and mythological concepts, represent a persistent counterculture movement.

Our entire Christian-European civilization has been based on the belief that the coming of Christ established a quasi-absolute line of demarcation between what mankind was before and what it became after this historical event. What came before Christianity was considered pagan and unworthy of being retained, except that part of the Hebrew historical tradition and mentality which could be interpreted as a preparation for the age of Christian truth and glory, plus the more intellectual aspects of Greek philosophy used to provide a rational framework for the superrational mystery of the Incarnation and Resurrection. Everything else had to be eradicated from the mind of a new Christian humanity—the books burnt, the statues and temples destroyed.

When such a wholesale orgy of destruction occurs—and this often happens when a new culture is born or imposed upon a disintegrating society—the inevitable reaction is an underground attempt to sustain and perpetuate some at least of the more essential features of the almost entirely destroyed past culture or cultures. Such attempts may be, and probably are, inspired and at first led by men who have a direct connection with what may have been kept intact of the core of the old culture. These men and their successors have to go "underground"; and anything that is able to maintain itself and grow under such conditions has certain inevitable characteristics. It must develop a great deal of mental as well as physical toughness. It has to give absolute value to the past—to the "tradition"; it must have an inbred resistance to change, a profound spiritual as well as mental "inertia" (in the true sense of the term). In most cases a group dedicated to the preservation of the past must remain secret and jealously guard its secrecy. It can nevertheless, from time to time, allow some of its members to try directly or indirectly to influence at least a section of the official culture which may contain a number of dissatisfied and restless individuals. Perhaps under the cover of some kind of social and cultural device—and by utilizing either a fashionable wave of enthusiasm for some unusual idea or phenomenon or a socio-political crisis which impels people to ask disturbing questions— "emissaries" of the secret group may be able to reintroduce into the mainstream of the culture ideas which constitute a vital challenge to the official mentality and the socioeducational Establishment.

If these ideas arouse the enthusiasm of even a small but dynamic section of the people, the term "countercultural movement" is applicable, the appearance of this phenomenon on the outer stage of history can be traced to a number of factors—social, economic, political and, recently, industrial—with which the official historian is accustomed to deal. But these existential factors may also be related to a deeper cause, that is, to the hidden ("occult") fact that the time has come for a change of rhythm—a "structural" or functional change—in the cyclic process underlying the evolution of a civilization; just as puberty and the change of life mark basic functional changes in the biopsychic rhythm of an individual human being, regardless of the external conditions and pressures affecting his outer life.

We might give as an example the outstanding coun-terculture which for a time flourished in Southern France during the twelfth and early thirteenth centuries, especially around the town of Albi. This Albigenses culture can be considered a counterculture because it developed on the basis of ancient near-Eastern concepts which had been repudiated by the Catholic Church and its powerful political supporters. It was a beautiful movement giving rise to a new and idealistic approach to womanhood and love, which for a time influenced even the Northerners' way of life. Many social and political factors—especially the first Crusades—contributed to the development of the movement. But it was ruthlessly destroyed during what historians call the Crusade against the Albigenses. This was engineered by the French King and the Pope, then the two main powers in control of the mainstream of medieval European culture. Soon after, the Templars, who had been deeply influenced by some of the traditions of the old Mediterranean religions which Christianity had fought against and rejected, were also relentlessly persecuted and killed.

Later on, the communalistic movement begun by the Bohemian, John Huss, was also violently eradicated by Popes and kings. Alchemists and Rosicrucians escaped persecution because they lived a two-level existence, keeping their beliefs and the true nature of their work secret. The guilds of operative masons from which the Free Masonry of the eighteenth century emerged as an influential force in the sociopolitical field were, at least to some extent, manifestations of a countercultural trend hidden behind their "operative" activities. Here and there this trend also produced mystical groups and out-standing individuals who, while still accepting outwardly the religious framework of the Church and the main teachings of the universities, actually challenged the dogmatic structures of the official European civilization.

The Romantic movement of the nineteenth century, pioneered toward the end of the eighteenth by men like

Jean-Jacques Rousseau, Blake, the young Goethe, Beethoven, and the more mysterious Mesmer, strongly reacted against the intellect-worshiping rationalism of the preceding century naively calling itself "the Enlightenment." After 1840 in America the Spiritualistic movement opened wide a mist-enshrouded door separating the world of rationally explainable phenomena from some vast unknown realm already being catalogued by official philosophers and psychologists as "the Unconscious." When, in 1874-75, H. P. Blavatsky appeared on the American scene, she had to use the Spiritualists' approach in order to gain some kind of public recognition. Soon afterward she declared herself the emissary of a trans-Himalayan Occult Brotherhood. In this capacity, she became the fountainhead and inspirer of a movement which, in its original form, struck at the very roots of Euro-American orthodoxy in religion and science.

The Transcendentalist movement in New England had already opened a channel of communication with the philosophy of India, which also inspired the founder of Christian Science, Mary Baker Eddy, though she later repudiated this influence. The young disciples who gathered in Chicago around the Parliament of Religion—close to the time of Blavatsky's death (1891) and that of the Persian Prophet, Baha'u'llah who had proclaimed himself the Divine manifestation for the New Age (1892)—provided a multiheaded start for the New Thought movement. Soon thereafter Swami Vivekananda who, with the young Buddhist Anagarika Dhammaphala, brought an extraordinarily vivid breath of Indian spirituality to the Parliament, initiated the Vedanta Movement in New England. Though Vivekananda died in 1902, the Vedanta Movement survived him, and not only developed many branches, but became an inspiration for the growth of many more recent attempts made by Hindu Holy Men to build *ashrams* or spiritual communities—the earliest being the movement begun by

Swami Yogananda which is still flourishing.

The term "counterculture" has lately been used with reference to the quite extraordinary upsurge of the American and, to some extent, European youth which has embodied in a number of ways the deepseated dissatisfaction and rebellion of the new generation against the very foundations on which our official Western civilization was built. Numerous causes for this youth-movement can be and have been advanced. The revolt against the Viet Nam war added much fuel to the fire of discontent against an increasingly intellectualized, technologized, automated, and hypocritical society whose religious and political leaders still mouth sanctimonious statements belied by their everyday behavior and greed. The spreading use of L.S.D. and other psychedelic drugs (however deplorable some of their effects) had undoubtedly a powerful cathartic effect, breaking open doors of the mind and the usual ego-defences built by our traditional culture. The sense of impending catastrophe related to the possibility of an all-out nuclear war has helped greatly to break down a collective ego-built confidence in the values of our society. Even the ambiguous and as yet unsolved mystery of the U.F.O. ("flying saucers") added to the underlying psychic unsettlement—and this exactly one hundred years after the Fox sisters episodes which began the American Spiritualist Movement.[1]

During the last few years the young people once known as "Hippies" have to some extent disappeared. After an orgy of senseless publicity and an invasion of drug-peddlers, they had become food for the media's avidity for sensationalism. But to say, as some people in positions of educational and cultural importance self-complacently do, that the counterculture of the Sixties has faded out, or that the generation gap is now closed, is both naive and misleading. Many youth communes are still in existence and, if overt protests have largely stopped, it is because youth has learned that a premature revolution is not only futile, but meaningless. What has been learned also is that the real revolution is a revolution in consciousness, and that it can be—indeed, it must be—carried on within or at the fringe of the official culture by quietly sapping the latter's strength and credibility.

The field of action of the present aspect of counterculture is increasingly defined by "psychic" research of all kinds, and by the modernizing of old yoga techniques and spiritual-mental disciplines, most of the time under the direction of individuals claiming a more or less direct contact with—or inspiration from—occult centers in Asia or the Near East. The fascination with magic and witchcraft—good, bad, or indifferent as the practices may be—is certainly spreading; and the traditional main stream of popular predictive astrology, with its new pseudo-scientific concern for "serious" research and its—to my mind, misapplied—statistics, is discarded or scorned by a great many youths who are looking for a more "humanistic" and countercultural astrology or "cosmopsychology," providing psychological if not spiritual guidance and what Dr. Carl Jung would call symbols of salvation. The number of persons using or claiming clairvoyance and contacts with inner guides, spacepeople, or discarnate healers is steadily increasing. What is more, the people interested in all these manifestations of a countercultural trend, which most definitely—even if often hesitantly and only half-consciously—challenges the validity of our Euro-American cultural main stream and of all that it takes for granted, are increasingly recruited from the above-thirty and above-forty generations, and from the university and scientific field.

Counterculture is not dead; it has never been so important and significant. All the nearly unquestioned premises on which our Christian and rationalistic Euro-American tradition has been based are becoming increasingly empty of vital contents. Even the most conservative Churches are in deep crisis. And behind all this intense mental-psychic fermentation we can and should become aware that a cycle of civilization is nearing its end. Whether this end will have a cataclysmic aspect assuredly is not certain, in spite of all the psychic or even scientific prophecies of disaster flooding the collective mentality of a large section of our population. Predictions of the "end of the world" have occurred before; but though "the world" has not ended, some very recognizable kind of cycle has ended at the times indicated, and a new cultural impetus has been given. When the Millerites of America sold all their possessions and journeyed to Mt. Carmel near Haifa, Israel to witness the end of the world, our new industrial society was becoming established through the spread of telegraphic and rail communication. At exactly the expected time (May 1844), the first Persian Prophet, the Bab, was declaring that the Islamic era had come to an end and announcing the advent of the "Coming One" who, in 1963, proclaimed himself as Baha'u'llah, Founder of the first detailed system of world-organization.

I shall presently discuss the probable meaning of Baha'u'llah's manifestation, but it was mentioned here to point out the fact that a psychic sense of impending cataclysm marking the beginning of a new historical and planetary cycle of human evolution can be, at the same time, both correct and incorrect. In a similar sense, the facts of genuine Spiritualistic manifestations, and the dates relevant to genuine sightings of U.F.O., are susceptible to both correct and incorrect interpretations . When doors are open between two deeply different realms of existence and consciousness, attempts to explain what comes in and what goes out of the door are nearly always confused, for the explanation has to be formulated in terms of the culture which has developed on *our* side of the door. This happens inevitably when great mystics try to speak of their subliminal experiences, but also when Spiritualists or "psychics" interpret inner

COUNTERCULTURE—PAST AND PRESENT

happenings, the nature of which they want to convey and make intelligible *to their own conscious mind* as well as to others. The U.F.O. experiences most likely come into a similar category and may not deal with strictly material machines; but here also the question may well center on what meaning we attach to the word "material."

We cannot give a really valid and historically significant meaning to all such unusual phenomena—rationally unexplainable in terms of *our* Euro-American science and intellectual tradition—if we are not willing, ready, and even mentally able to consider them strong indications that we are living in a period of transition between the old Western civilization, which built our Euro-American society, and a new type of culture presumably of a global nature. What we now see at work is the "invasion" of our mainstream Euro-American culture by all that in its origins—especially during the early period of formation of the Catholic orthodoxy, and also during the Renaissance and Classical centuries—it had to repudiate in order to successfully assert its essential character.

To say this does *not* mean that this character is basically nefarious or invalid. It has been a necessary phase in the development of the *total* human person and of mankind as an organic whole. No one should be so emotionally upset by the destructive aspects of our Western civilization, and by its soil, air, water, and psyche polluting technology that he fails to see the greatness of its most significant achievement—making it *possible* for all men to experience their essential unity. Unfortunately however, our Western civilization has exaggerated the specialized character of that evolutionary phase; it has developed in an atmosphere of violence and fanaticism which probably could have been avoided.

Whether or not this is a fact is now beside the point. Our kind of scientific empirical knowledge has been enormously successful among materialistic and technological lines; but "nothing fails like success," and we now should know what such a statement means. It may not be too late to *apparently* retrace our steps and reincorporate what Europe for so long has branded heretic, devilish, and childishly archaic; but this *should* be only an "apparent" turnabout. What is needed is not a glorification of some past "golden age"—even if it ever existed at the physical level, which is far from certain—nor an emotional expectation of a Utopian millennium. The direction should not be behind or ahead, but toward center—or, we might also say, toward a *foundation* that is now, ever was, and will remain until the close of the vast lifespan of the Earth.

True Occultism (and I shall capitalize the word to differentiate it from all the occult or pseudo-occult doctrines and practices recently popularized) or Esotericism (which by definition should mean only what cannot be expressed in terms of our public mainstream culture) refers to this foundation. It is *eonic* because it remains what is throughout an entire cycle or "eon." Today we speak of a genetic code that is formed at the time of the ovum's impregnation by a spermatozoon; this genetic code, pattern, or formula, exists at the innermost core of every one of the millions of cells of an organism. It is and remains what it was "in the beginning." In a biological sense it is the Word in the beginning—for that particular organism.

Is there such a Word for humanity as a planetary organism? If there is, how can we develop the "electron microscope" within our mind that will be able to detect its presence—or are there other ways of recognizing this presence in terms of the various *functional activities* it produces in the several organs of the great body of mankind?

Let us try to explore these possibilities.

References and Notes

1. For the meaning of the century cycle, read in Part Two, "Planetary and Social Cycles."

2. THE ONE PLANETARY TRADITION AND THE MANY OPERATIVE TRADITIONS

At certain times in the development of a society and its culture, a strong and often very emotional appeal is made to return to "the Tradition" and to repudiate and discard what is then given the pejorative name of "modernism." The appeal is made by religious leaders, as well as by politicians. In a deeper and more "occult" sense it is also made by individuals who have become involved in a variety of more or less recently formed "esoteric" groups and perhaps wandered far afield in search of glamorous doctrines and exotic teachers. Intellectually confused as well as emotionally disappointed and more insecure than ever, these men and women seek—as psychologists might say—to "return to the womb" of their ancestral religion or, in a deeper spiritual sense, to go back to a Tradition that offers them what seems to be a well established and secure path leading through "initiation" to supreme spiritual realizations and perhaps even to personal immortality.

The term, Tradition, when capitalized, conveys indeed a feeling of stability and strength. We can speak here of "root strength," partly in the same sense that the strength of a tree, and even its capacity to produce flowers, resides in its roots, and partly because the men who are the true custodians of the deeper, more essential and esoteric aspects of the Tradition are invisible or at least difficult to find. They often may work in secret underneath a purely cultural, or even socially commonplace facade. The rootlet is the first part of the plant to come out of the seed as it breaks open. It has to be first because it is through its functional activity that the germ can obtain the raw chemicals of the soil needed for its sunward growth.

To go back to the source of the Tradition implies a return to the "original impulse"—the creative Word—at the very beginning of one's small or large cycle of existence. Unity is to be found at the source of the cycle. The fecundated ovum is but one cell; from this original cell the billions of cells of a human body will be formed by mitosis (or division). Each of these body cells carries at its core a complex pattern (or genetic code) which defines its particular and *specific function* by means of a subtle chemical (or rather "alchemical" or superphysical) combination of open and closed channels through which the one Life-force (prana) is allowed to operate or is restrained. But *potentially* the whole of the genetic code is present in every cell.

In an occult sense, this implies that Man, as an archetype—a specific pattern of relationships and a particular set of biopsychic possibilities of development of consciousness—is inherent in every human being. But this archetype is there *occultly*, as total human potentiality, *not* as an actual existential fact in the operative world of everyday living on our physical earth.

This distinction between archetypal and existential, and therefore between the potential and the actual, is of fundamental importance; yet for various reasons— some of which have a specific temporal validity—this distinction is usually glossed over or deliberately ignored by most esoteric groups. The general collective mentality of the West tends to ignore it and to confuse potentiality with actuality.

In its emotional and idealistic eagerness to stress, at least in theory, the concepts of social individualism and equalitarianism, the American mind does not accentuate significantly enough the distinction between the *spiritual identity* of an individual and his *functional place and purpose* in the existential world of human society.

This distinction, which I have discussed at some

length in my recent book *We Can Begin Again—Together*[1] is of extreme importance for a real understanding of what can be meant by "the Tradition." This term can indeed be defined at two different levels—an archetypal and an operative level. And the operative level branches out in a number of specific directions in order to fill diverse, even though interrelated and presumably interdependent, functions.

Archetypally and potentially, humanity is "one"; but existentially, functionally, and in terms of sociocultural and religious conditioning—and also in terms of geographical locality and historical timing—humanity is "many." It has become fashionable to state that all religions and cultures have basic elements in common. Aldous Huxley spoke of a *perennial philosophy,* but, in fact, the historical knowledge he and our historians had limited the validity of the concept. Theosophists speak of a "Universal Tradition" and "original Revelation," but unless these terms are understood in their archetypal meaning, I believe they can be misleading. What they actually are meant to imply is that today we are in a period of history in which it is *spiritually essential* for all men to realize that we are slowly approaching the closing period of a planetary cycle which affords men the possibility of experiencing— not merely dreaming of or intellectually postulating—a state of conscious unanimity. It is this fact which gives its basic meaning to what happened during the last half of the nineteenth century in the field of occultism, and particularly to H. P. Blavatsky's work and *The Secret Doctrine.*

There are two kinds of unanimity—and the word simply means "of one soul." The original kind is compulsive and instinctual; it operates basically in the unconscious of a collectivity of human beings. It is the type of unanimity experienced in the pure tribal state of society, a state in which the tribal whole and not the individual person is the unit, a state of relative psychic undifferentiation in which life and its organic functions are the supreme rulers. The other kind of unanimity demands of *all* who participate in it that they be individually conscious and able to carry the responsibility of their function of destiny—their *dharma*. The first kind refers to the *alpha* condition of society; the second to the *omega* state. This omega state is still in the future, but the type of mental energy required for its actualization has been operative for some time. An esotericist, Alice Bailey, personalized it as "the Avatar of Synthesis."

The spirit of synthesis may operate within relatively narrow limits, or globally in a planetary sense. It may operate strongly at one level, or only in special circumstances, and remain ineffectual in most existential situations, whether at the personal or the national-collective level. The *potentiality* is there—or we might say the "availability" of the energy required for its actualization at one level or another is present. Yet this does not tell us much about the degree or quality of the actualization. Mankind is moving toward what I call the state of "multi-unity"—often referred to as "unity in diversity." Because of this cyclo-historical fact (which has a concrete manifestation in the technological wonders potentially enabling every human being to communicate with all others) individuals dream of, long for, unification or integration at one level or another. And this dreaming inevitably evokes in the depths of the consciousness an ancestral (perhaps genetic as well as psychospiritual) feeling of some preindividual, thus mostly undifferentiated, condition of unity. Confused by the separativeness, glamor, and alien quality of the variety of unprovable claims and special techniques now made available to them, many Euro-American men and women—no longer able to find spiritual, mental, or emotional sustenance in their churches or even in an unorthodox type of group or community—yearn for a return to a "state of innocence," the symbolic Edenic state before the Fall into duality and division.

If they are sincere and strong, they may find a line of

approach leading them to individuals who still represent a truly ancient and primordial Tradition unsullied by the pride of mental achievement and the excitement of emotional cravings. But will it be, *can* it be, the one Tradition? Can anything that is formulated in terms of a specific culture, however ancient, and in a particular language and symbols be the *one* Tradition? One should face these questions in every possible manner and at almost any cost; and the way one approaches the possibility of giving them a valid answer is bound to influence the seeker's entire spiritual life and his peace of mind and soul.

Hindu philosophers, during the great Age of Philosophy, gave us a most revealing way of approaching such an issue. They postulated six possible basic approaches to the Self, that is, to the essential reality of existence. Six great Schools of Philosophy were defined and classified, each representing one of these approaches. A human Soul, in the course of successive incarnations, was said gradually to experience all that was existentially and intellectually implied in each of these six approaches, after which it would be ready to experience the seventh, *Atma Vidya*. But this seventh approach is *not* to be considered a "School." What it leads to is ineffable, unformulatable except perhaps in geometrical symbols which are but a framework for direct experience. Nothing can be put in words about it except that it *is*, because any kind of definition would reduce it to a cultural level where multiplicity is the basic fact.

This simply means that beyond, yet at the core, of all great Traditions, we can conceive and perhaps to some extent experience, at least in its reflections, That which is in relation to these few basic Traditions as Light is to the colors of the spectrum. Esotericists may want to identify these several Traditions with the now much publicized "seven Rays"; but the Rays have confused students' minds as much as, fifty years earlier, Globes, Rounds,

Races, subraces, and family-races puzzled those who read about them. The number seven is itself the greatest of all occult enigmas because, in any sevenfold classification, it has a most ambiguous character. In Hindu philosophy there were only six Darshanas, six approaches to existential knowledge. The seventh is everywhere, in everything, and as well "nowhere." For the Buddhist it is *Sunya*, the Nothing that, at the core of everything, simply *is*.

Everything that is human contains, yet is absorbed in Man. *The* one Tradition is in every great occult Tradition and in the multiplicity of lesser cultural traditions. If one is a weary, confused, and disappointed searcher after mysterious and exotic truths, one may long for some stabilizing, reassuring, illuminating knowledge of that one Tradition. But looking for it in any particular place, according to any special technique, and in terms of Sanskrit, Arabic, Chinese, Tibetan, Greek, or Hebrew is, I believe, hardly the way to find it. The moment one depends upon specific "traditional" techniques and particular words or mantrams, one is outside of *the* one Tradition, even though there may be direct reflections of it everywhere.

What then can one do? If one wants to clearly or at least meaningfully *think* about what *the* Tradition is, it seems to me that the first thing to do is to understand what is *not;* then one should try to envision a cosmic or planetary frame of reference in relation to which it has a fundamental significance because it occupies a central place and function therein. This place and function no doubt have to be considered to a large extent symbolic, but symbols can be powerful levers to displace whatever blocks the path to inner experiences or intuitive realizations at the level of ideas and archetypes. If the Tradition is everywhere (yet nowhere) its presence within the human mind must have inspired great images and myths. These can indeed be found in many mythologies and religions. They are particularly in evidence, at least for Western individuals, in the Greek myth of Prometheus, and in the many references in Hindu mythology to the Kumaras. H.P. Blavatsky's *The Secret Doctrine*,[2] presents us with vivid imagery what we may take to be definite factual information concerning an event that took place on this Earth millions of years ago and which implanted in the animal-like organism of man the *potentiality* of self-conscious intelligence, or what is often spoken of as a spark of the divine Fire.

In the Greek legend, Prometheus was a Titan who stole this divine Fire and, out of compassion, gave sparks of it to human beings, allowing them *potentially* to become godlike. This "theft" aroused the anger of the gods; Jupiter threw his thunderbolts at the unhappy Prometheus and chained him to the Caucasus mountains, where a vulture perpetually tore his breast and ate his liver, which was constantly reformed and eaten again. This torture lasted until Hercules, the solar man, delivered Prometheus from his chains.

While this essentially tragic Prometheus myth seems to refer more particularly to the fate and the spiritual character of our Western humanity, which can be said to begin with the earliest development of Greek Culture, the coming of the Kumaras to our planet during prehistoric times and on what is spoken of as the Lemurian continent, has a much more planetary and all-human meaning. There are many ways of interpreting this coming of the Kumaric host and particularly of the four or seven Kumaras whose leader is named *Sanat* from the planet Venus, but a few points must be emphasized.

Venus may or may not be the physical planet described by our astronomers and now being investigated by our space probes. H. P. Blavatsky speaks of it as the "alter-ego" and spiritual twin of our Earth, on which it bestows one-third of the light it receives from the Sun; and we are told that the Earth is not, or not yet, a "Sacred planet."

What seems implied in such statements, and in many others scattered through esoteric and mythological

literature, is that at the close of one of its cycles of
development (it may have been about eleven million
years ago) the type of humanlike consciousness
developed on Venus was ready to "sow" itself into the
soil of a less evolved planet—ours. The Kumaras would
then represent spiritual seeds falling into the animal soil
of earthly mankind and therefore implanting *the true
pattern of MAN* (in a spiritual sense) in the as yet passive
and unself-conscious mentality of early mankind. In a
somewhat different sense we can also liken this process
to the grafting of a cultivated tree bearing excellent fruit
to a wild tree of the same species.

All such images, and even the more occult tales of "incarnation" of some of the Kumaras into human beings,
are symbols trying to convey the meaning of a particular
phase of the vast process of evolution of mankind as a
functional part of the planet Earth, and in relation to
what I call the Heliocosm (the solar system as an organic
cosmic whole). We might get a more concrete (though
not exact) grasp of what such a phase of development on
a planetary scale could mean if we thought of what the
crisis of puberty means to a human adolescent. Some
deep-seated change takes place which is *both* biological
and psychomental. New capacities *begin* to develop; and
these may be used "for better or for worse." They can be
a curse as well as a blessing; the interesting anagram-
matic relationship between the terms Sanat and Satan is
no doubt a most revealing symbolic indication. *The
Secret Doctrine* repeatedly refers to the concept of
"Fallen Angels" and the manner in which "Jupiterian"
religions and their leaders have considered as enemies of
the gods those Promethean beings who, cycle after cycle,
have sought to arouse in the masses of men this divine
Fire of self-conscious creativity and responsibility, and
have been crucified for their self-sacrificial attempts.

This divine Fire gives man the possibility of choosing
between "good and evil," of making at least relatively
free decisions, of learning wisdom through sorrow,

deprivation, and repeated crises of growth brought about by the use of these new powers of self-consciousness and self-will. The truly *human* way is, perhaps inevitably, the *via negativa* spoken of by many mystics—the way that brings a person to the knowledge of what he *is* as a result of revulsion from the experience of what he is-not. This is the tragic way, and the Promethean way, for in ancient times the liver was considered the seat of biological urges (of the "living soul") and the vulture is the devourer of all that has died of frustration and despair. Yet it need not always be a tragic way, because the ever-repeated sacrificial incarnations of the Kumaric beings keep open "the Path" that may lead the pure-in-heart (in whom the "higher mind" also operates) to the fabled Shamballah. This is the "place" where the "pattern of Man", at whose center the inextinguishable Flame of the divine creative Mind burns, is to be found. This pattern of Man is *the* one Tradition. And because Man is the microcosmic image of *his* universe, this Tradition implies also a cosmology such as *The Secret Doctrine* attempted to outline.

But what really is Shamballah? If we can speak of it as a "place," it is in the same sense in which Hindu scriptures state that Atman is in the cave of the Heart. If Central Asia is the Heartland of *our* present human world—as the English and German geopoliticians of the period between the two World Wars claimed—then Shamballah may well be located in the Gobi desert. But if so, it almost certainly does not have what we call a "physical" existence—unless we extend the term "physical" to include what is usually called "etheric." We have also to consider the possibility of fourth or fifth dimensional space and of interpenetrating universes or "globes."[3]

We may wish to think of Sanat Kumara as a divine Person; but the term "person," even if capitalized, is likely to produce confusion. "He" is a person to the extent that we, human personalities, think of or imagine

"Him" as a Person. Is *wheathood* a person? Wheathood "is" as the condition of existence of every stalk of wheat, and it specifically manifests at the core of every seed of wheat, because the vegetable species has its "esoteric" being in the long sequence of generations of seeds, while "exoterically" it takes the form of germinating, growing, maturing, and decaying plants. The Kumara essence is the seedhood of Man as a planetary being, producer of a long series of cultures, each of which *focuses on a particular aspect of life in the Earth's Biosphere*—an aspect which it is the culture's task to incorporate in energy-releasing symbols and meaningful generalizations at the level of the "higher" mind.

These symbols and the basic attitudes of mind which, at the end of the cultural cycle, can be transferred as a seed-harvest, or grafted upon new wild growths, embody archetypal principles or form, functional interrelationship, structural development, and personal behavior. These are variegated manifestations of *the* one Tradition, for they result from different ways of throwing light upon the various aspects of the planetary "pattern of Man." Each aspect responds to the light in its own characteristic manner, hence the various colorings characterizing the many human cultures.

Let me repeat that this pattern of Man represents all that is potential in humanity since the coming of the Kumaras. Each culture has actualized, today actualizes, and in the future will actualize an aspect of this human potential. Each culture has its exoteric traditions, and behind at least the most significant and basic cultural-religious traditions an occult Tradition stands—a particular aspect of the one planetary Tradition. Each cultural tradition develops as a specific answer to the particular need of a collectivity of people living in a particular locality of the earth's surface, small or extensive as this locality may be. Every culture has a *local biospheric character*, conditioned by geography, climate, telluric magnetism, flora and fauna, as these exist at the time of its formation. Every human being born within that culture has his or her psychic, biological, and mental capacities deeply conditioned and, most of the time—at least at the collective-unconscious level—actually determined by the great images, symbols and ideals of the culture, and first of all by a particular language or mode of social communication.

When a modern individual, deeply disappointed by the fading values of his culture and the empty verbiage used by the men charged at all costs to preserve its old institutions, starts on a search for an occult Tradition which, he may have heard, still exists in purity "somewhere," he may be led to its living Custodians, or to men who claim to be their representatives. The meeting can be a radically transforming experience; it may also be an answer to the emotional immaturity and intellectual naivete or confusion of the seeker—an answer therefore wrapped in multicolored glamor and imaginary claims. At best the would-be disciple may come in touch with men who truly live and think in terms of *a* Tradition, occult as it may appear to be. But it is not *the* one Tradition, even though it may accurately incorporate an aspect of, or mental reflection from, the latter.

This is certainly NOT to say that this particular occult Tradition is not valuable. It may be precisely what the seeker needs, at least at the time of his search. But it should also be clear that the moment the words, the symbols, and the divine Names of a certain language, and the mantrams, types of meditation, and techniques of a specific "School," are imposed upon the seeker as conditions of his acceptance, he is dealing only with *an* occult Tradition. He is dealing with a *root-knowledge* based upon something that has occurred *in the past*—an old seed-revelation that has long ago germinated into a plant whose vitality may have been exhausted or nearly so, and whose outer forms have perhaps become degenerated or empty of vital energy after having been

used by many generations of human beings depending
on them for spiritual food—perhaps now fermented food
that excites rather than satisfies and energizes.

One of the problems that meets the knowledgeable
seeker, once the first phase of enthrallment is past, is
that a claim is nearly always made that this Tradition is
the original one, more real and effectual than any other.
Such a claim may be inevitable because, by temperament
as well as because of the character of their work, the
Custodians of the pure ancient Tradition must be conservative and to some extent dogmatic. They embody a
form of spiritual inertia, because they have to resist all
attempts at introducing changes in the past
"Revelation." H. P. Blavatsky spoke of "the inertia of
spirit." This means that the original impulse at the
beginning of a large cycle of existence has to be maintained during the progress to outer growth in which an
immense variety of relationships are bound to induce
centrifugal types of thinking, feeling, and behavior. The
divine *alpha* state has to be reproduced in the spiritual
harvest of the *omega* state. The seedhood has to remain
invariant during growth. If there is to be a mutation it
can only be during the winter period of the seed—its
pralaya. But this applies only to what, strictly speaking,
one may call the "spiritual" scheme of existence; and, as
The Secret Doctrine powerfully states, there are *three*
basic evolutionary schemes or levels.[4]

The spiritual or "monadic" scheme is really not an
evolution because the essential part of what is called a
monad does not change—and there is really but one
Monad. What occurs at that level can be symbolized by
the circle. This circle becomes a spiral, thanks to the
operation of mind wedded to compassion. It is because
the Promethean beings constantly challenge the inertial
circularity of "pure spirit" by exerting a centrifugal
pressure that the ever-repetitive circle becomes a spiral.
This pressure should include both love and knowledge,
since these are expressions of significant and har-

monious relationship—real knowledge being based on a
holistic realization of the relation of everything with
everything else, and true love being in its universal sense
the encompassing of all beings in an act of total in-
clusion. If the love aspect does not prevail, the
knowledge element becomes "satanic."

This satanic element has been particularly strong in
our Western civilization because since the late Greek
period an unparalleled emphasis has been placed upon
that aspect of the mind that deals with material values
and the concrete embodiment of form into material
organisms. As matter represents the pole of
multiplicity—while spirit stands for the principle of
unity— any mind fascinated by matter, or even intent
upon the transformation of matter, must tend to become
analytical and separative and, in most cases, the servant
and justifier of materialistic values and desires. The
coming of Christ was evidently meant to release the
power of a universalistic and unifying divine Love that
could offset the intellectualistic search for mere
knowledge which had become emphasized by Greek
culture, and as well the intellectual egocentricity and
hard-headedness of the Hebraic tradition. But
Christianity lost its collective Soul during the first centuries A.D., and soon after the Papacy succumbed to the
lure of political power. Christianity lost its collective
Soul because it repudiated all that had been the spiritual
tradition of Asia and Egypt in an attempt to focus man's
attention exclusively upon the new Christ Revelation.
But this meant a total dependence upon the Hebraic
past, emphasized by Paul, and the Greek intellectuality
of the Alexandrian Fathers of the Church. On the one
hand the emotion-rousing dogma of salvation by divine
atonement for an original Sin perverted the entire pattern of cosmic evolution and induced a wholesale
neurotic sense of guilt, and on the other hand an
Aristotelian formalism and empiricism led to the one-
pointed development of a science and technology almost

exclusively concerned with materialistic concepts and material well-being.

The proud exclusiveness and ruthless expansionism of our Western civilization required a still more rigid state of secrecy. The old Traditions were forced in most places to go underground and to hide what remained of the spiritual harvest of the past cultures of mankind. In the "Introductory" of *The Secret Doctrine* (p. xxviii and following) we find most intriguing statements as to the preservation of such a harvest in the form of hidden libraries. Other assertions which undoubtedly appear to have a strong dogmatic character have produced diverse reactions among readers, discouraging all but a few who tend to become rather fanatic devotees. Theosophy was brought to the West a century ago, and now another hundred year period is beginning.

According to H. P. Blavatsky, the new century is to be marked by a new endeavor by the Kumaric beings to once more "fecundate" the collective mind of mankind, and it may be possible to reinterpret these seemingly dogmatic assertions in the light of what has been said in the preceding pages. This, however, can be done only if we try to ascertain as objectively as possible the nature of the source of the messages and the writings which seem to flow *through* H. P. B., as she came to be called, far more than *from* her unusual person, as well as the character of her mission at the particular historical time and in the particular places witnessing her activities. It will be especially important to discuss the nature of the collective human need which called for the release of the far-reaching and inclusive type of "information" that she gave, especially to the Western world, for the very first thing to be understood and clearly realized is that any new outpouring of knowledge from spiritual-occult sources always come in answer to a definite need, related to a particular phase in the process of development of a culture, and seemingly now of the whole of mankind.

References and Notes

1.   Omen Press, Tucson, 1974.

2.   cf. *The Secret Doctrine* (original or facsimile editions) II, 244 et seq. 519 et seq.

3.   The "globes" mentioned in *The Mahatma Letters to A.P. Sinnett* are not seperated in a three-dimensional space, as many illustrations erroneously suggest. They are said to ḅe "in co-adunation but not consubstantiality" (cf. *The Secret Doctrine;* Vol I, p. 157), whatever this exactly means.

4.   cf. *Secret Doctrine* I, p. 181 for a clear statement concerning "three separate schemes of evolution which in our system are inextricably interwoven and interblended at every point . . . the Monadic (or spiritual), the Intellectual (represented by the . . . givers of intelligence and consciousness to man), and the Physical represented by the *chhayas* (or astral shadows or webs of energy. D.R.) round which Nature has concreted the present physical body . . . Each of these three systems has its own laws, and is ruled and guided by different sets of the highest Dhyanis or "Logoi." Each is represented in the constitution of man, the Microcosm of the great Macrocosm, and "it is the union of these three streams in him which makes him the complete being he now is"—to which I would add *in potentiality*.

3. H. P. BLAVATSKY, THE TRANS-HIMALAYAN OCCULT BROTHERHOOD, AND THE NINETEENTH CENTURY

Helena Petrovna von Hahn was born at Ekaterinoslav in Southern Russia during the night of August 11-12, 1831 (July 30-31 in the old style Russian calendar), probably around 2 A.M.; thus bringing the 13th or 14th degree of Cancer and the great star Sirius to the Eastern horizon of her birth-chart—this being the celestial location of the Sun on July 4, 1776: an interesting correlation. At the time of her birth her father was a Captain in the Horse Artillery. His family came originally from Mecklenburg, Germany. An ancestor, a Teutonic knight, had adopted the name von Hahn (cock) because one night while fighting in the Holy Land, the crowing of a cock had awakened him just in time to save him from sudden enemy attack. Helena's mother, a novelist and feminist, came from a highly placed aristocratic Russian family. She died of tuberculosis when her daughter was eleven years old. From the first years of her life, the young Helena displayed both a powerful will and unusual psychic abilities. As the result of a dare, when only 17 years old, she married Nikifor Vassilyevich Blavatsky, the elderly Vice-Governor of the Province of Erivan in the Caucasus. After three months of resistance to the consummation of the marriage, she managed to escape, finally arriving in Constantinople. There she began a long series of travels which led her first to Egypt, where she studied with a renowned old Copt occultist. Her father, finally accepting the fact that his daughter would never live with her husband (from whom, eventually, she became divorced), supplied her with money.

From childhood, Helena had had visions of the tall Rajput Indian who has become known as the Master Morya. When in London, perhaps in 1850, she met him physically; presumably he had come there as a member of the Nepal Embassy. According to her, however, a more important meeting took place at Ramsgate (only a symbolic name!) on August 12, 1851, on her twentieth birthday. As she died in May of 1891, the mission with which she was entrusted by the powerful member of the trans-Himalayan Occult Brotherhood lasted almost exactly forty years—a significant period. Compare, for instance, the forty years during which Moses led the Hebrews in the Wilderness before they entered the Promised Land; the forty years' imprisonment of Abdul Baha in the Turkish city of Akka (a word referring to the womb) in Palestine, etc. Madame Blavatsky passed the first half of her forty-year mission in preparation, her *public* work having begun only after she reached New York in 1873.

The significance of all that this preparation entailed is not understood by most people because they fail to distinguish between direct *physical* contact with *planetary centers* in which occult Brotherhoods exist (a matter which I shall discuss further) and *psychic or mental* communications with Adepts. The travels of Occultists, or even of individuals definitely charged with occult (and thus at least to some extent "planetary") missions are most revealing, for they touch certain points on the globe to which such missions may be related and which perhaps they contact for special purposes. Helena Petrovna's travels link Egypt (and the Coptic descendants of the ancient culture) with London, North America, Central and South America (the Mayan and Incan centers), Java, Northern India, and Tibet—to mention only what is publicly known. She had also, as an adolescent, studied piano in Paris and was an excellent musician and performer. A trip by covered wagon from Chicago to San Francisco in 1855 was a prelude to her second and successful (perhaps because she was disguised) attempt to reach Tibet and the occult Brotherhood, a first attempt a year or two earlier having met with insuperable obstacles.

She returned to Russia in 1858; there she displayed for her relatives and friends what today we call powers of ESP, including clairvoyance, telepathy, telekinesis, astral projection, and materialization of messages in locked boxes. After a mysterious illness she resumed her travels through the Balkans, Egypt, Syria, and Italy. In 1867 she joined the forces of Garibaldi fighting for Italy's nationhood against the French and Papal forces. She was wounded in the bloody battle of Mentana. Some students of esotericism believe that her body was actually killed during this battle, but that it was "resurrected" to become a focal point for the power of her Brotherhood.

In *The Mahatma Letters to A. P. Sinnett* there are somewhat mysterious references to H.P.B.'s condition of existence after the years of occult training in Tibet, references which may throw some light not only on what, later on, became her often disconcerting temperamental characteristics as she came under attack as the originator and teacher of the Theosophical Movement, but also on the drastic consequences of being a "messenger" or agent of an Occult Brotherhood. In a letter received in Simla in 1881, in the blue ink writing of K.H., the following statement is made:

> I am painfully aware of the fact that the habitual incoherence of her statements—especially when excited—and her strange ways make her in your opinion a very undesirable transmitter of our messages . . . . Notwithstanding that the time is not quite ripe to let you entirely into the secret; and that you are hardly prepared to understand the great Mystery, even if I told of it, owing to the great injustice and wrong done, I am empowered to allow you a glimpse behind the veil. This state of hers is intimately connected with her occult training in

Tibet, and due to her being sent out alone into the world to gradually prepare the way for others. After nearly a century of fruitless search, our chiefs had to avail themselves of the only opportunity to send out a European *body* upon European soil to serve as a connecting link between that country and our own. You do not understand? Of course not. Please then, remember what she tried to explain, and what you gathered tolerably well from her, namely the fact of the *seven* principles in the *complete* human being. Now, no man or woman, unless he be an initiate of the "fifth circle," can leave the precincts of *Bod-Las* and return back into the world in his integral whole—if I may use the expression. *One,* at least of his seven satellites has to remain behind for two reasons: the first to form the necessary connecting link, the wire of transmission—the second as the safest warranter that certain things will never be divulged. She is no exception to the rule, and you have seen another exemplar—a highly intellectual man—who had to leave one of his skins behind; hence, is considered highly eccentric. The bearing and status of the remaining *six* depend upon the inherent   qualities,   the   psycho-physiological peculiarities of the person, especially upon the idiosyncracies transmitted by what modern science calls "atavism." Acting in accordance with my wishes, my brother M. made to you through her a certain offer, if you remember. You had but to accept it, and at any time you liked, you would have had for an hour or more, the real *biatchooly* to converse with, instead of the psychological cripple you generally have to deal with now.[2]

Exactly what is meant by this quotation must be left to the student's intuition, bolstered up by the proper kind of study and concentration. It may at least suggest how difficult it is to be certain with whom one may have to

deal when contacting a person whose activities and reactions may seem, from our normal sociocultural point of
view, at least relatively irrational. This is especially true
when one has reason to believe that these activities are
connected with the "occult world."

Whatever may have happened occultly to the being
born as Helena von Hahn—either in Italy or in India and
Tibet where she lived for three years with her
Masters—she later found herself faced with the dark
aspect of her karma, particularly in Alexandria, the city
where long ago Christianity became to a large extent
distorted and dogmatized. In 1873, while in Paris, she
received definite directions from the Brotherhood, in-
structing her to go to New York. It is said that on
reaching her embarkation point, seeing a sobbing
woman with children who had been cheated of their fare
to New York, H.P.B. promptly exchanged her first class
ticket for steerage accommodations for herself and the
defrauded family. After a peculiar karmic episode in
Philadelphia, she met Colonel Henry S. Olcott who was
investigating some spiritualistic phenomena in Chit-
tenden, Vermont. In 1875, H.P.B., Colonel Olcott,
William Q. Judge, and a few others founded The
Theosophical Society. Most of the members of this new
organization were deeply intrigued by H.P.B.'s occult
powers and were eager to investigate the nature of the
mysterious phenomena she produced. Nevertheless, the
fundamental aim of the Society was officially stated to be
the eventual formation of "the nucleus of a Universal
Brotherhood," which in time would encompass the
whole of mankind.

In 1877 H.P.B. published *Isis Unveiled*, which
brought her at once fame and enemies. She became an
American citizen on July 8, 1878—a fact few persons
seem to know. But in December of the same year she left
with Colonel Olcott for India by way of England,
arriving eventually in Bombay. The magazine *The
Theosophist* appeared in October 1879. H.P.B. soon

made the acquaintance of A. P. Sinnett and, through him, of A. O. Hume; and both became the recipients of letters occultly "precipitated" by the two members of the trans-Himalayan Brotherhood, Morya and Koot-Hoomi. It seems that these two had taken the main responsibility for the beginning, through H.P.B., of the Theosophical Movement. It was an attempt to establish a psychomental "link" between their occult level of existence and the Western world of the materialistic nineteenth century, and thereby to allow some of the ancient and eternal "seed ideas" of *the* one planetary Tradition (begun with the coming of the Kumuras) to fecundate the collective mind of Western man.

Isis Unveiled deals particularly with the religion and the various unorthodox and occult movements of the European world. The book sought to establish the underground existence of a Countercultural Movement (though H.P.B. did not use such a term) which remained active through many more or less secret societies drawing their inspiration from Near-Eastern traditions (Hermetic, Gnostic, Kabbalist, Sufi, Druzes, and later Alchemical, Rosicrucian, and Masonic). The book also had the perhaps less obvious purpose of showing the essential difference between the path of at least relatively passive *mediumship* and that of positive and deliberate *adeptship*. It was this aspect of her constant remarks in conversation with others, which aroused the enmity of the Spiritualists, and eventually led to a tragic episode. This was the careless and essentially biased "investigation" of H.P.B.'s activities at Adyar, headquarters of The Theosophical Society, by Richard Hodgson, an agent of the Society for Psychical Research. Hodgson accepted uncritically "evidence" fabricated by the Coulombs who were housekeepers of the Adyar building. H.P.B. was not in India at the time, and when she returned she found such a tense and inimical atmosphere—and particularly hatred among the Catholic missionaries—that she returned to Europe. In December

1885 the *Proceeding of the Society for Psychical Research* branded her "one of the most accomplished, ingenious and interesting impostors of history."[3]

The last six years of H.P.B.'s life were devoted to writing *The Secret Doctrine, The Key to Theosophy, The Voice of the Silence, The Theosophical Glossary,* and numerous articles. She was ill most of the time, and at least once, when death was momentarily expected, was miraculously healed. She died suddenly in London during an influenza epidemic on May 8, 1891.

The foregoing outline of Helena Petrovna Blavatsky's tempestuous life is obviously most sketchy. Nevertheless it may be sufficient to show that the one fundamental factor in trying to reach a deep understanding of the meaning and purpose of that life is the meaning and purpose of the occult trans-Himalayan Brotherhood whose agent she claimed to be. It may be impossible scientifically to prove the validity of that claim; it is as impossible to prove it was a hoax, considering the quite outstanding individuals who had firsthand experiential knowledge of the validity of her assertions. Even more convincing is the astounding character of the contents of her large books, especially *The Secret Doctrine,* which no ordinary mind could have produced without passing dozens of years studying and collating an immense mass of verifiable documents in many great libraries. At the same time, it is evident that H.P. Blavatsky, the woman, spent her life away from universities and national libraries.

What *The Secret Doctrine* primarily sought to show was that, at the core of the basic teachings found in all or most of the world's religions *which have left visible and intelligible records,* there exists a Universal Tradition—also called "Wisdom Religion"—and that, through all times and in all continents, this Tradition had been preserved by an uninterrupted line of Custodians and interpreters organized in occult brotherhoods.

However, if one accepts this as a fundamental claim,

one should be careful not to jump to premature or unnecessary conclusions. The first and most essential realization is that a mind trained by our Western civilization is unable to pass judgment on the validity and implications of such claims *unless* it be willing to set aside its life-long conditioning by the local point of view characteristic of our Western culture and religion, and learn to function on an all-human, planetary level, free to judge on their own merits the ideas and values which all cultures have contributed, and are contributing, to the evolution of mankind.

If there is a Universal Tradition, then only a universal mind can hope to adequately understand its nature and its planetary source. This cannot be a cultural, religious source, because—as I have tried to show—the sources of all particular cultures and institutionalized religions (with their distinctive symbols, ideologies, practices, and dogmas) are the manifestations of local conditions. No doubt the consciousness of the founders of the more recent "great religions" (as we call them), especially Gautama the Buddha and Jesus the Christ, was illumined by culture-transcending and "universal" experiences, and by divine love and compassion. But none of these prophets or Avatars built *a* religion, as an institution depending on formulas expressed in a particular language, with dogmas and rituals answering to the specific and characteristic *needs* of a particular people. Their disciples did; and the development of such religions involved endless arguments, compromises, and pressures from political and socio-cultural forces. At the same time their religions came in answer to the disintegration or crystallization of previous religions and cultural institutions.

A Tradition that could truly be called "universal" must therefore have its being essentially beyond the cultural level; it must be transcultural, in the sense that while it may operate through any culture, it is not bound to, limited by, or essentially conditioned by any

one culture or by local factors. Its custodians, just because they are "universal" or planetary beings, aware
of the need for a new release of their knowledge and
intervention, are inwardly compelled out of love for
humanity to answer this particular need in whatever way
makes the answer most effectual. As this happens,
what I have called *the* one Tradition is seen operating
in the aspect which is specifically able, ready, and willing to exteriorize the spiritual-mental answer. It operates through an Occult Brotherhood.

There was not only one Occult Brotherhood when, in
1883, the Mahatma K.H. wrote in *The Mahatma Letters:*

As the course of the river depends upon the nature
of its basin, so the channel of communication of
Knowledge must conform itself to surrounding circumstances.   The   Egyptian   Hierophant,   the
Chaldean Mage, the Arhat and the Rishi, were
bound in days of yore on the same voyage of
discovery and ultimately arrived at the same goal,
though by different tracks. There are even at the
present moment three centers of the Occult
Brotherhood in existence, widely separated
geographically, and as widely *exoterically*—the true
esoteric doctrine being identical in substance,
though differing in terms; all aiming at the same
grand object, but no two agreeing *seemingly* in the
details of procedure . . . . The only object to be
striven for is the amelioration of the condition of
MAN by the spread of truth suited to the various
stages of his development and that of the country he
inhabits and belongs to.[4]

From this statement, every sentence of which should
be carefully studied, one can deduce that there is but one
Occult Brotherhood with three centers widely separated
geographically. But here *we deal with a semantic* matter.
A similar issue arose when Annie Besant, after H.P.B.'s
death, seemingly took upon herself to change the word-
ing of the first object of The Theosophical Society from

"to form the nucleus of *a* Universal Brotherhood of humanity" to to form "a nucleus of *the* Universal Brotherhood of humanity." As it undoubtedly was Annie Besant's purpose to popularize Theosophy all over the globe, the change may have been valid *at that time*. A still deeper change in the concept of the Masters can be noted when one compares the over-all picture that emerges from *The Mahatma Letters* with that which has prevailed in theosophical circles during the 20th century. Perhaps the need to conform to what is "suited to the various stages of (man's) development" is the deepest reason one can present for such a change.

The nature of "the three centers" to which K.H. refers can be known only by a mind able to operate at the truly occult level. It is nevertheless an acknowledged fact that, during the first stage of H.P.B.'s work in America, a strong contact existed between her and what has been referred to as the "Hungarian Lodge" directed by the Master R. and the "Egyptian Lodge" headed by "Serapis." The former is said to have been the inspiration of secret European societies such as the original Rosicrucians and early Free Masonry in the eighteenth century; the latter may have been the true and original Brotherhood of Luxor of which H.P.B. was apparently a member.[5] Yet these "Lodges" and the trans-Himalayan Brotherhood almost certainly were not the only centers of occult activity. One of the three mentioned by K.H. may have been related to the Andes and the remains of the Inca and the pre-Inca civilizations. Some time after World War I an American occultist, Brown Landone in Florida, asserted that most of the greatest Adepts who had lived in the Himalayas and Tibet had moved to the Andean region of Lake Titicaca. What occurred in Tibet some fifteen years ago and the resulting disruption of the ancient Tibetan way of life give validity to the story, which I personally had confirmed by another seemingly knowledgeable source.

In the book *A Collection of Esoteric Writings* by Subba Row, a very valuable book for students, some "Notes" by H.P.B. speak most interestingly of the "Aryan-Chaldeo-Tibetan doctrine, or Universal WISDOM Religion," relating, and nearly identifying, the trans-Himalayan esoteric doctrine with the Chaldeo-Tibetan traditions. There seems indeed to have been a close connection between Chaldea (or Syria and Babylonia) and Tibet. Recently, Sufi-oriented students taught by a Chilean occultist, Mr. Ichazo, and to some extent related to the movement that had been started by Gurdjieff who studied with Dervish Teachers, speak of the Hindu Kush as the seat of an Occult Brotherhood. Sufism itself may be traced in its origin to the ancient teachings of some of the Hebrew Kabbalists; but the Kabbalah may well have had its origin in the Jews' captivity in Babylon, which leads us again to that region—an important one in the development of *one branch* of our present humanity.

All such matters are evidently speculative; and in the Theosophical Movement and other esoteric groups which branched from the original impulse given in 1875 by H.P.B. and those behind her mysterious personality, there is a tendency to provide the interested seeker with exciting bits of information which tend to *personalize* currents of force, magnetic centers of the earth, and the beginnings and ends of cycles, rather than to try to make people "feel" and intuitively envision the vast rhythmic sweep of cosmic, planetary, and even historical sociocultural *processes*. The various phases of these processes certainly can be personified; but there is a fundamental difference between an approach to existence according to which cyclic activities are produced *by* divine superhuman or human beings, and another approach leading one to realize that these activities operate *through* these beings serving as focal points for the release of the transforming energy of cosmic evolution.

These two approaches are manifestations of what recent "philosophers of science" have labelled atomism and holism.[6] Broadly speaking, throughout the nineteenth century, the Western mind interpreted all experiences basically from an atomistic point of view, while the developing trend during the twentieth century (especially after World War I) has been toward holistic concepts. The spread of the German concept of *gestalt* (a word perhaps best translated as "configuration") belongs to the latter development. It obviously had antecedents in earlier philosophical thinking; but, at least since the Renaissance, atomism in science and individualism in the sociopolitical and cultural fields have dominated the consciousness of Europe and America and what I call the "Euromind." The individual ego of human beings and the collective ego of nations—with their attendant pride and greed for power, wealth, and material comfort—have been blatantly in the spotlight. The most basic types of thinking and feeling have focused upon some kind of *individual entity,* at the supposedly spiritual as well as the most materialistic and physical level. Distinctly differentiated and essentially separate characteristics have been attributed to each one of billions of monads, souls, and citizens— to each nation, atom, or element. In America, personal emotions and opinions have come to dominate everything, including family relationships and education. Yet in a peculiar manner these supposedly "personal" factors and needs have proven to be most easily and collectively manipulatable by the media and propaganda. However, these manipulations belong especially to our twentieth century with its new emphasis on social consciousness and on "groups" endowed with a kind of mystique.

If we are trying objectively to think of the esoteric movements of the last hundred years, it is first of all most important to realize that the release of occult knowledge has always to conform to the nature of the general mentality of the potential students of that knowledge. For this reason, *nothing* can be transformed except by someone who has been and at least externally remains a part of that which requires transformation.

This is why a great Adept who is a member of an Occult Brotherhood cannot directly and publicly operate in a society in need of spiritual transformation, especially one as materialistic and individualistic as our Western society was in the nineteenth century. Someone who to some extent belongs to the two realms of knowledge (occult and cultural) must serve as an intermediary or channel for communication. This must be an individual able to withstand *both* the downflow of occult power through his organism, and the scorn, indifference, or attacks of individuals and institutions of the society in which he was born, but from which *his consciousness and will* have emerged in at least relative freedom. Only such a person can serve as a link between an occult Brotherhood and the collectivity whose time for transformation has come, according to some planetary cycle. Occasionally there are individuals who prematurely attempt to introduce radically new ideas or modes of energy-release into their society. For example, *The Secret Doctrine* mentions J.W. Keely who, a hundred years ago, tried to commercialize a mysterious force through a most ingenious motor of his invention. But such premature attempts achieve no results because the time has not yet come for what has somehow been discovered. Even if the time had really come, the intermediary could at first usually affect but relatively few people. *All natural processes are hierarchical.*

What this all means is that, while what the Theosophical Movement released through H.P.B. and a few others should be considered as the direct manifestation of an aspect of *the* Universal Tradition of Man, it is nevertheless only one aspect, initiated by the trans-Himalayan Brotherhood through a Russian woman whose individual karma, as well as the karma of European nations, inevitably gave a particular character and definite limits to the release. Theosophy—and all that has during this century, developed along related lines— has therefore necessarily a two-fold nature. It is stamped with the need of the nineteenth century in the Western World, with some of the character of Helena Petrovna von Hahn and (it would seem) of the main sources of her knowledge, the Brothers K.H. and M. But its essential Source is *the* one occult Tradition whose spiritual origin can be referred back to the coming of the Kumaras, and particularly to that aspect of the Kumaric "descent" to which the name Sanat is given.

H.P. Blavatsky was selected by the trans-Himalayan Brotherhood "after nearly a century of fruitless search" (cf. the quotation on page 32) as "the only opportunity to send out a European *body* upon European soil to serve as a connecting link between that country and our own" (i.e. the Tibetan Himalayas). She was selected from an ancestral lineage which presumably had genetically developed certain psychic powers.[7] These powers later on had to be brought under conscious training during her stay in Tibet, if not before, because she had first to deal with a society and culture in which the only wide-open door to anything beyond physical matter was the spiritualistic movement. Spiritualism had to be used, dangerous as such a use proved to be, because it established a point of contact.

In the background, another point of contact was also available—what remained of the movement started by Anton Mesmer during the last quarter of the eighteenth century. The kind of vital energy which Mesmer was trying to reveal to the narrowly rationalistic public (what he called "animal magnetism") had been scorned by an official Commission of learned personages, including Benjamin Franklin, then U.S. ambassador to France, and the scientist Lavoisier. Nevertheless disciples of Mesmer in France and in the United States carried on along the lines of inquiry he had opened. They led not only through Phineas Quinby to Christian Science, but also to the psychological experiments of the Nancy School in France, which started Freud on his career. This "Mesmeric" contact was used in India by Colonel

Olcott who became widely known as a magnetic healer.

The Spiritualist movement had opened a door to the "astral" realm, but while some of the phenomena were no doubt genuine, the interpretation given to them was, according to H.P.B., erroneous. *Isis Unveiled* was written, at least partly, to disprove the validity of the Spiritualists' claim to be in touch with the real spiritual individuality of departed men and women; and this, as we have already seen, led to tragic misunderstandings and bitter enmity which adversely affected the Theosophical Movement. An interesting and perhaps significant fact is that the Spiritualist movement—which began with the mediumistic phenomena produced in 1848 by the Fox sisters at Hydeville, N.Y. and soon spread wildly throughout the States—has a parallel, almost exactly 100 years later, in the U.F.O. (flying saucers) movement which, for a while at least, also gained a vast number of adherents claiming direct experiences.

While in the nineteenth century Spiritualism sought to establish the existence of human minds and soul-entities beyond the borderline of the physical world, the twentieth century U.F.O. movement—which also produced a wide variety of "communications" from "Space-people"—attempts to show that "men" from other planets or solar systems exist. It is maintained that these "Space-people" can break through the barrier that seemingly has isolated our planet and its gravitational field from other cosmic regions, where other kinds of "humanity" live and are able to develop technologies superior to our own. Both movements therefore have a common aim: to break down man's basic sense of isolation and loneliness—Spiritualism in terms of the possibility of communication with physically dead human persons who nevertheless exist in a different realm, and the U.F.O. movement in terms of the possibility of establishing physical and mental contact with other humanities.[8]

Both movements represent an attempt at expanding consciousness and human contacts, and it will be interesting to see whether, after 1975, the occult "messenger" announced by H.P.B. will *use* the U.F.O. concept to gain public notice, and soon after also show that the usual interpretation given to flying saucers and space-people is not the correct one.[9]

In its most advanced form since the days of Planck and Einstein and the beginning of our present century, Western science has experienced a most basic change of mind. Top physicists, chemists, biologists can hardly any longer be called materialists, yet their training and the pressure of official institutions and academic thinking often make it impossible for them to draw certain kinds of philosophical and even metaphysical conclusions. This is true both from the level of "material" activity which is the subject of their studies and as concerns the essentially symbolic character of the mathematical symbols which they use as a highly complex and actually transcendental language. The basic problem today is that the inertia of past Euro-American sociocultural, economic, and political institutions is obstinately resisting acceptance of the radically new approach to man, and to cosmic, planetary, and biopsychic energies. Such a new approach *alone* could repolarize the collective consciousness of the directing managerial and intellectual elite, and establish it at a level where it could openly *resonate* to the universalistic concepts and vibrations of the occult world.

This occult world can *now* appear in a somewhat different light to the minds of men able to think in planetary all-human terms. As long as man's thinking was conditioned by but a *partial and local* response to the basic factors in his earthly evolution, the glamor of mythological or transcendent events and personages was necessary to allow the devotees of particular cultures and religious institutions to transcend (literally: to take a step ahead of) their institutionalized consciousness.

However, now that man is at least potentially able to think holistically in terms of the whole of mankind and of the earth as a vast organism with many "globes" or levels of existence, the world of true Occultism need not be thought of in remote, mysterious, and utterly super-natural terms—and even less in terms of the miraculous. In its concrete, external manifestations, it is the world of humanity-as-a-whole beyond all localisms, and beyond (though at the core of) all cultures and organized religions. It is a world of planetary activities dealing with the whole sweep of the cycle of evolution in the solar system. These activities are totally inclusive; they do not select this individual or that particular tribe or race as especially—or, even less, exclusively—important, except when, at a particular time, it can serve as a focalizing lens through which new energies of a planetary character can be released.

The true Occultist lives, thinks, and essentially acts in a planetary (and at times superplanetary and "heliocosmic") world of forces, which constitute the true "astral" realm—a world of energies guided by the archetypal patterns of the so-called "casual" aspect of the cosmic and planetary Mind. He works for humanity rather than for individuals, save in exceptional cases and for more-than-personal purposes. His work is moved by a deep unfaltering love for mankind. Throughout *The Mahatma Letters,* and in countless statements made by H.P.B. and William Q. Judge (who was instrumental in the formation of the then Esoteric Section of The Theosophical Society), the basic keynote for entrance upon the path that leads to the true Occultism of the Elder Brothers is sounded forth: consecrated service for humanity in a total surrender of the ego and its lesser goals and narrow possessive loves. In *The Mahatma Letters,* in a letter from Morya, one reads: "It is he alone who has the love of humanity at heart, who is capable of grasping thoroughly the idea of a regenerating practical Brotherhood who is entitled to the possession of our secrets. He alone, such a man, will never misuse his powers and there will be no fear that he should turn them to selfish ends. A man who places not the good of mankind above his own good is not worthy of becoming even our chela—he is not worthy of becoming brighter in knowledge than his neighbour."[10] This is the acid test of the kind of Occultism of which H.P.B. became the emissary. Any other kind will sooner or later lead to the dark path of the "Brothers of the Shadow."

Let me repeat here what has already been said concerning the Kumaras or Promethean Spirits. In their nature, Love and Knowledge are two poles from whose interaction power is released. If they are eager to break through the inertial Ring of Saturn and the all-too-spiritual glory of King Jupiter so that evolution can forever go on along its essential spiral path, and if they are ready to suffer the nearly inevitable consequences of their compassionate involvement in the development of self-consciousness and responsibility in Man, it is because of their boundless compassion; this compassion encompasses all who are able to resonate to their everlasting Call. This ability to resonate and respond is inherent, though so often undeveloped, in all human beings since the most ancient coming of these exalted beings and the sacrificial grafting of their power of universal Love and occult Knowledge onto the wild animal-like nature of earthbound mankind.

This power is for us all consciously to use at this crucial period of human evolution. It is a time which, at the level of the strictly human consciousness, repeats the great transformation that was induced at an unconscious level *in the Earth's biosphere* millions of years ago under the impact of the Venusian Host. It is for Man now consciously to choose between the way of spiritual integration through Love and that of slow gradual decay through selfishness, fears, greed, and lust.

We are coming to the turning point. Everything depends on the clarity of our knowing and the purity and compassion of our loving. Knowledge and Love are both essential. Knowledge alone is dark; Love alone is possessively blind. All deep and radical spiritual transformations able to alter the total reality of Man require an illumined mind and an all-encompassing heart.

References and Notes

1. There are several biographies of H.P. Blavatsky, but most of the material mentioned here is taken from an excellent short biographical chapter included in a remarkable book *Damodar and the Pioneers of the Theosophical Movement* compiled by Sven Eek (Theosophical Publishing House, Adyar, 1960).

2. *The Mahatma Letters to A. P. Sinnett,* pp. 203-4, 2nd ed.; p. 201, 3rd ed.

3. More recently the SPR has officially affirmed that responsibility for the statements about H.P.B. rested solely with the author of the report (Richard Hodgson) and not with the Society for Psychical Research.

4. P. 399, 2nd ed.; p. 393, 3rd ed.

5. Afterward a group that took the name of the Brotherhood of Luxor became active in Europe and the United States, but H.P.B. said that it was not the ancient one rooted in the occult past of the earliest Egyptian civilization.

6. The words, holism and holistic (from the Greek term for "whole") are now used extensively, but to my knowledge, were not, or but very rarely, used until the publication after World War I of a remarkable book *Holism and Evolution* by the great South African statesman and thinker, General Jan Smuts. Yet his name is hardly ever mentioned by the people using the adjective, holistic. However, I would mention here a very significant book by Lancelot Whyte, *Accent on Form* (Harper and Brothers, N.Y. 1954). I might also refer the interested reader to my books *The Astrology of Personality* and *Person-Centered Astrology.*

7. Presumably her paternal line, because her father's daughter from a second marriage after Helena's mother had died, had also in early youth strong psychic powers which disappeared as she grew older (cf. *Damodar*, p. 541).

8. The astrologer will easily relate these two movements with the character of the two planets, Neptune and Pluto. Spiritualism is Neptunian in its ambiguity and glamor; the U.F.O. concept is Plutonian in all it portends, superphysically and yet concretely.

9. In this connection one would do well to read a quite fascinating article by Jacques Vallee in the February 1974 issue of the excellent magazine PSYCHIC published in San Francisco: "UFO: The Psychic Component."

10. P. 252, 2nd ed.; p. 248, 3rd. ed.

4. A PLANETARY FRAME OF REFERENCE

Because the consciousness and the emotional response of most human beings today revolve around the ego, and their minds refer most experiences to an irreducible feeling of "I myself," it is very difficult for them to come to a vivid existential realization that the person they "know" themselves to be is only a transient phase in a vast process of unfoldment of human potential—a process which can never be fully understood unless it is seen to encompass the whole of mankind on this planet. This knowledge of being a particular person centered around a self, definable in terms of everyday experiences, seems to most individuals of our time fundamental and irreducible because it no longer operates within a powerfully compelling and larger frame of reference. Even in old Europe the family, the ancestral religion, and the national culture constituted unquestioned frames of reference in relation to which the "I" was given some kind of function and purpose—if only that of perpetuating the family, the racial inheritance, and the cultural and religious tradition.

Now, especially in America, the "I" has acquired a quasi-absolute character and value, thus an unrelated significance in a pluralistic universe which to the spiritually oriented is ultimately reducible to an immense number of independent spiritual "monads." These monads, in some ancient metaphysical systems, are considered to be coeternal and absolute; but to the christian theologian and philosopher—and still to most ordinary people in the Euro-American world—they are created *ex nihilo* (out of nothing) by a mysterious all-powerful God of Whom they are, in some sense at least, the spiritual progeny. Thus the one essential relationship to which these centers of consciousness and will can and should respond is their relationship to their divine Father. All other relationships are usually regarded as transient means to "learn lessons" which most often involve conflict and pain in the process of developing love and overcoming pride, greed, and possessiveness.

Christianity no doubt officially believes in the Brotherhood of Man as well as the Fatherhood of God; all men theoretically are "brothers" inasmuch as all are "sons" of God. But the record of our Western society and of the Christian religion assuredly fails to present a glowing picture of "brotherly love" between Christians and non-Christians, and even between Catholics and Protestants. This is usually attributed to the still spiritually and morally unevolved character of the immense majority of human beings or to the inherent sinfulness of human nature since the "Fall of Man." However, back of such concepts, and giving them power and meaning, we are actually dealing with a more basic metaphysical belief in the irreducible separateness of individual Souls and/or monads. This belief almost inevitably leads to and strongly supports a personalistic and sociocultural glorification of the ego, as well as the "sovereign" state and national entity. The cult of the ego and, at least in theory, the dogmatic assertion of the prerogatives of the individual person as a social "atom"—the citizen—were bound to generate a collective mentality which, as soon as the binding moral framework of family tradition and religious beliefs lost its credibility and effectiveness, would give rise to an anguished and widespread sense of separateness and alienation.

Perhaps this is the inevitable shadow of the light produced by the "gift of Fire" made by the Kumaras to human beings. As self-consciousness grows in the human organism and every experience becomes referred to a center—an interior "I"—the habitual responses of this center become organized as an egostructure. Eventually the pride of personal achievement produces an increased reliance upon this controlling ego-structure; and, as it is the very nature of life to expand, and the human being is still dominated by the compulsive instincts of organic living in the earth's biosphere, this ego-structure also tends to expand. This ego-expansion requires, and indeed receives, the services of the mind's capacity for organization.

It is the mind that can provide frames of reference for man's experiences and impulses, and for his aspirations and personal desires. Religions and philosophies build such frames of reference. At the collective level of society these become the "traditions"; they always have a local character when referring to the products of particular cultures and societies. But there is a level which is higher, because more inclusive, than that of relatively local cultures and even of "Races" (in the theosophical sense of the term) and continents. It is at this level that the Promethean or Kumaric fire of self-consciousness and individual responsibility operated when, millions of years ago, it was brought to Man; and it has never ceased to operate at that level— the level of the earth as *a planetary organism*. At that level, Mind does not operate as the servant of the egos of individuals, or of any situations in historical time or local space. It operates in terms of the evolution of the entire solar system—or "heliocosm"—and in relation to the galactic whole of which this heliocosm is but a small cellular unit. It operates in terms of planetary consciousness.

The coming of the Kumaras and, according to Occultism, the special relationship between Venus and the Earth, are factors that have meaning in terms of the evolution of the whole solar system as an organized field of interrelated and interdependent activities. For human beings who cannot operate beyond the planetary field of the earth (but now man has begun to take a transcendent step in overcoming this limitation) the *inplanetarization* (rather than incarnation) of the Kumaras and the start of the process of individualization of Man are global events. They are phases of a planetary process; phases which cannot really be understood unless the whole process is studied and its over-all structure discovered. This requires at least the start of a planetary type of knowledge. That knowledge can be acquired only by planetary beings. They can transmit it only to individuals who, in some manner, have developed minds whose intuitional perceptions encompass processes of a planetary scope.

This is the reason why *The Secret Doctrine* and the very existence of Adepts who inspired H.P.B. *could not* be publicly revealed—i.e. revealed to the collective mentality of our Western humanity—before human beings had at least begun to circumnavigate and physically experience the whole globe of the earth and become related to all the sociocultural collectivites at present in existence. The Industrial Revolution of the first part of the nineteenth century made such global concrete experiences possible. Thus it brought to the fore *the need for a planetary type of knowledge,* and also for the kind of "universal Love" which the humanitarian movements of the 1840s at least forshadowed. Blavatsky's travels around the world are *ritualistic symbols* of a globe-encompassing all-human awareness. They herald the actual emergence of a planetary consciousness, which our two World Wars have precipitated under baptisms of blood.

Actually the first public impact of the new potentiality of existence of integrally organized all-human society came with the proclamation in 1863 by the Persian Prophet-Avatar, Baha'u'llah, of his worldwide mission as Law-giver for a New Age society. This proclamation was sent also in the form of "Letters" to the then ruling Kings of the main nations of the world. At the close of this book I shall try to interpret the relation between the

Theosophical Movement and the Baha'i Faith. But at this point I should state that the Theosophical Movement has essentially operated at the level of the higher Mind and in terms of occult knowledge, rather than as a world-wide social-religious organization. The aim of the early Theosophical Movement actually was to present a planetary-cosmic frame of reference for the then imminent development of a new science and psychology; above all, it has continued to stress fully conscious growth of a spirit of all-human brotherhood made possible by the breaking down of cultural boundaries and religious dogmas.

The recently developing scientific attitude deals holistically with *processes* more than atomistically with isolated and unrelated *entities*. In its own hesitant and empirical way it is reaching intangible and nonmaterial bodies or objects. Science even at times abandons the very idea of "substance" as a concrete factor, and interprets existence in terms of "pure forms," which are closely related to the archetypes of occult philosophy.

Late in life, H.P.B. told her disciples that the task of Theosophy was to "change the mind of the twentieth century." It is no doubt difficult to establish a causal connection between what she taught and the progress of electronic and atomic physics and chemistry; but who can tell how *mind currents* operate and which seeds hidden invisibly in the damp autumnal soil and covered by the winter's snow become, in springtime, the causes of the emergence of new plants?

Unfortunately the Western mind has an avid curiosity for new phenomena and for events extending the scope of its perception or stimulating its remarkable ability to correlate, rationally classify, and describe what the senses experience. H.P.B.'s followers were greedy for new information and overeager to claim the capacities required to become disciples of those whose consciousness and behavior are ineradicably rooted in the patterns of *the* occult Tradition, the original answer to the need of Man and the Earth. Very few among these would-be disciples had developed anything like a planetary consciousness. They wanted, usually on their own terms, direct contacts with the Masters; and we can read in *The Mahatma Letters* what were the results of such an attitude, particularly in the case of Mr. A.O. Hume.[1] They wanted the kind of knowledge which the European mind has been brilliantly able—for better or for worse—to put to use, but knowledge without spiritual-moral responsibility, knowledge unintegrated with universal Love.

During the countless millennia of the prehistoric as well as historical past of mankind, knowledge had always been understood as being hierarchical. It flowed from beings of a higher type to the most devoted, intrepid, and willful members of a culture. It had a hierarchical, secret character. It flowed through what might be called a vertical line of transmission. The religious person of our society speaks of the "Fatherhood of God"; but the occultist of the past received his knowledge from a quasi-divine personage who, in turn, had received it from his guru—the long chain of transmission *(guruampara)* extending, at least ideally, to Man's divine Instructors. He received more than knowledge, for its very possession necessitates that the "divine spark" of Kumara Fire should be made to flame forth—and the oxygen needed for this flaming forth, if the source of the transmission was pure, was divine Love and infinite compassion for Man—the essence of what I have called planetary consciousness.

Such a hierarchical and "vertical" kind of transmission has almost inevitably a restricted field of application. Whoever was actually ready to receive the knowledge became drawn to the particular aspect of the Tradition which, because of his cultural upbringing and condition of birth, constituted an answer to his personal need and, at least to some extent, to the needs of his society. His actual readiness was tested in all sorts of ways to safeguard so far as possible both the knowledge and the line of transmission.

What today we call empirical and scientific knowledge has a totally different character. It develops "horizontally" through the free sharing of informaton between minds able to extract from a multiplicity of classified data and from shared new discoveries what they need for their effective operation. These minds, even though they evidently differ in quality and ability to organize and apply information, are nevertheless theoretically on the same level of consciousness. The process of transmission has no longer an essentially hierarchical character; it is "democratic"—even though the vanguard of active searchers and discoverers constitute an "elite" which tends to perpetuate itself in relative isolation from the mass of people whom, deliberately or not, they at least indirectly control. When such a control becomes rigid and truly aristocratic—in the traditional European sense of the term—we see the rise of a technocracy. The typical technocrat is a man able to use a definite amount of knowledge and technological skill with little or no consideration for the actual welfare—and even less for the spiritual-individual development—of the persons who will be affected by this use. It is knowledge without love for humanity—even if the knower is able to display personal affection for one or a few intimates.

Because the Theosophical Movement of the Nineteenth century had to some extent to deal with persons who held that type of love-deprived knowledge and merely were eager to obtain more of the same kind, provided it was new, spectacular, and fascinating, the trans-Himalayan adepts, working through H.P.B., placed the formation of a Universal Brotherhood founded on the love of humanity as the first and most basic of their aims. At the "horizontal" level brotherhood was to be the keynote or, one might say, the common ground. Without such a "ground" ready to receive seeds of the higher occult knowledge, the sowing of such seeds was neither safe nor even possible except in a very general manner.

Yet the trans-Himalayan Brothers had to formulate the concepts which they transmitted in writing in terms of the essentially atomistic and individualistic taken-for-granted beliefs held by the collective Western mentality. They had to use intellectual, analytical means to bring credence to the vast cyclic realizations of true Occultism, which deals essentially with forces and processes, and only secondarily with the myriad of entities of the mythological world, whose "names" symbolize the many phases of the world-process. What H.P.B.'s *The Secret Doctrine* intended to do was to show that all these mythological names and stories (for instance, the creation myth of various cultures and the many confused references to "Fallen Angels" and human Progenitors of various types) were derived from a common Source of occult Knowledge; and that only that Source and those whose consciousness was *identified* with it could provide modern individuals with the structural sequence of the phases of "cyclocosmic" processes and the true character, meaning, and purposes of each phase with reference to the whole.

While occult knowledge is fundamentally holistic, it assuredly does not play down the role and significance of individual entities. Yet, the concept of "monads," which presumably originated in the mind of the German philosopher, Leibnitz, in the seventeenth century, has, I believe, been greatly misunderstood. References can be found in *The Mahatma Letters* and elsewhere to the effect that actually there is only one Monad, or that the term applies as well to an atom as to a human individual, a solar system, or a whole universe. The term, *atma,* has also been used in a confusing manner, without regard to H.P.B.'s or K.H.'s repeated statement that *atma* can "exist" only in relation to *buddhi.* The concepts of "monadic place" and "monadic evolution" are indeed ambiguous, as we read that the monad itself cannot be said to "evolve."

Likewise the sketch repeated in many books pur-porting to show how the "Life-wave" passes from Globe to Globe in a planetary Scheme is also sure to create con-fusion, for the Globes have a common center, and may even be said to exist in different "dimensions," whatever this exactly means! All such concepts were presented in a manner which seemed the most acceptable to the culturally set minds of men like Sinnett and Hume; they were conditioned by the "Euro-mind" of the time and the very words were, as K.H. once wrote, picked out of Sinnett's mind. This is inevitable. I repeat that *The Secret Doctrine* as a book is a compromise with the nineteenth century mentality. Even some of its claims, which have offended people who have not understood the psychological reason for them, were meant *to convey the necessity of a certain approach to the study of the book,* and of Occult knowledge in general—an approach wholeheartedly accepting the inevitable character of the vertical transmission of knowledge from the keepers of the Tradition to those who seek to be initiated into its secrets.

For these reasons, and considering the fact that the Source of the knowledge presented by H.P.B. was *one of the several Occult Brotherhoods* operating in the nineteenth century, and whose collective dharma it presumably was to try to establish a connection with the Western society and *in the English language,* it should be clear that what H.P.B. wrote under direction, yet *through* the cerebral processes of her body, is not a manifestation of the wholeness of knowledge within *the* one planetary Tradition, but only of the apsect of *It* for-mulated in terms of a karmic relationship between a cer-tain group of Adept-Brothers and the need of humanity—particularly Western humanity—in the nineteenth century. This does not make the work of H.P.B. less important, but it may enable one to see the whole issue of the value and character of *The Secret Doc-*

trine in a broader perspective. This, however, is not said to justify many of the claims made since H.P.B.'s death—claims of direct and literal transmission by the Adepts who sent her into the world.

Everything dealing with Occultism—white or black —is ambiguous and paradoxical. H.P.B. repeatedly stated that she was not allowed to give out the whole truth and that "blinds" had to be used so long as Universal Brotherhood was not a realized fact. As I see it, what really matters are not fascinating details to be memorized by the curious mind, but the gaining of a whole view of cosmic, planetary, and human evolution. It is to be able to "see" or even feel this evolution, with its interconnecting cycles and subcycles, microcosmic as well as macrocosmic. As long as the mind thinks atomistically and tries to classify entities and their many names in computerized brains, and as long as it is not able to have clear and sequential experiences of supermental "seeing," it can only stand, confused and befuddled, at the threshold of a "door of perception" whose transparency is impaired by fog and dirt. Above all, what the would-be Occultist needs is the ability adequately to formulate his superintellectual experiences or intuitions in concepts and words which at least approximate what he has "seen" or "felt."

The formulating process is the key to whether or not what is imparted to others is valid. For such a process to be not merely intellectual information and fascinating stories, but an inspiration for a transformation of consciousness and greater living, it is essential that the mind of the formulator should be able to deal directly with "whole ideas" founded upon metaphysical and cyclocosmic principles, and thus to develop what I have called "clairthinking." Any other process will lead to episodic formulations.

A really holistic approach must be able not only to produce concepts that embrace a totality of data or experiences and reveal their internal "form," but it must

release vibrant and potentially transforming ideas in-
fused with the love of Man. One can never repeat enough
that there can be no true Occultism without a "heart"
filled with transpersonal and sacrificial Love. Without
this Love, woe to him who seeks to tread the path of Occultism and to break through the threshold!

I have spoken of vertically transmitted and horizontally shared knowledge. I should like to conclude these
pages by stressing again the fact that what has come to
us during the last hundred years from Occult Sources
has been in answer to the newly developed and growing
possibility of using a planetary frame of reference for our
conceptions. It is the time when an Occult Messenger
comes, and the environmental conditions through which
he or she has to operate are the surest clues to the
meaning, validity, importance, and scope of the mission.
One should not separate *The Secret Doctrine* from the
nineteenth century. Only a thorough understanding of
the *time-space situation* in which H.P.B.'s works were
produced can make us evaluate within a larger and
holistic frame of reference the meaning, *not* of the fundamental principles which *The Secret Doctrine* presents
(these are "eonic" and inherent in *the* Tradition and the
cosmos seen from the Earth's point of view), but of the
formulation given to these principles and their effects
upon the existence of Man at his various levels.

Moreover, as H.P.B. came and worked as an emissary
of one of the several Occult Brotherhoods, it should also
be most important to understand what place this trans-
Himalayan Brotherhood occupies in the total organism
of the planet, Earth, and the function it performs—not
even mentioning the even more difficult grasp of the
Earth's place and function within the heliocosm, and of
the latter in our galaxy. I do not see how such an understanding is possible without the realization that the
Earth is indeed a cosmic organism, and that it has not
only a physical globe as its material body, but also an
electromagnetic "ethero-astral body," and still higher

"fields of existence" in which mental and spiritual forces and dynamic centers operate.

Such an assertion is obviously undemonstrable from a strictly scientific point of view, though modern physics is now studying planetary currents of magnetism and the Earth's reactions to "solar winds" and a myriad of other atomic or superatomic energies. Yet today Occultism makes little sense without the realization that this occult world deals with planetary forces and centers rather than with mysterious personages performing actions which, to our perceptions and interpretative minds utterly conditioned by the prejudices of our local culture, appear miraculous. We can no more understand the meaning of the Occult Brotherhoods without referring them to the Earth-as-a-whole than we can grasp the rationale of yogic exercises and modes of concentration of pranic energy without accepting as a fact the existence of the *chakras*.

The chakras are pictured by clairvoyants as whorls of forces existing in the superphysical "etheric body," which resembles the normally invisible electromagnetic field surrounding a magnet. They are invisible to the average human eyes, but are described in some detail by Hindu yogis and by Western clairvoyants, the number of whom seem to be greatly increasing. H.P.B. spoke of three systems of chakras: the exoteric ones which are related to and permeate some large nerve plexuses (those existing along the vertebral spine from the coccygeal region to the top of the head) and what she called "master chakras" within the head or above. More recent information concerning the chakras speaks mainly, or exclusively, of those along the spine and within the head.

If the Earth is a cosmic organism, it must also have within its total being (or "auric egg"), which may extend as far as the Moon's orbit, whorls of planetary energy, planetary chakras. Ancient as well as modern occultists have spoken of "sacred mountains" or highly magnetic centers—perhaps "holy places"—on the Earth's surface. It seems also that high mountains, some of which are apparently especially "sacred," are to be considered as the Sources of invisible currents of mental-spiritual inspiration for the cultures developing below their peaks. One can think especially of the Himalayas above India, of the Caucasus above Persia, Mesopotamia, and Asia Minor, of the Alps above Italy, of the Carpathian mountains above Austria-Hungary, of the Andes in relation to the Incas, and of some North American mountains "sacred" to Indian tribes—some of them, such as Mt. Shasta and the Tetons, having acquired quite a name in modern American esotericism. There are also high mountains in Africa, and the two branches of the "sacred" Nile flow from some of them.

It naturally comes to mind that the Occult Brotherhoods have some definite connection with these mountains. The activities of these Brotherhoods may well be related to the operation of the Earth's chakras, which in turn affect changes in the Earth's biosphere and, as a result, the evolution of human races and cultures. The idea at least seems logical and valid provided it is not materialized by thinking of our planet merely as a mass of physical matter. Its main value consists in the fact that it could reinterpret what to mystics appears totally transcendent and essentially ineffable, bringing their experience to a level comprehensible to the holistic mind for which the Earth in its total being is a vast, living, thinking organism in which *all* kingdoms of life perform interrelated and interdependent functions.

These kingdoms do not include merely the mineral, vegetable, animal, and human kingdoms. One must add oceanic, atmospheric, and stratospheric currents, ionospheric fields and Van Allen belts, and even less perceptible forms of energy pervading the Earth's aura, for this aura exists within the vaster aura of the solar system which in turn operates in the space-field of the galaxy. One should not dismiss as fairy-tales a "deva kingdom" which seems to refer to non-individualized beings possibly related to solar forces and servants of the "will" of a planetary or solar center of consciousness. One should also speak of a superhuman (or "fifth") kingdom whose cosmic Source is the Kumara Host which gave to animal man the Fire of self-consciousness and responsible will.

All these "kingdoms" and levels of energy-release or energy-control are integral and organic parts of the Earth. Each has a definite function to perform. Humanity has a definite organic function to perform—a function probably similar to that of the three nervous systems of the human body (sympathetic, parasympathetic and cerebrospinal), or at least of the brain (old and new). The Occult Brotherhoods also have definite functions to perform, the main one at a level beyond man's normal perception. This is the level of *akasha* at which a "Master" has his true "mahatmic" being, if we believe many of K.H.'s remarks in *The Mahatma Letters*.

The human body operates in a hierarchical manner. Not only does it originate from one fecundated ovum, which through a series of subdivisions produces the trillions of its cells, but it operates under a very rigid system of controls along a hierarchical line of command. Similarly, the esotericist speaks of a "planetary Hierarchy" with an equally definite line of command, or at least control. There has been a tendency of esotericism to glorify—or at least glamorize—the Masters. But if one reads *The Mahatma Letters* one gets a very different impression of what the members of an Occult Brotherhood are like. K.H. repeatedly stresses his total obedience to *his* Master, the Chohan, and his inability to use more than a certain amount of "occult power" in his dealing with the members of The Theosophical Society unless authorized by the Chohan, who apparently is the Head of the Brotherhood—of this particular trans-Himalayan Brotherhood, let us not forget.

It would be attractive to be able to correlate the three main chakras, the much publicized "Rays," and the regions of the Earth; but as already stated, a higher type of knowledge would be required. It may nevertheless seem possible, or likely, that the Trans-Himalayan Brotherhood corresponds to the Ajna center back of the human forehead which synthesizes the operations of the "lower" spinal centers, and perhaps directs them— somewhat as the pituitary glands direct the activities of other glands by releasing powerful hormones. One might also suggest that the fabled Shamballah may correspond to either the heart chakra or the "Sahasrara" chakra above the head, and imagine a pulsating connection between the Shamballa center in central Asia (the Heartland of the Earth?) and the Himalayan center. If so, and if it is true that most of the highest members of the trans-Himalayan center have moved to the Andes, might this not indicate a relatively imminent (which may mean decades or even centuries away) shift in the polar axis readjusting the relationship between *perhaps immovable* ethero-astral whorls of energies and continental localities at the surface of the globe?

These are only speculations. What may be more significant to discuss is the existence of a certain amount of confusion in the minds of esotericists between what they call "the planetary Hierarchy" and "the White Lodge." One can think of the Hierarchy in terms of divine or quasi-divine "Beings" to whom names and specific characteristics are given; this is the mythological, and also the "atomistic," because individualizing approach. If a human being enters into relation to this Hierarchy he will presumably do so in terms of a contact, at whatever level it may be, with some mysterious personage who may remain an ever-present influence and guide. But one may also think of the Hierarchy as a progressively more complex pyramidal series of "offices" or of centers of activity having *a functional character* in the existence ana evolution of the planet, Earth, and of Man as an organic part of the planet. This is the "holistic" approach in which process is the most essential factor, even though evidently each phase of the process can be personified into a great being who has become identified with it. From this point of view Masterhood is primary; the individual human being who, as a Master, manifests the power and activity of this Masterhood is secondary. Fire is the essential reality, even though its existence implies flame after flame. And it is in that sense that *the* one Tradition exists *through and within* every great Occult tradition formulated by a particular Occult Brotherhood.

If one thinks of the Hierarchy as a planetary web or field forming the innermost structure of the dynamic astromental body of the Earth, one will at once realize that the great beings who "manage" these offices must have reached a basic high level of planetary consciousness; at that level they operate—at least in their "Mahatmic" condition—in a condition of essential unanimity. They constitute therefore a "pleroma" of beings—the omega state of the cyclic evolution of the Earth. It is a state of *multi-unity.* This pleroma state of multi-unity IS "the Great Lodge." It is a state of consciousness and power. On the other hand, the Heirarchy is a spiritual-mental *organization* of offices or planetary functions. Every member of the Hierarchy must be able to operate at the level of consciousness which is the Great Lodge, but every member of the Great Lodge need not be a member of the Hierarchy.

It is said that Gautama, the Buddha, "reorganized" this Lodge. This has puzzled many students, but presumably it means that, being what has been called a "sixth-Rounder" he brought to the planet the *potentiality* of manifesting the cosmic vibration of Number 6; whereas the Kumaric Mind vibrates essentially in a fivefold rhythm, and self-conscious Man is the Pentagram, the five-pointed star.

In *The Mahtma Letters* definite references are made not only to Gautama and Sankaracharya as "Sixth-Rounders," but to Gautama (and after him Tsung Ka

Pa, reformer of Buddhism in Tibet) having been the first human being able to penetrate beyond the "Ring-Pass-Not" of the solar system.[2]

Mention is made also of "Fifth-Rounders" who are divided into three classes *(The Mahatma Letters:* p. 117): "The natural-born Seers and clairvoyants of Mrs. Anna Kingsford and Mr. Maitland's types—the great Adepts of whatever country—the geniuses, whether in arts, politics or religious reform."

These terms, Fifth-Rounders and Sixth-Rounders, may seem very mysterious to a person unacquainted with the apparently complex system of Schemes, Rounds, Root Races, Subraces, and Family Races taught by K.H. to A.P. Sinnett in long letters appearing at the beginning of *The Mahatma Letters*— a system on which the English writer based his book, *Esoteric Buddhism.* But these terms simply refer to divisions of time—just as seconds, minutes, hours, days, years do. Time is the structuring power which divides the universal world-process into wholes within wholes within wholes; or as a modern thinker, Julius Stulman, expresses it, "fields within fields within fields. . . "

What many modern teachings do not clearly enough state is the manner in which these cycles, subcycles and sub-subcycles *interpenetrate.* At least tentatively, to understand this interpenetration requires the ability to think in terms of pure numerical abstractions. This leads one to a type of consciousness, as it were, *beyond the dimesions of measurable time*—which does NOT mean beyond what H.P.B. calls "infinite Duration." We have then to deal with numbers as implying what, for lack of better terms, I might call "vibratory qualities."[3]

A first Round operates in such a manner that, at the core of and through all the manifestations of existence during its vast time-span, the vibratory quality of Number 1 operates. But this same vibratory quality operates also—yet in a *less fundamental* manner—during the first

Root Race of the second, third, fourth, etc. Rounds. And by Root Race is meant *a specific type of humanity* rather than what today we call a race. In other words, what is called "round" refers to the Fundamental Tone of the total manifestation of existence on the planet, Earth, during an extremely long period, lasting millions or even billions of years as we presently interpret that word. During such a period seven Root Races are said to operate, theoretically succeeding one another, yet in many ways also interpenetrating during a large part of their lifespan. The vibratory quality of these Root Races does not erase the vibratory quality of the Round of which they are parts, but "tops" the latter—just as in music overtones *add themselves* to the Fundamental Tones without obliterating them.

Thus a fifth Root Race of, say, the fourth Round—which is the planetary set-up defining the character of our present humanity—reveals the operation of the vibratory quality 4 as Fundamental, and *over it and interpenetrating it,* the activity of the vibratory quality 5.

This obviously is not all; for our Western civilization is also said to characterize the fifth subrace of the fifth Root Race. Thus, in our civilization, the vibratory quality 5 of our fifth Root Race, is reinforced by the vibratory quality 5 of the present subrace. As a result, the total "tone" of mankind at present can be determined by a Fundamental tone 4, and two levels of Overtones vibrating to the Number 5.

What this means is that the basic tone of *Earth-nature as a whole*—a tone on which the music of China was officially based—vibrates with a quality which can be symbolized by the Number 4. This is therefore also the basic vibration of human nature throughout this fourth Round. Every human being inescapably vibrates to it at the genetic root of his being; but if this human being actually is able—because of parentage, environment and, above all, "past karma" as a spiritual Entity—to *resonate to and embody* in his consciousness, feeling, and behavior, the vibratory quality 5, the root-vibrations of "human nature" become modified by his or her individual character and consciousness. He basically remains a Fourth-Rounder, but with an individualized Fifth Root Race consciousness; and to the latter may be superadded a further accentuation of the five, if the individual (or a whole collectivity) responds to it as a manifestation of what the coming of the fifth subrace *has made possible* for all human beings born within it.

The coming of a new vibratory quality does not necessarily mean that all the members of a Root Race or subrace will fully embody it; it merely opens up a new genetic and sociocultural set of possibilities. For a similiar reason, there may be *individual cases* revealing that an individualized Soul-entity (not a mere personality) has somehow anticipated the change in vibratory quality of the planet-as-a-whole and thus of human nature-in-mass. This is possible only, it would seem, when a new vibratory quality begins to develop as an overtone of the Fundamental 4.

For instance, the fifth Root Race in a sense began when the fifth subrace of the fourth Root Race was in existence because the vibration of 5 of that subrace— to a very small extent—opened up the *possibility* of a basic change from fourth-Root-Race-consciousness to fifth-Root-Race-consciousness. Only a few individual Souls in the fabled Atlantis (fourth Root Race) were ready *to modulate* from the 4 to the 5. In a similar manner, an even deeper "modulation" (or change of level of consciousness and spiritual-mental rhythm) became possible when the fifth subrace vibration strengthened further the 5 of the fifth Root Race. A few individuals, to whom the above quotation from *The Mahatma Letters* referred, began to operate *in their minds* as Fifth Rounders. As higher Minds, they had become able to *radically* change their vibratory quality from the Fundamental Tone 4 to the Fundamental Tone 5. The change however does not imply an overt *physical* change, because *as bodies* these Fifth-Rounders still belong to the fourth Round, still in existence at the level of the Earth and of human nature as a whole. They are therefore, in a sense, ahead of their planetary time. They are, as K.H. wrote, "a few drops of rain that announce the future coming of the monsoon."

If now we think of the vibratory quality 6, it should be clear that the beginning of the sixth subrace of the present fifth Root Race will slightly open a door through which an even more radical transformation of human beings will be made possible. We are told, however, that the change from a Fundamental 4 to a Fundamental 6—that is, moving ahead more than one number—is not possible except as a result of a "Mystery," the "Mystery of the Buddha." What this Mystery is remains unexplained, though some have tried to explain it; but Gautama the Buddha, and his successor, Sri Sankaracharya—who in a sense "opposed" (that is, polarized) the exoteric doctrines of developing Buddhism—are said to be Sixth Rounders.[4]

What this means is therefore simply that, for some "mysterious" reason, at a time of the Earth's fourth Round at which the vibratory quality 6 was due to start operating in an active manner (at least at the higher mental levels of the one planetary Mind) Gautama was born with the capacity to bring to a focus in a body of Earth-matter, the Root-manifestation of that quality. Sri Sankaracharya, founder of the Adwaita School of Hindu philosophy, was apparently the polarizing aspect of that manifestation, and thus is also called a Sixth Rounder. Through the Buddha, the release of this vibratory quality 6 affected "the White Lodge"—that is, the state of consciousness of those who were to become the Pleroma, (the spiritual Seed Harvest) of Humanity. It is also said, after he had discarded his physical body, the "inner vehicles" of Gautama were mysteriously "kept" to become those used in the incarnation of the Christ.

Whether or not this refers to an occult fact, it should

be clear that a definite relationship exists between the Buddha and the Christ—in whatever way one interprets such a relationship according to one's philosophical-occult outlook. This relationship has a simple historical and spiritual character. Buddhist missionaries were sent by the great Buddhist king of India, Asoka, to the shores of the Dead Sea in Palestine (third century B.C.); and it is not impossible that the community to which Jesus belonged (H.P.B. said it was not the Essenes, but a sect called "the Poor" which refused any possessions) received its original inspiration from these Buddhist missionaries.

In a deeper sense, Buddha in the sixth century B.C. represents the Seed of a long precessional cycle, while Christ symbolizes the Germ of a new cycle. Buddha stands for all-encompassing Wisdom; Christ for the Redeeming Love that alone can heal and "save" human beings distraught by the responsibility of an individualized consciousness burdened with the power to make "free" choices. This power implies as well the possibility and therefore ultimately the responsibility to radically transfigure the fourth Round character of human nature. This transformation, if it is total, begins with higher Knowledge and individualizing power of vibration 5 (the Kumara Mind), but it needs the release of universal love and compassion abstractly symbolized by Number 6 in order to bring an individual human being to the level of the consciousness of the White Lodge.

The initial manifestation, public and collective, of such an exalted state of consciousness demands the formation of a planetary type of society. This possibility of it is now with us, and it is the reason for the development of the Western mentality and our recent technology. The greatness of our Euro-American civilization fundamentally resides in its ability to bring any human being anywhere in contact with all others and to escape the gravitational pull of this physical globe of matter, thus allowing men to clearly see and experience the Earth as an external objective entity supporting, yet not irrevocably binding, the consciousness of Man.

I repeat that it is *because* of the development of the actual, concrete possibility which <u>Man has now acquired to</u> <u>become an integrated whole *in conscious and physical*</u> <u>*fact* that the occult revelation of the last hundred years</u> <u>has taken place.</u> This revelation, mainly through Theosophy, has limits and a specific character conditioned by the need and as well the relatively narrow receptivity of the people to whom it has been addressed, and of the individuals through whom it could only be formulated; but such limitations are inescapable. They simply have to be understood, if the revelation is to make sense and to lead to a further release of consciousness and power which, according to H.P.B. <u>is now imminent.</u>

References and Notes

1. The contact with the Masters was broken by this remarkably proud Englishman; yet his real abilities found their use in the more mundane political field and he became the prime mover of the Indian Congress which played a historical role in freeing India from British rule.

2. cf. *The Mahatma Letters,* p. 43, 96-117.

3. This is the foundation of a true Numerology, of what I called long ago *Arithmosophy.*

4. An unfortunate confusion apparently exists between the original Sankaracharya—the first of a long series of leaders of the movement he had initiated in Southern India who all took the same name—and a much later Sankaracharya who reformed the movement. Orientalists insist that this latter Sankaracharya who lived in the 8th century A.D. is the original one; but an initiated member of this branch of Hinduism, Subba Row—one of the early members of The Theosophical Society in India—brought forth a seemingly convincing rebuttal of the Orientalists' claim. He shows that the original Sankaracharya "was born in the year 510 B.C., 51 years and two months after the date of the Buddha's Nirvana as 477 B.C. Buddhists also refer to Buddha's nirvana and his ParaNirvana at his death. cf. *The Esoteric Writings of Subba Row,* p. 162 and 163 (Theosophical Publishing House, 1910).

PART TWO

Of Time and Cycles

5. TIME AND THE CYCLIC STRUCTURE OF COSMIC PROCESSES

Man's most primary experience is the experience of change. It is a disturbing experience for the mind that wants to establish itself in a secure and dependable position from which it can objectively consider, remember and give value to the mass of impacts, sensations, and feelings which unceasingly reach the consciousness. In human beings consciousness becomes what Teilhard de Chardin has called "reflective consciousness," a consciousness able to sufficiently separate itself from the data it receives to consider that data as something apart and thus reflect on it. Such a consciousness in order to function adequately must acquire an at least relatively unchanging frame of reference; and no frame of reference can appear securely stable unless it is centered around some kind of fundamental realization or intuitive feeling—the feeling that there is an "I" which is the experiencer of the ever-changing impressions reaching the consciousness.

In its attempts to maintain its position of at least relative changelessness while coming to terms with its experience of unceasing change, the human I-consciousness and its tool, the mind, devised—or became receptive to—the idea of "time." Time is the universal experience of change transformed by the mind into an abstract concept. In becoming an abstract concept time seems to refer to something within which actual, perceptible changes occur. Thus time is made by the abstract mind to be the "container" of changing events. In the same way, the concept of space arises in order to attribute an external "place" to sets of experiences which it seems necessary to bind together into entities essentially different from "I, myself." Relationships of a particular character had also to be established between the "I" and the other entities in order that the mind would know how to come to terms with them. Space therefore was thought of as some kind of container within which relationships with external entities occupying a definite place could be given definite values.

The concept of space is an abstraction of the experience of relationship, just as the concept of time is an abstraction of the experience of change. As relationships also change, man had therefore to think of change in terms of time and space. A further abstraction led to the concept of "process." This concept refers to changes which have repeatedly been known to occur in a clearly definable sequence in which each change is structurally and purposefully related to all others in the series.

Strictly speaking, the concept of process implies a *closed* series of activities requiring a more or less definite expenditure of energy for a definable purpose. If we speak of "life processes" it is because we are referring to series of activities performing an organic function within some kind of organism. The term organism, however, should be extended to any (at least relatively) closed system of interrelated and interdependent activities having some overall purpose—for instance, that of perpetuating its specific character and rhythm of operation, of expanding the scope of its activities through increasing productivity, and in most cases of reproducing itself or creating multiple reflections of its own image by following characteristic procedures or techniques.

It should be obvious—though it does not seem to be so for some philosophers, so confused and ambiguous is the concept of time—that there can be no sequence of activities, thus no process, without time; that is, without one event or phase of a process succeeding and preceding another. Change—actual, perceptible, feeling-engendering change—not only implies time; it *is* time in operation within some kind of field of energies acting upon substantial units at whatever level of substance this may be—from the grossest matter to the most subtle and imponderable "primordial stuff" which, in comparison, we are likely to think of as "spiritual."

When the Hindu philosopher speaks of an endless series of *manvantaras* and *pralayas* (states of cosmic manifestation and nonmanifestation), and of "the Great Breath"—the exhalations and inhalations of a Creative God—then speaks of time and the sequence of past, present, and future as an illusion, he is simply attempting to force the student to modify his strictly human and experiential concept of time by confronting him with a paradox—a technique often used in occult teaching and spiritual development. H.P.B.'s *The Secret Doctrine* is full of such a procedure which is traditional and particularly used in Zen Buddhism. We find it also in Christian Gospel, especially in the Beatitudes and related sayings.

This technique implies that the way the mind *interprets and conceptualizes its basic experiences* must be transformed when the consciousness passes from one level of activity and organization to the next. *Nothing* at the level of the vibrational quality 5 can be apprehended, understood and formulated in the same manner as at the 4 level. A change of basic frame of reference must occur—a metanoia—and this requires "taking a step ahead" in man's evolution. The whole of Indian philosophy and yoga is polarized by that one purpose— taking the next step ahead. Everything else—including what we in the West usually mean by "truth"—is secondary, in spite of many references to a capitalized Truth. This Truth is simply the particular frame of reference as far as anything in the solar system is concerned —unless an individual mind somehow succeeds in piercing through the Ring-Pass-Not of our heliocosm and begins to resonate the galactic level of truth. But what must appear "universal" for entities that are "cells" operating within this heliocosmic field of activity, becomes a *particular* statement and interpretation of existential fact for Minds that would operate at the level of galaxies.

We seem to have to pass from particular to universal values and interpretations—of spirit, matter, time, space, process etc.—as our consciousness expands according to its normal and steady rhythm of expansion and always greater inclusiveness—but in fact the change is one that leads from a' narrower particular to a wider particular. Yet there are critical points in this process leading from level to level at which the mind may suddenly break through the boundaries of the lesser field and become illumined by the realization of the transcending character of existence in the greater Whole. This is what most likely is meant by *satori,* or the experience of "the unitive state" experienced by the mystic. It may be a deep realization of what essentially wholeness means; or a feeling-experience (to use inadequate terms) of the light and activity of the greater Whole flooding—or reflected upon—the consciousness of the mystic.

What the mystic confusingly calls the timeless state, or "the instant" of illumination, is no denial of the existence of time as normally experienced by human beings in the Earth's biosphere. When the mystic "returns" to the normal state of the human mind in this fourth Round of the Earth's evolution he finds that his clock has not stopped, nor has the Earth-globe ceased rotating according to his day-night rhythm of revolving around the Sun (the cycle of the year). Earth-time has not been affected, but the individual consciousness has temporarily transcended it by becoming *attuned and responsive to a quality of existence* far more inclusive than these Earth-rhythms. In the Bible and other Sacred Books, it is stated that a Day of the Lord is like a thousand years of men. Thus is accepted the fact that time exists also in the "divine" world of existence. Time must exist if this is a world of activity; whether we call that activity cosmic, mental, or spiritual does not matter as long as there is action and therefore change of some sort. But the character of this divine time must evidently differ from that of our human time, and the processes operating in the divine world inevitably have to be of a nature which it is most difficult, if not impossible, for us, as humans, to conceive.

One may nevertheless imagine a divine world in which time would have no past, in the sense that to the consciousness operating in that world there are only creative processes in which what is released "in the beginning" as seed-potentiality of existence unfolds in a straight line—or as many radii emanating from one center—in progressive stages of actualization until what is potential in the beginning (alpha state) becomes perfectly actualized (omega state), and therefore activity totally ceases. In such a divine time-sequence, there would be no looking back and no regressive step. Activity would exclusively be the exteriorization or expression of an initial impulse containing in latency all that would gradually unfold in creative time.

We could likewise imagine a kind of space measurable only by the intensity and direction of the divine, creative intent. If at any particular moment, God seeks relationship with any entity in the universe (or in *His* universe), at once God *is there*. In such a space, distance becomes determined by intention, and attention. In a sense it is a one-dimensional space, but this dimension can operate in any desired direction. Activity is always straightforward, even if conceivably it could be multilinear should the divine consciousness be able to intend to act simultaneously in several directions.

We could likewise imagine a kind of space measurable only by the intensity and direction of the divine, creative intent. If at any particular moment, God seeks relationship with any entity in the universe (or in *His* universe), at once God *is there*. In such a space, distance becomes determined by intention, and attention. In a sense it is a one-dimensional space, but this dimension can operate in any desired direction. Activity is always straight-forward, even if conceivably it could be multilinear should the divine consciousness be able to intend to act simultaneously in several directions.

In contrast to this we can think of time as absolutely cyclic and totally repetitive, and of space as rigidly bound by unbreakable boundaries. This would be the time of Nietzsche's Eternal Return, according to which every aspect of a one and only universal cycle of existence would be infinitely repeated without any possibility of change. Undoubtedly some ancient philosophers, perhaps in India and most likely in Greece, have presen-ted such a concept of time; but it is difficult to know the real reasons for their doing so and to what extent they ac-tually believed in its absolute character. It is a typically rationalistic concept produced by a type of mind which, as it were, worships its own power of formulation and definition. It is a mind intent upon bringing every phase of human experience to a clear and logical focus, and dismissing any possibility not included in a definite form. This form could be immense and cosmic, or it might be individualized by a particular set of human cir-cumstances and conditioning; but in either case it would be finite, definitely structured according to rational prin-ciples (however suprarational and cosmic these might be), measurable and inescapable.

Unfortunately, when the intellectually college-trained person of our century is confronted with the concept of "cycle," his or her first reaction is to think of it in terms of the Nietzschean Eternal Return, and usually to dis-miss it. Since the Council of Constantinople in the fifth century A.D. the concepts of cyclic activity and cyclic process have been repudiated by the church and the of-ficial mentality of the Euro-American culture, having been declared heretical. This repudiation had very grave results in the development of our Western thought. It was part of an attempt to make the coming of Christ a unique event dividing the history of mankind into a radically different "before" and "after." In so doing the Fathers of the Church followed the Jewish tradition which also gave to the Exodus and relationship between a personal God and Moses, his Lawgiver, a definitely historical character—history being conceived as a straight line, unidirectional movement. During the nineteenth century, as men's minds were glowing with pride in the achievements of science, this movement took the form of irrevocable "progress" from barbarism to ever more glorious and expansive manifestations of civilization; but unfortunately our Western world understood and interpreted such a linear development almost exclusively in terms of material well-being and inflated technological productivity. This interpretation made of it a tragic shadow of the divine world of spontaneous and radiant creativity—thus evoking satanic powers and perversions of the mind which may lead to "black magic" on a large scale.

It became essential therefore to try to reinterpret the linear straightforward motion of evolutionary progress at a spiritual level, and to show how that movement of the divine time-process could be integrated with the circular movement of time. The result of this integration is the concept of time as a logarithmic spiral which is the true representation of the world-process. In this world-process spiritual creativity—straightforward motion operating in many directions (many universes, many dimensions of cosmic existence)—is constantly associated with the circularity of the formative Mind and its processes of focalization and functional integration. Thus three fundamental types of motion, and therefore three essential modes of activity, are found represented in man's experience of change and process, an experience which at least *reflects* the basic realities of the cosmos.

To these three kinds (or modalities) of time, three different concepts (or modes of apprehension) of space correspond: (1) multilinear space defined by the character and intensity of intentional relationship, and in which distance is qualitative rather than quantitative and measurable; (2) three dimensional space in which every existential unit occupies a definable and measurable place and at some distance (minute as it may be) from other units; and (3) space in which the *interpenetration* of everything by everything else is an essential factor in the development of ever more inclusive and "plenary" modes of relatedness and interdependence, the motive power of which is universal Love.

H.P.B. in *The Secret Doctrine* speaks of three schemes of universal evolution: spiritual, intellectual and physical.[1] These can be related to the three basic concepts of time and space just mentioned; and to the experiences which have given rise to these concepts. It is also stated that "each [of these three systems] is represented in the constitution of man, the Microcosm of the great Macrocosm; and it is the union of these three streams which makes him the complex being he now is."

Circularity and cyclicness are related to mind, but to the mind which establishes order in the apparent chaos of "chance happenings" in a world in constant change. One may call this mind *cosmogenic* because it generates order and also beauty (the two main meanings of the Greek term, cosmos) in the human consciousness. It relates the confusing and apparently irrational sequence of life-events—that is, what Western man calls and almost worships as "chance"—to basic principles establishing a cosmic frame of reference. Science tries to discover such principles, referring to them as "Laws of Nature"—an awkward term for scientists who refuse to believe in a Lawgiver—but modern science shies from making of them the expression of an overall purpose that would relate end to beginning, and postulates an *omega* state to polarize an *alpha* state now appearing in scientific theories as a "Big Bang" starting the universe.

It is the end of a process that makes the start of it meaningful. The value of the world outlook presented by the eminent Jesuit philosopher-scientist, Teilhard de Chardin, resides in his providing a meaningful end to evolution. But such an outlook essentially is a reflection of the ancient traditional occult picture of the universe upon the inspired mind of a Catholic thinker—and interestingly enough much of this outlook took form while Teilhard lived for many years, as an anthropologist, in or near Central Asia.

The ancient picture of world-processes recurring at an always new level (or dimension) gives a far greater and more enlightening meaning to human experience because it is holistic. The vast cosmic cycle is reflected and multiplied almost *ad infinitum* in a myriad of smaller cycles, which form a hierarchy of manifestations extending from the level of unity to that of ever increasing multiplicity, until the "bottom" of the process is reached and multiplicity is transformed into unity through a series of periodical integrations, and thus through the gradual *simplification of relationships* between the Many.

Each phase of a cosmic process begins in a new— though secondary, tertiary, quaternary, etc.—release of spiritual energy. Each of these releases (or "quanta") of energy has a unitarian character, reflecting at a new level the original One that started the entire cosmic process. It manifests or expresses a spiritual quality. This quality can be personified as an Entity. Being a reflection of the One Source, it can be called a "Monad." A name can be given to it symbolizing the "quality" it characterizes within the entire world-process. Thus Occultism speaks of a multitudinous hierarchy of Beings each having specific attributes and a sacred (and secret) Name. Yet, at a more abstract and esoteric level of understanding, it is the phase of the process which is the essential reality. Then the cosmic Office is emphasized rather than the Officient who performs the activities required by the Office: the particular type of Mastery, rather than the being who, when he occupies the position of Master, ceases to be, strickly speaking, an "individual" in the sense that he has become identified with a phase of the process and thus with a cosmic or planetary quality. Nevertheless, he appears as an individual person if he has to deal with and affect men who are still at the level of individualized egos.[2]

The value of such an "occult" picture of the world-process resides in giving to *all* activities at all levels of space and time the character of identifiable phases of processes of different scope and length. Each of these activities, as a phase of a structure and purposeful process, has a particular meaning. This meaning can be perceived by the mind who thinks in terms of process and cyclic phases. Such a type of thinking brings to man's consciousness intellectual understanding. It should be associated with an intuitive grasp of the ever-present reality of the creative straightforward motion of spirit lest it lead to the Nietzschean concept of ever-repeating identical sequences of events. This Nietzschean concept denies that there are infinite possibilities of solutions to the problems of existence. It denies the infinite capacity of the Divine Mind to "imagine" always different universes for Its manifestation. Geometrically speaking, it reduces all spirals to closed circles.

The seed that ends a cycle is always potentially susceptible of mutation. But while there undoubtedly are wild mutations produced by a polluted environment or (at a human level) a perversion of the spiritual power of imagination, mutations normally occur according to a pattern of cosmic (whether microcosmic or macrocosmic) order. They significantly lead to new phases of the process of activity according to an archetypal "plan" defining the structural order of *activity-sequences* and the character of the *agents* able to bring to a focus the precise quality of action required for the operation of every particular phase.

The structures of cycles are, in the occult sense of the term, archetypes. Archetypal knowledge does not deal with events *per se* but with their structural sequence. It is indeed most important to differentiate between "archetypal" and "existential." The same archetypal structure may link—"contain" would be a rather inadequate term—very different events. To these different events it gives the same cyclic meaning. The rose blossoming on the rosebush in the spring 1975 is not a combination of *the same* molecules and atoms which formed roses on the same bush in 1974; and if the 1975 weather is bad, the new roses may be imperfect. Yet they will still embody the archetypal quality, Rosehood, and will still be spring-time in the year-cycle.

We should never forget these facts when we think of cycles or try to draw conclusions from a knowledge of cycles. This knowledge does not allow us to accurately predict all events, but only the structural relationship between events. It helps us, if we are a gardener or botanist, to envision the oak in the seed; but too many possibilities concerning the relationship of a particular oak to its total enviroment may become precipitated into concrete events affecting the growth of the tree to allow us to be certain of the exact character of each phase of this growth. We can be sure nevertheless that the acorn will not grow into a plum tree.

Cyclic knowledge is mind-knowledge—however vast and encompassing the mind may be. It is structural knowledge. It is only one mode of knowing; but this mode is all-important in situations where disorder, confusion, and emotional biases prevail. It does not take the place of direct experience, whether at the personal or the spiritual level; but it enables the experiencer to place his experience in a frame of reference which reveals their eonic significance—i.e. the function they occupy within the entire life-span. And many a mystical vision or peak-experience results in no permanent, basic transformation of the consciousness because it cannot be formulated and assimilated. It does not "belong" anywhere. It may turn into toxic material for the confused and unstructured consciousness.

Such a possibility became most evident as a result of the Industrial Revolution of last century. This produced a definite psychological need, and this need has increased a hundredfold during the last decades. The ancient concept of cyclic time which was declared heretic some fifteen centuries ago has to be revitalized and expanded to meet that collective need of Western humanity. As the traditional frames of reference of the Euro-American culture are shattered by the relentless surge of new creative spiritual currents, of which our society reveals so far mostly the dark materialistic reflection in its insane worship of unstructured "growth" and productivity at all cost, the study of cycles can bring back to distraught individuals a new, deeper, yet also intensely personal, sense of order.

Order, meaning, beauty and the inner sustainment arising from the conviction that one has a place and function to perform within a vast planetary process whose essential nature is rhythm and harmony regardless of the grinding noise of passing dissonances—what could be more valuable for men, women and children of our civilization headed toward chaos?

References and Notes

1. *The Secret Doctrine* I. 181 "There exists in Nature a triple evolutionary scheme for the formation of three periodical Upadhis; or rather three separate schemes of evolution, which in our system are inextricably interwoven and interblended at every point. These are the Monadic (or spiritual), the intellectual and the physical evolutions .... Each of these three systems has its own laws, and is ruled and guided by different sets of the highest Dhyanis or Logoi." The term, intellectual, may however be confusing. It refers here to the higher Mind and is said to be represented by the givers of intelligence and consciousness to man—the Promethean Spirits of Kumaras.

2.   cf. *The Secret Doctrine* I, p. 174. "Metaphysically speaking, it is of
     course an absurdity to talk of the 'development' of a Monad, or to say
     that it becomes 'Man.' But any attempt to preserve metaphysical
     accuracy of language in the use of such a tongue as English would
     necessitate at least three extra volumes of this work and would entail an
     amount of verbal repetition which would be wearisome in the extreme.
     It stands to reason that a *Monad* cannot either progress or develop, or
     even be affected by the changes it passes through . . ."

     Yet H.P.B. differentiates "three great classes" of Monads and the
     "stages" they pass through. Later on (p. 177) she writes: "As the
     spiritual Monad is One, Universal, Boundless and Impartite, whose
     rays, nevertheless, form what we, to our ignorance, call the "Individual
     Monad" of men . . . It would be very misleading to imagine a Monad as
     a separate Entity trailing its slow way in a distinct path through the
     lower Kingdoms, etc." (p. 178) Yet it is what many books seem to
     describe.

6. HUMAN CYCLES OF UNFOLDMENT

When one deals with human beings, two basic sets of factors have to be considered. A third no doubt exists which, however, transcends ordinary knowledge and cannot be discussed here. A man or woman is first of all a *human* organism, operating at the level of human nature, which itself has to be considered part of the Earth's biosphere and subject to planet-wide rhythms and influences. Then this man or woman may present characteristics indicating that an individualizing process has been operating, not merely in terms of surface modifications of a particular type of human nature, conditioned also by environmental sociocultural patterns, but in terms of truly individual responses to events and everyday pressures.

In my book *Fire out of the Stone,* a reformulation of the basic images of our Christian Tradition (1950-1961), I spoke of three souls in man, or three fundamental levels at which what we call "Soul"—the essential power of integration operating wherever there are organic manifestations of life—can operate: living soul, individual soul, and divine soul. The existence of these three stages of Soul-evolution which exist at least in potentiality in the human kingdom are clearly indicated in the Bible. In Genesis 2, God operating under the symbolic name of JHVH (Jehovah or Yahweh) endows man with a "living soul." This living soul does not basically differ at first from the soul of animals and it is given the same name. But in man the potentiality of a higher mode of Soul-activity was latent even at the beginning of human evolution in the passive Edenic state. It was latent in the ability Adam—a symbol for the early Root-Races of theosophical lore—had to *name* everything he saw or met. This potentiality of objective consciousness became developed through various crises in consciousness, and particularly with the coming to the Earth of the *Ben-Elohim* (the "Sons of God-Elohim") who "married" the daughters of men. These were the Promethean or Kumaric Spirits who gave to Man the fiery spark of self-consciousness, self-determination and, therefore, moral responsibility. The result turned out to be largely destructive, leading to the Deluge and a totally new humanity (the fifth Root-Race, born, according to *The Secret Doctrine*, in central Asia a million years ago).

The development of the "individual soul" is symbolized in the Biblical tradition by Moses's meeting with God in His aspect of "I Am That I Am"—which means God as the spiritual-cosmic Principle of Individualization. With the coming of Christ, the possibility for mankind as a whole to develop the "divine soul" was revealed. But very few individual human beings have actualized such a potentiality in their lives. According to the symbolism of number briefly mentioned in a preceding chapter, the living soul vibrates to 4, the individual soul to 5, and the divine soul to 6. The student of Theosophy will no doubt identify these numbers with the fourth, fifth and sixth "principles" in the constitution of man—*kama, manas,* and *buddhi.*

As already stated, because we are in a fourth Round—and the American Indian traditions speak of "the fourth world"—the fundamental vibration of human nature (and of the Earth's biosphere as a whole) is 4. It is the vibration to which life on our planet generically responds. It is the vibration of man's living soul. And students of occult philosophy should know that Number 4, by a process known as "Kabbalistic addition," becomes 10 (1+2+3+4 equals 10). At the level of the living soul 10 is therefore a highly important number and the basis of the decimal system of measurement, soon to be universally adopted.

Another number, 7, figures prominently in occult tradition. It is seen to be definitely related to the most basic patterns of evolutionary unfoldment, at least in our present world system. It can also be shown to refer to the most important cycle in the development of a human being at all levels, as the pattern of man is a microcosmic reflection of the pattern of the great cosmos. Around a circle, and tangent to it, six circles of the same size and tangent to each other can be drawn. This illustrates the relationship between the six and a central seed-unit which is the seventh—or the first, depending on the way one looks at the situation, i.e. pastward back to the One, or futureward in terms of a synthesizing process (a harvesting).

It is this seven-year cycle which we wish now to study. It should be stressed, however, that such a cycle does not imply that particular *events* repeat themselves every seven years; for, as already stated, cycles refer to structural patterns in the development of specific qualities of existence and of human faculties at particular levels, but not—or at least not essentially—to the actual events making possible or hindering this development. We shall discuss, first, the basic character of *any* seven-year cycle in a human life, according to which every year of the cycle can be given a very general, yet often most revealing, meaning; then we shall study the series of seven-year cycles during a man's life-span.

The length of the life-span of human beings obviously varies; yet traditionally one can speak of an archetypal life-span, whether or not any particular human being actually lives a shorter or longer period. We shall discuss, however, two archetypal life-spans: a 70-year period which refers specifically to the level of development of the "living soul," and an 84-year period in terms of the "individual soul."

THE SEVEN-YEAR PATTERN

In occult analysis a cycle of seven units can generally be divided into two hemicycles, each lasting 3½ units. The first hemicycle represents an involutionary sequence and the other a symmetrical evolutionary ascent. The involutionary descent operates through the three basic levels of cosmic energy—spirit, mind and life—and the movement of return (evolution) passes in reverse order through these same levels.

The figure shown below schematizes this wave-process; but while it assuredly helps to grasp something of the structure of the process, it also tends to crystallize an unfortunate picture of up-and-down movement—of spirit, mind, and life as separate layers. A better diagram would be produced by two spirals within a circle, one centrifugal (from center to circumference) and the other centripetal (the return movement); but it would be far more complex and still not really adequate in two dimensions.

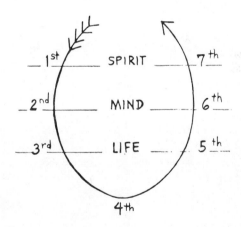

The first three years of the process—most of the *involutionary* hemicycle—represents the progressive unfoldment outward and clarification of the new cyclic impulse, and the gradual response of the new materials drawn into the field of energies produced by that creative or transforming impulse. The fourth year is the turning point, the bottom of the cycle— and this constitutes a probable critical state; the impulse may scatter itself and lead to disintegration and failure, or it may find in the integrated materials gathered into the field the organized concrete vehicle for complete actualization and fulfillment. The process of concrete actualization operates through the last three years of the seven-year cycle, the seventh year being both the seed-consummation of the cycle and the seed-foundation out of which the new cycle will unfold.

The year-by-year analysis which follows is made in as broad terms as possible; it has to be reformulated with reference to whatever the actual situation, heredity, and environment of the individual are in the particular instance being considered.

First year—(the first, eighth, fifteenth, twenty-second, etc. years of a human life). The type of development which will characterize the entire seven-year cycle manifests as a new impulse, or a new compulsion of destiny, on the basis of what has developed in the last year of the preceding cycle. The impulse, or new beginning, is usually not clear; even though some definite occurrence may set the stage for it. Very often, that year is peculiarly elusive and uncertain in character, or filled with emotional confusion. The real things which occur take place inside, below the level of individualized consciousness. Life seems neither one thing nor another. Yet in some cases there is great impulsiveness and emotional intensity; perhaps a sense of freedom and of new beginnings.

Second year—(the second, ninth, sixteenth, twenty-third, etc. years). On one hand, the new impulse and the new destiny should then begin to repolarize the life and the substance of the person's feelings; on the other hand, a great deal of resistance against the new is likely to manifest. What was developed in the preceding cycle may oppose the new trend; or else the new trend has to push through the old ideas step by step. Psychological conflicts may well occur. Decisions may have to be taken. Financial or social issues may arise.

Third year—(the third, tenth, seventeenth, twenty-fourth, etc. years). The new trend takes on a more definite form. The mind usually receives, clearly or not, the vision of what life offers to the individual. A definite period of exteriorization and action should begin, even though one may feel very lonely and the ideals may seem unrealizable and one's abilities most inadequate. This lack of technique and of adequate means is often acute; yet there is a deep sense that one has to go on, perhaps amounting to emotional, irrational enthusiasm or devotion.

Fourth year—(the fourth, eleventh, eighteenth, twenty-fifth, etc. years). This is theoretically the period of "embodiment" of the impulse-idea, the *leaf* stage of vegetation. But while new energies are likely to be released and new forms of living consolidated, it may also mean conflict and struggle—or at least a choice or decision at the core of a more or less acute personal or social crisis. At three and a half (i.e. at the mid point of the fourth, eleventh, eighteenth, etc. years of the life) a turning point may be experienced; yet it often need not take the form of a sharply defined event. Events are not actually what count, but rather what response we give to them; it is the quality of the response which will mean, at the end of the cycle, relative success or failure.

Fifth year—(the fifth, twelfth, nineteenth, etc. years). This is the symbolical stage of the *flower*. Theoretically, the "vision" phase of the third year now comes to a phase of actual manifestation and enjoyment— provided the growth has proceeded healthily! 5 on the "evolutionary" ascent balances 3 on the "involutionary" descent. If the process is completely negative, the five-pointed star is inverted, a symbol of destruction.

Sixth year—(the sixth, thirteenth, twentieth, etc. years). This is the symbolic stage of the *fruit*. The seeding process has begun within the flower; now the consciousness should begin to be aware of a "mystery," of deeper depths, of a center of spiritual energy, of the "God within." The urge should be to feed this transcendent realization, to "sacrifice" the past to the future. The creative impulse of the cycle, which has built the "plant" organism of consciousness and individuality (only with reference to this particular seven-year cycle of course!), is now drawn inward, towards the mothering of the seed of the future. Compassion and understanding should be cultivated at whatever level one is operating, and if difficult experiences come, they should be faced with inner strength and peace.

Seventh year—(the seventh, fourteenth, twenty-first, etc. years). This is the *seed* period when a particular seven-year cycle is being concluded and the need for some new life-values and a new phase of destiny or character-development should be felt. It may be experienced with poignant intensity, or in a confused way, or not at all if growth has been arrested or dormant. It could be a year of consummation witnessing some high points of consciousness, but in many cases negative factors may be as apparent as the positive ones, if the original impulse of the cycle has been weak and the pressure of family, group, society has been oppressive or repressive. This seventh-year is both an end and the implied promise (or at least possibility) of a new beginning—a synthesis and a prelude evoking or at least suggesting the main theme of the coming seven-year period. It is an important year because it requires at the same time the willingness to bring some past to a conclusion—as perfect and liberating a one as is possible under the circumstances —and a consciousness open, in inner expectancy and faith, to whatever prompting or intuition of possible development may appear upon the stilled and receptive mind.

Three Score and Ten Years

When one speaks of the "natural" life-span of man, one refers to the conditions prevailing at the particular stage of evolution in which our present mankind is unfolding its powers. In a sense the three score and ten year period (seventy years) often mentioned as the length of an archetypal human life, is a "myth"; that is to say, it expresses the symbolic, yet essential, relationship between human beings and the nature of the Earth's biosphere in which these beings live and from which they draw their sustenance and their strictly "natural" powers. But the nature of the biosphere undergoes gradual changes, and sometimes these are quite radical. It is also possible that, as H.P. Blavatsky stated in letters to A.P. Sinnett, the length of the year has been decreasing considerably since very ancient times, because our planet has been coming gradually closer to the sun. In terms of *existential* values—i.e. of sequences of concrete events —the year cycle should be considered a relative measure of time; yet the *archetypal* pattern—the seventy-year measure—could still be thought of as a permanent factor characterizing mankind at the generic biological level of activity. It can also be related to the ten lunar months of the gestation period—a *lunar* factor as it occurs within the mother's womb which, in this connection, reflects the broader *solar* pattern of ten. This pattern constitutes a formula of human development at the level of the "living soul"—that is, in terms of organic living in a natural state of existence in the biosphere. Organic living includes also the psychic overtones of the functional activities of man's organs, glands and nerves—and of currents of energies undertoning these activities.

This pattern, just as that of the simpler seven-year cycle which is its basic unit, must be wisely applied if it has to serve any purpose at all. As it is both a general and generic frame of reference, it does not deal with "particulars," but only with "universals." It can be used to *relate* events to one another as they follow one another; but *not to predict* any one particular actual event. It is a tool for understanding and for the discovery of meaning—and thus for the understanding of what either has already happened, is happening, or is just about to occur as the result of preceding causes which one can perceive and analyze. It could be used as we use a clock when we have to get ready to leave our office in time to get a good place in a restaurant at lunch time; but looking at the clock will not tell us what will happen on the way to the restaurant and who will sit at the table next to ours.

While the seven-year pattern is applicable to various stages of the development of man's life, the seventy-year cycle refers specifically to the factor of *age*. Because of social prejudices, which differ in various cultures and even at various times in the cyclic development of one culture, "age" is often a not clearly understood factor. At the level of human nature—thus as a factor in the life of every individual person, however "individualized" and unique he or she may be or consider himself or herself to be—age refers to what is now often called the "biological clock" whose rhythms control the interrelationship between all the constituent organs and cells of the organism. The way the clock works is moreover deeply affected by what occurs in the organism's environment; and today more than ever one must consider the sociocultural and political as well as the biospheric environment.

Nevertheless if one thinks of age only in terms of biological and environmental factors one misses the whole point which a study of the seventy-year cycle—and even more of the eighty-four-year cycle presently to be discussed—should reveal. What one does is to regard man as merely an animal organism. Yet the character of man's existence far transcends strictly animal biological values. Man's life on this Earth, even at the level of what I once called "man's common humanity"[1] is a process whose purpose it is *to extract meaning from all conceivable types of activities.* It can be regarded as a "seasonal" process, the entire lifespan being then divided into a number of "seasons of growth" and each of these having an archetypal character of its own.

It is to this archetypal character of the several seasons of growth that, at least in the occult sense, age refers. We are therefore not dealing here with the more or less appealing and socially or personally highly valued character of a certain age period. We are dealing with the specific character of ten basic age-periods whose archetypal functions are to contribute in specific ways to a total and final "harvest of meanings" to be gathered and assimilated by the Soul. Each age-period should provide its own characteristic contribution to this harvest, just as each human "culture-whole" contributes its own harvest of values and meanings—expressed through symbols, creative works and institutions—to the planetary consciousness and the one Mind of Man. Every human being, just because he is human, passes through ten stages of potential development—ten different personal "cultures," each of which vibrates to a basic keynote of human possibility of growth. Each should be evaluated in the light of its potential contribution to the whole life-process, without any abnormally glorified or scorned value being given to it because of sociocultural preconception or bias.

If we consider the life of an individual person we undoubtedly will observe an individualized series of events and developments which may considerably differ from the merely human archetype or generic norm. Growth may be accelerated or retarded in many ways and for many *karmic* reasons (both personal and social-collective karma), some of them producing dramatic or even spectacular results of a positive or negative character. But cyclic patterns do not directly refer to these results, except in the sense that they can help us to understand their meaning in terms of the karma and dharma (the "truth-of-being" or individual selfhood) of the individual Soul to which, generally speaking, the human organism has been karmically drawn through some kind of magnetic resonance. A deviation from the norm has a positive significance if it strengthens, steadies, or increases the individual's ability to actualize his birth-potential; it is negative if it hinders, weakens or disorients and perhaps perverts the process of actualization.

This process of actualization of the birth-potential is not accomplished by denying, ignoring, or trying to escape from the karma of both the individual past and the past of the racial-cultural community in which one is born and educated, but by *using* this karmic conditioning in an individualized and significant manner. Karma and dharma—the past and the future-in-the-making—are actually the two sides of the same coin. Dharma can be fulfilled only *through* the experience of karma. Spiritual living implies going through the karmic remains of the past and, very often, becoming what one is meant to be in spite of what one has been. Man can neutralize karma only by creating a new chain of causes, but such a creation has optimum results when performed in the clarity of a consciousness about to evaluate the archetypal meaning of the time and the season of the performance; and this with reference to the entire life-cycle.

Spiritual creation is always a response to a need. Such a response can be unconscious and spontaneous; but what we call spontaneity is very often only the expression of a superficial mood or emotion, conditioned either by the pressures of our society and its patterns of thinking, feeling, and behavior so long impressed upon our consciousness and our nervous system, or by the memories of our previous responses to life-challenges. This kind of spontaneity may also be purely instinctual and strictly determined by biopsychic factors referring to the common aspects of human nature. These are not to be denied without clearly individualized and conscious reasons; but they should be used, as any of our personal and social possessions have to be used, as our knowledge has to be used. It is always the use we make of knowledge—especially of occult and cyclic knowledge—which proves its validity *to us as individuals*.

All life-cycles should first be divided into two halves. The first hemicycle considered from the point of view of the creative power of spirit, can be called *involutionary* because (at whatever level it may be) it refers to the gradual actualization and embodiment in some kind of concrete substance (not necessarily physical substance) of an originating initial impulse, a creative Word. The first hemicycle is essentially a period of activity—activity leading, if all goes well, to the incorporation of the quality released by the original impulse in some kind of organism; and by organism is meant here any organized system of interrelated and interdependent activities having a definable purpose and life span.

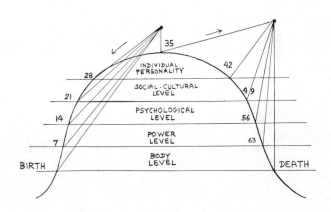

The second hemicycle is *evolutionary,* if seen from the point of view of the consciousness having developed within the organism. If all goes well, this consciousness then radiates in and through mental constructs: ideas, symbols, conceptual systems and theories, and any socio-cultural manifestations. Through these and the harvest of meaning they bring to focus, the human being gathers the material which will reach a point of synthesis at what the Hindus call "the last thought in death." This "thought"—or rather this moment of synthesized consciousness—is said to condition the karma of a future cycle of existence in a new human body.

According to such a cyclic pattern, the thirty-fifth birthday is the turning point. At that point in time the human being should normally reach maturity as a "living soul" able to focus its energies and its generic consciousness in a mind at least relatively well integrated, and thus able to participate in a mature and emotionally steady manner in the building of the higher socio-cultural aspect of his community, tribe, or nation. This man or woman may not be truly individualized in the sense of having actually transferred the center of his or her consciousness from the biopsychic to the mental-spiritual level; yet he or she can act as a mature person with a clearly distinct character in the fulfillment of whatever place and function he or she occupies in the social environment. The term "personality" is used here to mean the capacity a human being has to take a distinctive stand among the crowd and more or less forcefully and effectively to impress upon others the quality of thinking, feeling, or behavior this stand implies.

Theoretically, and indeed in most instances after thirty-five, the biological forces acting through the physical organism begin to lose some of their power. A slow process of *devolution* becomes set and eventually leads to crystallization and deterioration in old age, and perhaps to senility. But another process may and should begin to operate in an opposite and polar direction, and at another level. If it takes place at all, this process represents a *building in consciousness*, succeeding at a mental-social-cultural level the earlier process of building a concrete organism of personality, which theoretically reaches some kind of apex in the vicinity of the thirty-fifth birthday. Thus, during the first thirty-five years, the building forces in man operate biologically and psychologically at the physical-personal level; then, if the momentum has reached a proper basis of operation, they become *repolarized* at the sociocultural communal level along lines of forces established in the mind-field of human activity.

This repolarization could lead to a continual process of development until bodily death occurs, but if this should be the case it would be because the human being has been able to transfer the very center of his consciousness, the I-focus, from the biopsychic level of natural man vibrating to the planetary 4 to the mental-spiritual level of a *definitely individualized* person in whom the vibration 5 has become dominant. Such a dominance is needed if the entropy (or disintegrative trend) of the body energies and cellular substance is to be effectively counteracted after the age of fifty-six; but even then the counteraction may only be partial and fade out. If it succeeds in keeping the bodily instrumentality of consciousness—mainly the brain, but also the endocrine glands and the heart—responsive to the expanding and self-clarifying consciousness, this is ample proof that the person's life has become reorganized in mid-life and shifted to the rhythm of the eighty-four-year cycle. Such a shift undoubtedly was potential at birth, but the definite evidence of its having actually occurred in most cases should be looked for at some time during the late thirties—perhaps around the turning-point of the seven-year cycle from thirty-five to forty-two. Very often at that time some event or decision can be found pointing to a further change during "the dangerous forties."

If we should try to ascertain the character of each of the ten seven-year cycles within the whole life-span of the human being we should once more be sure to realize that only general trends or principles can be stated. These should help us to understand the meaning of actual events in a person's life but in no way should serve as a reliable basis for prediction.

The first seven years constitute above all a period of body-building but, in a deeper sense, they are concerned with the original and most basic *adjustment* of the innate potential of the newborn to the pressures of the environment. What at birth is a field of "pure potentiality" faces the constant challenge to define its main lines of response to body functions, family, society, school, etc. The child tries to find out how far he can go and retain his base of operation—this with reference to whatever he touches or experiences, especially with the parents whom he absolutely needs, yet whose psychological pressures he tries to resist at every step.

The second cycle (seven to fourteen) reveals the child normally more sure of himself (unless the environmental pressures have been unbearable) and eager to assert his urge to *active self-expression*. He is still one of the tribe, yet the energies of his nature demand to be released in their own way. The child not only responds to changing stimuli and pressures in a differentiated manner, he seeks to affirm his own biopsychic rhythm (which, however, must not be confused with the true individuality). We spoke of this level as that of power because it deals with the building of the ego as a focus for the release of life-power.

The third cycle (fourteen to twenty-one) starts with puberty and the rise of the sex urge. A mostly unconscious yet disturbing feeling of incompleteness forces the adolescent to seek a new orientation toward his associates, toward society in general, and the knowledge and traditions of his culture (high school and college years). This is the period during which the emotions dominate and control the ego-center of power.

The fourth cycle (twenty-one to twenty-eight) is one of

attempted consolidation and *fulfillment of ex-pectation*—or of great restlessness and rebellion against family and social demands. If the latter prevails, whether outwardly or within the consciousness stirred by the ego, the stage is set for the process of individualization. However, real individualization is not proved by one's eagerness to repudiate the past and assert one's ego-will in emotional outbursts against unbearable sociocultural situations. It can manifest in one's ability to transform oneself and to transfer one's center of consciousness to a conscious mind-level in at least relative freedom from biological and emotional compulsions.

We shall presently see the importance of age twenty-eight in the eighty-four-year long life-cycle, but in the seven year pattern it marks the possibility of focusing the results of one's experiences at the sociocultural level as a foundation for the building of a personal status, or even stature. The twenty-one to twenty-eight period is theoretically the one during which a human being finds himself attracted to, or deliberately selects the type of associates, comrades or companions with whom he feels he will be able to develop and stabilize his personality as a functional unit in the larger social process—and therefore this fourth seven-year period (twenty-one to twenty-eight) archetypally represents the natural time for marriage or its present-day equivalents. If, as is now so often the case, such a union of boy and girl occurs before age twenty-one, this tends to mean that the basic tone-quality of the marriage or steady companionship is con-ditioned by psychological factors and emotional needs or impulses rather than by the realization that the union has a procreative and/or sociocultural purpose, i.e. the perpetuation of the human race and/or of one's culture, religion, and family-tradition. Here again, from the point of view of such a study of life-cycles, what mat-ters is not the actual events in the associative process, but the quality of the performance and the character of the purpose with which it is associated.

With the fifth seven-year period (twenty-eight to thirty five) the creative potentiality inherent in the outcome of the four preceding periods should be released. However, there may be no creative or transforming release whatever, and the still young person simply becomes gradually more set as a replica—with only superficial modifications—of a particular human type and of the social pattern which his parents exemplified before him.

Whatever happens conditions the second half of the life. If maturity in the mid-thirties brings at least a relatively important development of the personalitized consciousness in terms of the traditional and quasi-official structure of culture and society, the human being is able to go on with that process, whose field of action is the mind associated with feeling responses. Such a person may make a real contribution to his or her society. At least he may effectively fill a role determined or conditioned by his or her karma. Yet that contribution usually has a crystallizing effect upon the character. In other cases, the period thirty-five to forty-two may witness some cathartic experiences, especially during the thirty-ninth year (after the thirty-eighth birthday), which *71-72* may contain in germ the crisis of the mid-forties.

During the "dangerous forties," either the individual settles to routine and a resigned acceptation of a life pattern which he or she seems unable or unwilling to alter, or a sharp revision of attitude may occur, especially toward one's intimates or one's religious beliefs. This very often leads to an emotional and often confused attempt to make a new start, or merely to an escape from a seemingly unbearable situation. This is the age period which used to send most people to psychiatrists and analysts; and it still does, except that now every age period seems to reveal a similar need for psychological problems and more or less real emotional crises.

After forty-nine mental crystallization often sets in, at least to a degree and as a limitation to the power of changing one's self image and accepting the possibility of

radical life changes. On the other hand, the socially successful person may then assume greater collective
responsibility as a managerial figure or executive. The
physical condition of the body and the state of the vital
forces largely determine what occurs after fifty-six and
especially sixty-three. Each particular case differs, the
more so the more the human being has experienced, even
to a small extent, the transforming power of the process
of individualization. One point nevertheless is worth
mentioning for, in many instances, it may help one to a
deeper understanding of what is taking place after thirty-five.

The basic concept is that the thirty-fifth birthday is
like a kind of hinge. What happens afterward can be
said to reflect the karmic imprint of what occurred from
thirty-five *back to birth*. This means that at thirty-six
and thirty-seven the life reflects some of the karma of
what occurred at thirty-four and thirty-three. Seven
years after thirty-five is related to seven years before thirty-five. Thus the eighteenth birthday is reflected in the
fifty-second birthday; the seventeenth in the fifty-third;
the sixteenth in the fifty-fourth, etc. At forty-nine one
reacts to the karma of what occurred at twenty-one,
because forty-nine is fourteen years after thirty-five; and
twenty-one, fourteen years before thirty-five. Age sixty-
three reflects age seven; and seventy reflects birth, as
the end of a cycle reflects its beginning.

There is no question at all here of similar events. The
connection between after thirty-five and before thirty-five
is subtle and can easily elude the mind conditioned by
thinking only of very specific, actual events. What is involved is the quality of the living, and the manner in
which past experiences and, even more, *events which
failed to happen* (man's "unlived life," as a psychologist
would say), affect the development of the later life. This
must not be taken as a general rule applying to every
year and every person's life, but many significant examples could be given.

Here the difficulty is that only a very intimate knowledge of the life of a person could reveal this type of connection. It is mostly a technique to be used by the person himself in order to gain a more holistic picture of his entire life and understand in a new way the complex ramifications interrelating its various phases. Moreover this seventy-year archetypal pattern tends to be modified or overshadowed by the rhythm of the eighty-four-year long life-cycle when, as is the case in our modern civilization glorifying individualism, the mid-point of the cycle shifts from age thirty-five to age forty-two.

This eighty-four-year cycle theoretically refers to the level of development of the individual soul; its basically mental rhythm at birth is merely a potentiality which in most instances develops only progressively. The numerical basis of this rhythm differs from that of the "living soul" (seventy-year) cycle. The eighty-four-year cycle—which turns out to be the length of a complete revolution of the planet, Uranus, around the Sun—should be divided into three twenty-eight-year sections. The cycle proceeds according to a three-phase rhythm, whereas the seventy-year pattern is basically twofold in structure. A two-beats rhythm is primarily biological; and at the level of the "living soul" in the Earth's biosphere the numbers 2, 4, and 10 are dominant. At the level of the mind, at which the process of individualization operates, numbers 3, 7, and 28 are the essential factors—and 7, by Kabbalistic addition, gives 28 $(1 + 2 + 3 + 4 + 5 + 6 + 7 = 28)$ which, occult tradition claims, is the number of Man.

The Uranian Cycle of Individualizing Transformations

The meaning of the eighty-four-year cycle as an archetype of man's life span has been discussed in various books to which the reader is referred.[2] Thus, during the first thirty-five years, the building forces in man operate biologically and psychologically at the physical-personal level. What should be emphasized here is the transformative character of the cycle. It becomes operative wherever man is either ready and willing to raise, at least to some extent, the level of the foundations of his consciousness, or is driven by the pressure of a civilization stressing intellectual faculties and artificial city-living to changes which his mind may not actually understand. When the vibrational quality of the 5 becomes accentuated as an overtone of the basic natural rhythm of the Earth's biosphere, the tendency consciously, or only half-consciously, to accept the Uranian-Promethean principle of transformation as a dominant factor is bound to appear. But it may take many forms.

The Vedas, whose earliest origin should be traced to the source of our Fifth Root-Race in central Asia— even if the recorded version known today was written at a much later date—are coded witnesses to the appearance of this principle of transformation; but they must be understood in the manner suggested by the modern Indian Seer, yogi, and poet, Sri Aurobindo, in his fascinating book *On the Veda.* In the *Upanishads* and subsequent writings, we see an intense drive toward biopsychic transformation and the emergence of consciousness at a transcendental level taking many forms, some quite extreme and based on a misunderstanding of what is to be accomplished—an accomplishment in which the whole of mankind should be involved in so far as that is possible.

Our Western civilization, since its origins in ancient Greece, has followed an approach to transformation which polarizes, and in this sense complements, the Aryan-Hindu approach. By stressing the development of the rational mind and of an aggressive individualism, European culture has aimed at effecting a theoretically universal transformation of natural man. The development of the typically American way of life, feverishly taking hold of the vast resources of a sparsely inhabited continent—and in the process destroying most of its natives—accentuated the European drive toward this universal transformation by glorifying ego-aggressiveness, material success, and in general all the *transferable products* of the operations of an intellect intent upon subjugating nature in order to satisfy man's craving for comfort and power. Money is transferable social power; and an education stressing the "how to" kind of knowledge—matter-bent, earth-bound, analytical and statistical, then computerized knowledge—is also transferable in the form of textbooks, and university degrees.

The whole atmosphere of American living has been blatant with an ever accelerated drive for change and instant fulfillment at the material-social level; but it is an intoxicating atmosphere which has spread around an increasingly polluted and often devastated biosphere. Intoxication and pollution are inseparable; and so is the artificial prolongation of man's natural life-span inseparable from overpopulation and the exhaustion of natural resources. Considering our present state of affairs it certainly would seem that mass-individualization—as we have sought it—is not the solution. The kind of equalitarianism which actually turns out to be equality between egos, does not usually reflect the ideal of spiritual equality of which Buddha and Christ spoke. The transformation of humanity inevitably must have a hierarchical character, if it is based on individual efforts and understanding, and is not dependent upon transferable recipes for every one sheepishly to memorize and apply in a spirit of competition and greed for success and social prestige.

Individual transformation operates, exceptions notwithstanding, in a dialectical sequence of three phases. These phases, archetypally considered, last twenty-eight years; and, as already stated, 28 is the number of Man for it expands at the level of the conscious mind the implications inherent in number 7. Twenty-eight is also four times 7, and eighty-four is twelve times 7—12 being the symbol of cosmic completion, whether one deals with macrocosmic or microcosmic processes.

The first twenty-eight years begin with physical birth and the embodiment of consciousness in a world of bodies. The second twenty-eight years begins with a more or less accentuated kind of rebirth, and we may speak of "birth in individuality." However, in a great many cases, the human person is not able to experience such a rebirth; if so, the rhythm of the seventy-year pattern is the only one worth considering. Even if the process of individualization has begun, the natural rhythm of generic man still keeps operating at the bio-psychic level of unconscious activities, but the individualizing mind and the ego-will nevertheless can begin to gain strength as overtones of the fundamental vibrations of human nature. Gradually they are able to assert their power of transformation and to offset to some extent the entropy of natural processes.

Around the age of twenty-eight, two important astrological cycles are concluded: the cycle of the "progressed Moon" (twenty-seven and one-third years long) and that of Saturn's revolution around the Sun (twenty-nine and one-half years long). Both refer to the parental past, the Moon being the Mother-symbol, the Sun the symbol of the Father-image—that is, the image which a person makes of his or her father as a result of experiences in family-living. These experiences may be either positive (fulfilling the natural need for a father) or negative (frustrating the fulfillment of the need). What this means is that from age twenty-seven to age thirty the "would-be-individual" is potentially able to become completely objective toward his physical parents, his racial ancestry, and even his culture; and being objective, he can be free from the compulsive pull of the past. He can act as a *creative source of the future.*

This does not mean that he has to (or that he may want to) entirely repudiate all natural attachments to his past. He may even cease, at that time, to indulge in a subjective and emotionally compulsive rebellion—fashionable or ego-motivated—against this past, because, having become more objective to the situation, he may be able to gain a better perspective on the actions of the protagonists involved in it. Nevertheless we can speak of the second twenty-eight-year period of the gradually self-transforming and consciousness-repolarizing individual person as the "antithesis succeeding the thesis represented by the first period of his life." The thesis is human nature in its generic mass vibration, or the collective tradition, the particular society, culture, and religion in which the individual has grown up. The antithesis represents an attempt at a basic differentiation and individualization of consciousness, feelings, and behavior. Such an attempt inevitably implies a separation from what the individual is emerging from; but the separation need not be physical for it refers essentially to the level of consciousness and self-realization.

The stage of "synthesis" theoretically occurs with the start, at age fifty-six, of the third twenty-eight-year period, though evidently in most cases the new emergence (third birth) is a gradual process requiring a gestation period. I have spoken of it as "birth in light" for in the white light of the sun all the colors exist in a state of unity or multiunity.

In the light of the *spiritualized* consciousness, the preceding phases of thesis and antithesis are seen to interpenetrate and interblend. The person is no less an individual for realizing then more clearly and vibrantly his dedication to humanity. In this realization, the ego surrenders *its opacity* and becomes a clear lens focusing into personalized consciousness and activity the *quality of existence* (or, one might say, the mission or dharma) which, from the very beginning of his existence as a particular human organism, it has been his potential destiny to actualize.

Most human beings are not able to experience a truly effectual "third birth." Indeed, even those whose minds are repolarized through a really individual process of rebirth around the age of twenty-eight still constitute a relatively small minority if one considers the entire population of the globe. Yet, in some manner, what remains a potentiality may cast fleeting and at times perhaps quite definite reflections upon the consciousness of still opaque and rigidly bound egos. The Saturnian father-image that took form during childhood and adolescence can be transmuted into the inner center of a personality to some extent responding to the still clouded presence of the Father within of whom Jesus spoke, and that Presence may be increasingly felt during the second Saturn cycle from age twenty-nine to fifty-eight or fity-nine.

At the age of about sixty, Saturn and Jupiter return to the approximate zodiacal positions they occupied at birth; and because these two planets symbolize the social consciousness of a person—and, at a higher level, his approach to religion and the integrative energies of his psyche—their joint cyclic reappearance at their natal places evokes the possibility of a new beginning at a new level of mind and soul activity. As the possibility of establishing the center of his being at the level of the "divine soul" is inherent in every man—remote as this possibility is for most human beings in our present society—that age of sixty may witness the hesitant beginnings of such a spiritualizing process, open to individuals of all races and cultures. It may of course begin much earlier in supernormal cases.

Many persons after sixty—and not a few before—display crystallizing tendencies in mind and feelings, together with a loss of vitality and organic resilience. These are natural tendencies; but these manifestations of biological entropy can be given a harder and more actively negative form if there has been a real degree of individualization during the second twenty-eight-year cycle and if this individualization has allowed the shadow aspect of egocentricity to take control or has led to frustrating and embittering experiences. Then "old age" can lose the glow of radiance of wisdom it so often has in a society and culture built on the overtones of natural living; it can lead to depression, hostility, and tragic sense of futility, emptiness, boredom, and alienation from the life that still surges ever fresh in the new generations. This then is the negative or shadow aspect of the spiritualizing possibility available to all human beings.

Each of the three twenty-eight-year periods in this archetypal eighty-four-year life-cycle not only unfolds its potential in four seven-year subcycles, but the patterns of the latter often display revealing correspondences. In other words, the internal structure of the subcycle from birth to age seven finds itself potentially repeated in the one from twenty-eight to thirty-five at the new level of individualization. In a usually less noticeable manner the period from fifty-six to sixty-three may also reveal corresponding developments at the new level of synthesis of ancestral-collective and individual values. There is also an often clearly recognizable connection between age fourteen and age forty-two (twenty-eight plus fourteen). One can truly think of the much publicized "change of life" (psychological even more than biological, and in males as well as females) as a kind of *puberty in reverse*. The emotional tensions which had followed puberty often are reflected at the level of the mentalized consciousness by an equally emotional crisis in the mid or late forties.

At twenty-one a young person is—or at least was until recently—"coming of age;" and at forty-nine or fifty the active member of society may see his life socially realized, perhaps as an executive. In the third twenty-eight-year cycle this corresponds to age seventy-seven. Death may be impending; but in some instances these last years of the archetypal life-pattern may witness spiritual experiences and the transcendence of death at the level of a mind totally free from the natural entropy which dominates our biosphere.

Correspondences may or may not be revealing to the

mind studying the archetypal patterns—revealing, that is, in terms of the meaning they can give to specific remembered events. But even if there are no apparently significant correlations and reflections, the very attempt to think of one's life in such cyclic terms should help to develop an objective approach and a consciousness of this life-as-a-whole. This whole may be experienced as an unfolding melody, whose tonality reveals the essential character and quality of the purpose of having been born in a particular time and place.

Natal astrology can also be a means to reach a revelatory experience of the meaning of one's life-as-a-whole. Astrology deals with individual cases, and it can help us to follow year by year, or even month by month, the manner in which the basic functional activities in a man's biopsychic organism operate in their constant interrelationships and interblendings. These basic functional activities are symbolized by the ten astrological planets (including the apparently moving Sun and the Moon), each of which moves at a different speed because their orbits occupy different places in the solar system (or heliocosm). It is these places which fundamentally determine the symbolical meanings of the planets, either from a heliocentric or a geocentric point of view, or both.

Astrology can deal with actual events far better than the type of cyclic symbology discussed in this chapter, because it deals with functional activities *at the existential level.* Cyclic patterns that refer to human life in its most universal aspect have, I repeat, the character of archetypes. They show what is possible for every human being simply because of the fact that he or she is human—a representative of the genus *homo sapiens,* but from the occult point of view, even more a microcosm of the universal macrocosm.

The study of these all-human cycles can also throw some very basic light upon the character and significance or purpose of important events—markers in the pattern of destiny—merely because of their occurring at a particular age. One of such events might be marriage, child-bearing for a woman, or even death itself. The fact that such an event occurs during the first, second, or fourth, or seventh year of any *one* of the seven-year cycles can be highly significant. <u>The numerological meaning of the year will normally *undertone* the meaning each partner</u> gives to the marriage. Marriage during the twenty-fifth year (after the twenty-fourth birthday) may be seen to carry the deep impress of vibration 4. It may lead to a critical revaluation of the partner's consciousness and life, also perhaps to conflicts which nevertheless can be harmonized and become the foundation for a self-transformative process. Marriage during a seventh year carries the meaning of "seed" realization, out of which a new life can assuredly be expected sooner or later to emerge.

In most cases the ages of the partners vibrate to different cyclic notes. Today, however, because of our type of school education in which boys and girls of the same age are thrown together in daily contacts, marriage—whether legal or extralegal—often unites two partners of the same age. Thus the numerical vibration undertoning the marriage is reinforced. This occurs also when two people marry who are seven years—or a multiple of seven years—apart. These usually are quite significant cases because every new year alters in the same way the character of the union, especially if the birthdays are close to each other.

If marriage occurs before twenty-one it is likely to have a more "psychological" meaning than if it occurs between twenty-one and twenty-eight, the "social" level in the seven-year cycle. If it occurs after thirty-five it may well be an answer to some life-development which took place as many years before thirty-five. Marriage at forty-nine would tend to reflect what, at twenty-one, brought either psychological pressures and frustrations or some achievement which eventually made this marriage possible. When an eighty-four-year life-pattern applies, such a marriage at forty-nine may resonate to what occurred in the individualized life at age twenty-one—because forty-nine equals twenty-eight plus twenty-one.

This is not the place to discuss individual case histories which, I repeat, generally speaking are only for the individual person to study and evaluate; and what was said about marriage can be applied to any event deeply affecting the manner in which the life-pattern becomes filled with existential and perhaps transforming events. The main purpose of this chapter is to show how a whole life can be scrutinized from an objective and detached point of view—an approach which should clarify and intensify the meaning of basic changes in one's life experience, if pursued in a constructive spirit and not with a literal mind. This discussion was also meant to stress the importance of the age factor to comtemporary men and women, whose attitude towards themselves as well as towards others is mainly personal and hypnotized by facts, small occurrences, and strictly existential values.

In our youth-glorifying American society and with children and adolescents rushing feverishly toward experiences which their nervous system and emotional nature are not able to handle significantly and constructively, or even less assimilate, the values inherent in every age-period are most often forgotten, or thought of in a culturally biased and morally prejudiced manner. By trying to see everything at every time through the heavily colored glasses of equalitarianism denying the *functional differences* which allow for harmonic interaction of individuals within an organic society and culture, modern men and women, young and old, have lost the most basic sense of human and planetary value.

In the operation of any whole organism, every function is essential and valuable. There should be no question of "superior" or "inferior," whether racial or functional. In an organic democracy every cell and organ—every individual and every healthfully operating group and institution—is equally important, necessary, and to be protected as well as valued. But every function is different. No individual should be compelled, urged, or subtly forced to occupy a function which is not his or her own by right of individual destiny (dharma or truth-of-being); yet in a well organized society every individual should consider the welfare of the whole above his own individual welfare. Childhood, adolescence, maturity, old age have different functions; and it is tragic to see any of these ignored, overpraised or scorned, and above all confused.

To grasp the significance of every phase of the age-pattern has indeed become an urgent task in order to bring sanity to our social, educational, and business processes. This however is assuredly not a call for a return to old traditional patterns of family or social behavior! One should always look ahead and be intent on creating the future. Yet creation demands understanding: understanding requires wisdom rather than the kind of knowledge our factories of learning provide for a high price. And there can be no wisdom where the mind is not able to operate in terms of universal principles intuitively sensed and reverently applied.

References and Notes

1.   cf. *The Faith that Gives Meaning to Victory* (N.Y. 1942).

2.   cf. Rudhyar's *New Mansions for New Men*, Part One, *The Astrology of Personality* (p. 212-222 Doubleday edition); *The Astrological Houses* (p. 144-150).

7. PLANETARY AND SOCIAL CYCLES

The study of cycles is very complex and elusive. Cyclic activities are found at all levels of existence, from the cosmic to the atomic level. The physicist and the ecologist concerned with fall-out and atomic waste products speak of the "half-cycle" of radioactive materials; the biologist studies what is now called the biological clocks establishing the rhythms of all life-species; the astrologer analyzes the patterns of unfoldment of planetary cycles, of which there are many and of different types; historians who are not content with collecting information seek to outline the cyclic rhythm of growth, maturation, and decay of human societies; and, should he be following a hint given by H.P. Blavatsky, the theosophically oriented student of occult processes concerning the activities of at least the trans-Himalayan Brotherhood pays attention to the century cycle.

All these cycles are of different lengths. Because they refer to very different kinds of processes, they unfold presumably according to different rhythmic patterns. We have already spoken of a seven-fold rhythm in the lives of human beings; and, according to *The Secret Doctrine* and other occult treatises, this sevenfold division of cycles is basic in the operations of what has been called "the Life-wave." It defines the succession of Rounds, Races, sub-races, etc.

On the other hand, in many instances, particularly in the case of seasonal activity during the year-cycle, the process of cyclic activity is best understood in terms of a fourfold operation. Because the zodiac essentially is a projection of the year-pattern upon the sky, as seen by human beings living in relatively temperate zones of the Earth's surface, it has primarily a fourfold character. But a threefold division of cycles is also well known, which in combination with the fourfold pattern produces a rhythm of twelve beats, from which we draw the measure of the months of the year and the zodiacal signs.

The periods of revolution of the planets around the Sun—when considered *in relation to that of the Earth's revolution,* let us not forget—in several instances reveal such simple rhythms at work. Jupiter's revolution lasts close to twelve of our years; Saturn, thirty years; Uranus, eighty-four (7 x 12) years. The revolution of the Moon around the Earth lasts close to twenty-eight (4 x 7) days. If one takes Uranus' period as a unit, Neptune's cycle has twice, and Pluto's cycle three times its length. However, these figures are not strictly exact, and no cycle *at the existential level* seems ever to be measurable in terms of precisely an integral number of shorter cycles; a coefficient of uncertainty always exists wherever *a relationship* between two cosmic factors is at stake. Simple numbers and geometrical figures belong only to the realm of archetypes.

The second of the "Three Fundamental Propositions" on which, according to H.P.B., the Secret Doctrine of Occultism is based, refers to the universality of cycles. She writes:

> The Secret Doctrine affirms: (2) The Eternity of the Universe *in toto* as a boundless plane . . . the absolute universality of that law of periodicity, of flux and reflux, ebb and flow, which physical science has observed and recorded in all departments of nature. An alternation such as that of Day and Night, Life and Death, Sleeping and Waking, is a fact so common, so perfectly universal and without exception, that it is easy to comprehend that in it we see the absolutely fundamental law of the universe.
>
> (PROEM, p. 16-17)

This universal pattern of periodical flux and reflux refers to the already mentioned differentiation of an involutionary hemicycle—the descent of Spirit, level after level, into ever more crudely material conditions of concretization—and an evolutionary hemicycle representing an ascent of consciousness through a differentiated form or material structure (i.e. a "body" at the level of the Earth's biosphere). Such a twofold pattern is essentially dualistic and demonstrates the operation of two principles, which Chinese philosophy names Yang and Yin. These principles alternatively wax and wane within an at least relatively closed *system of activity* (an organism), one of them waxing as the other wanes.

This type of dualistic pattern is typified by the cycle of the year. In my book *The Pulse of Life* (Shambala Publications, Berkeley, California), I have spoken of the two Yang and Yin principles as the "Day-Force" and the "Night-Force," because during six months of the year (from the winter solstice around December 21 to the summer solstice around June 21) the length of the day increases as that of the night decreases; and the reverse process operates during the six months from the summer to the winter solstices. Such a rhythm produces four characteristic moments dividing the course of the entire cyclic process into four sections. In the year cycle there are the four seasons respectively beginning at the four crucial moments of the year, the two solstices and the two equinoxes. The solstices are times of greatest disequilibrium between the day force and the night force; while at the equinoxes of spring and autumn these two forces are of equal strength. However, at the vernal equinox the day force is mounting in power and thus is the dynamic and dominant force, as far as all external manifestations of life are concerned; while at the fall equinox this day force has a subsiding negative character, and it is the night force which is the positively dynamic factor.

The equinoctial and solstitial moments of the year

cycle establish the fourfold pattern which most typically characterizes the zodiac. A similar fourfold pattern referring essentially—though this is not usually understood—to the space surrounding the newborn is shown in the birth-chart with its four "Angles" produced by the horizon and the meridian.[2]

Though it is a space pattern, it can also be referred (and is most often related by astrologers) to the daily rotation of the Earth around its axis—a rotation which produces the alternation of days and nights, of the waking and the sleeping (and dreaming) states of consciousness. Night consciousness is "subjective"; day consciousness, "objective." There again we can speak of two polar principles, subjectivity and objectivity, which can also be referred to the coupling, darkness and light—or again, in the Chinese world-view, Yin and Yang.

This daily rhythm has been "cosmified" by India's vulgarizers of the esoteric doctrines into the Days and Nights of Brahma, the Creator. These refer to immensely long periods of cosmic Manifestation, and equally long periods (though here one can no longer speak of time in our human sense) of non-Manifestation. The state of Manifestation *(Manvantara)* constitutes what we call "existence." All existence ceases during non-Manifestation *(Pralaya)*. Yet the mind can make a conceptual picture of a process, no longer of existence, but of "in-istence," referring to the Pralaya state, the cosmic Sleep, which can also be symbolized at the biological level by the state of hibernation.

At a more transcendentally human level, we can also consider as a Pralaya condition of the human consciousness, the period between death to the *physically objective* world of bodies and a new birth defined by the karma (positive as well as negative) of the past. "Existence" refers to the exteriorization of consciousness as the result of *a particular relationship* between (1) a Soul and (2) a human body produced by the long evolution of material organisms on the biosphere. This particular relationship is made possible by (3) the integrative power of a monadic spark of the Divine. Therefore the Occultist speaks of man's threefold nature, and more generally of *three schemes of evolution.*

When this relationship is dissolved, the Soul and the body each goes its own way—the Soul to a condition of subjectivity, the body (and this includes all its psychic overtones) to a condition of reabsorption into the material (the "humus") of the biospheric "ground"— a ground, the matter of which is not only physical-molecular, but also includes a kind of *planetary psychic stuff* filled with the decay of all strictly "personal" and non-spiritualizable aspects of the human being during the life just ended. Death therefore brings about a definitely dualistic state of affairs in which Spirit and matter are seemingly completely separated. That separation, however, can only be temporary in a world founded upon the harmony of two polar principles. After a relatively subjective state of consciousness in which the Soul experiences itself within itself (the Devachan state of theosophical literature), it is compulsively drawn by the Law of Harmony (which is what karma is) toward a new manifestation, that is, a new relationship to a new human organism.

Mythological cosmologies speak of Brahma's "desire to be" as the cause of the creation of a new universe, but this is personalizing what to the Occultist is simply the operation of an impersonal metacosmic principle of absolute Harmony, whose polarities are Subjectivity and Objectivity. Likewise, it is sometimes said that the Soul "chooses" a new personality before it is embryonic in a human mother's womb. Very likely at a relatively high level of spiritual development such a possibilty of "choice" may exist, but back of it stands the karmic Law, which simply refers to the momentum of past successes and failures and the unexpended energy involved in them. It is only as this momentum is exhausted that the condition of Nirvana may be reached. But then another and more inclusive type of dualism arises, opposing those who succeed in reaching that state and those who fail and drop along the path—or who became positive expressions of Darkness, while the Nirvanee merged into the Light of pure subjectivity.

This same basic process operates everywhere and at every level, but evidently in infinitely varied forms. It is, for the Hindu mystic, a Play—the *lila* of Brahma. To the Western mind it seems more like a drama; or to the ancient Greek, a tragedy. Each drama or tragedy has a certain number of acts. If complete, it has also a prologue and an epilogue, because nothing begins except it be born out of some past, and it leads toward a more or less distant future. The dramatist selects a specific situation as the main theme of the play. He starts the action at a certain moment, when the personages of the play have reached a definite and potentially dramatic (or hilarious, if it is a comic farce) condition of interrelationship. Yet somehow he has to explain how everyone in the cast came to that significant moment in their interconnecting lives, and this is stated in the prologue.

The student of cyclic processes faces a related problem when he is attempting to understand the character and meaning of the cosmic, natural, or historical events or situations which he is able to perceive as phases of a cyclic process. This problem is the determination of what is to be considered *the beginning of a cycle.* The nature of such a problem can most easily be understood when we consider the cycle produced by the yearly revolution of the Earth around the Sun, and the manner in which such a cycle affects the type of vegetation which most characteristically reflects this seasonal rhythm of change. When should we say that the year cycle begins?

We have only to look at the various calendars in existence today to realize that the question can be answered in several ways. It seems, however, that most of the answers use one of the four cardinal moments of the year as the at least approximate starting point of the year cycle; yet I personally do not know of any society using the summer solstice, or a day near it, as New Year. In our Western world the year begins after the winter solstice: the Jewish year starts around the fall equinox, and many ancient countries and the recent Baha'i Movement—together with the astrologers of today and of old—use the spring equinox as New Year day, speaking of it usually as the beginning of "Nature's year."

The meanings attributed to the various phases of cycles inevitably reflect the character of the collective experience of the people whose culture formulated and symbolized such meanings. Human beings find in the vegetable kingdom their basic sustenance, either directly in the vegetarian mode, or indirectly by eating animals which have fed on products of the vegetable kingdom. The trees of that kingdom have also been responsibile for the development of an oxygen-rich atmosphere needed for man's breathing. The vegetable kingdom is the foundation of biospheric activity, and this activity is dominated by the rhythm of the seasons, and of related atmospheric and climatic changes of a cyclic character. The cycle of life on Earth can therefore significantly be symbolized by the seasonal changes in vegetation; but in order to understand these changes and what they symbolize one has to realize that the life of a plant—and more characteristically an annual or deciduous plant—manifests in two modes, represented by the *seed* and the *leaf*.

Every aspect of the plant's life outside of the seed can be referred to the leaf and the development of its pattern. Even the trees which develop trunk and branches, and a complex root system balancing them underground, are essentially modifications of the leaf pattern. The seed, on the other hand, has a character and shape all of its own. It serves a function totally different from that of the leaf and its derivatives, which include the flowers and fruits. Seeds are mostly invisible except for a very brief period when they drop upon the soil; leaves and flowers are visible and have a direct relationship with the sunlight and all the lives that use them as food. The leaf's chlorophyll, which gives a basic green tonality to the biosphere, fulfills through the process of photosynthesis an absolutely fundamental function in the development of the biosphere of our planet. The leaf becomes transfigured into the flower, whose color and fragrance attracts insects who help in the fertilizing process, insuring the perpetuation of the species. After fertilization, the new seed is reformed under the protection of various enveloping membranes, which in many cases develop into succulent fruits. As the fruit decays, the seeds contained within its womb are released, some falling heavily upon the ground; others, endowed with wings, are carried by the wind to give them a better chance to fall on fertile soil.

The realm of the leaf and all its derivatives is the realm of *existential manifestation*. The realm of the seed refers to at least relatively unmanifested essence. The seed is an agency through which the archetypal reality of a vegetable species reaches and is able to affect the existential world of the Earth's biosphere. Through the seed the species acts, focusing the specific type of energy and structuring forces which characterize this generic form of life. *Within* the seed a tiny reflection of a transcendent reality vibrates.

Whatever belongs to the realm of the leaf must disintegrate at the close of the cycle, but the seed has the power to retain its identity and remain as a potentiality of creative renewal after the cycle's end. Eventually it will perform the sacrifice of the seed to the new vegetation. It will die so that new life once more may arise and ascend toward the Sun; but that kind of death is a victory over nature's entropy, of Spirit over all material forms. New leaves will unfold and in turn become the flowery womb for a multiplied harvest of seeds.

This should not be interpreted as a picture of exact cyclic recurrence insofar as existential realities are concerned. The molecules and atoms in the rose that grew on a bush in 1974 will not be the same atoms as those in the rose of spring 1975. Besides, from one seed germinating into a plant a vastly increased number of seeds may grow; and on this power of self-multiplication all agriculture, and also cattle-breeding, is based. The *archetypal* structure of the process remains the same, but the *existential* products structured by it may not only produce an increase of substance—an increase affecting the whole environment—but they may lead to creative mutations.

Mutations occur only in the seed—perhaps at the time of the symbolical Christmas, when the Sun begins to "move Northward" (in declination) and days gradually lengthen. Some mutations are the answer of the species-as-a-whole to new challenges of the environment and are constructive; others reflect the onslaught of destructive forces upon the integrity of the biosphere. The patterns of change are never exactly repeated, for forces are constantly at work produced by the essentially unpredictable results of various types of existential relationships; "vertical" relationships between lesser wholes that are organic parts of greater wholes—and "horizontal" relationships between wholes operating at the same level.

It is by establishing the distinction between the seed-realm and the leaf-realm that we can gain a deeper understanding of why certain societies felt the urge to begin their year with the onset of spring, fall, or winter. Cultures which sought to attune themselves fully to the natural biospheric rhythm of annual transformation, and to glorify existential realities as direct reflections of a divine Power projecting itself and fecundating them, chose the symbolic time of germination—the beginning of spring—as their most sacred time for a celebration of life. Other cultures (for instance, the Hebrew) use the fall equinox as their approximate New Year because they sought deeply to respond to *the occult potency of the seed in Man;* and that seed is the mind and its power of symbolic self-multiplication in an ever increasing harvest of ideas and social forms. This seed-mind is the foundation of the sense of personal identity—thus, of the realization "I am" and of the process of individualization and intellectual analysis which has dominated our Western civilization since the days of Moses and ancient Greece.

Yet European culture, under the influence of Christianity, has used as the start of the year the days following the winter solstice—the time when the Promise of a future rebirth of life and vegetation is given by the rising arc of the Sun's motion across the sky; a Promise only and one which Christianity, invaded by the ghosts of the Roman empire and torn by the old Hebraic sense of guilt and sinfulness, actually was not able to fulfill. Christianity was intended to compensate for, balance and illumine the new evolutionary trend toward individualistic and intellectual self-assertion, and indeed autarchy; yet it was unable to significantly offset the fateful power of such a trend. Still, the attempt remains alive in the symbol of a New Year associated with the winter solstice and the symbolic birth of the solar Christ.

H.P. Blavatsky stated that January 4 should be considered the esotericist's New Year, and to my knowledge little has been added to this statement. It nevertheless seems probable that in some manner that day has a direct or indirect reference to the coming of the Kumaras and thus the beginning in man of "reflective consciousness" or the consciousness of being conscious—truly a momentous "mutation." It is, moreover, significant that the polar opposite of January 4 is July 4, celebrated as the birthday of the American nation. And, according to at least some of its true Founders, the United States of America was not to be merely another nation in the European style, but the beginning of a new kind of society exemplifying a new way of living—*Novum*

Ordo Seclorum (a new order of the centuries).[3]

Whether or not America has succeeded in being true to her essential or archetypal destiny is a highly disputable matter; but the cyclic connection between January 4 and July 4 is deeply significant and an unmet spiritual challenge. The two dates are related as the Ascendant of an astrological birth-chart is related to the principle of relatedness; this also means the beginning of a cycle is related to the mid-point (or "bottom") of the cycle. The occult solar promise in the zodiacal sign Capricorn is related to the building in Cancer of both the home and the concretely integrated personality. What is occultly envisioned within the "Christed" consciousness in darkness of winter (the "midnight Sun" of Masonry) should become fully actualized in early summer. Then within the small fruit developing at the center of what had been a beautiful flower the seed is being reconstituted. It could become the symbolical Child, the Body of Immortality—also called the Diamond Body or the Body of Resurrection—in whom man would experience his seed-victory over natural entropy and death.

The symbolism which has been attached to the yearly process of vegetation has had the most profound influence on the development of man's consciousness since the ancient days of what has been called the Vitalistic Age, when human society was completely polarized in everyday living by agriculture and/or cattle-raising, and the ritualistic worship of the two poles of the life-energy, male and female, gave collective forms to man's aspirations toward a creative state of total survival in self-multiplication and self-transcendence through attunement with biospheric and solar-lunar rhythms.

Astrology was, if not born, at least codified in its multiple forms during the millennia of such a vitalistic evolution—and evolution not yet completed in most places—and took from the dominant preoccupation of the epoch its basic tenets, including the starting point of the year cycle at the vernal equinox, "Nature's birthday." This became "the first Point in Aries," the beginning of the zodiac. Yet there seem to have been regions in which the time of the harvest and possibly the star Spica were given precedence, because of the climatic and harvest conditions prevailing in such regions less susceptible to the changes in seasons of the temperate zone of the Northern Hemisphere.

It is evident that a correct solution given to the problem of ascertaining the most significant starting point in a complete cyclic process—which in an archetypal sense has no beginning or end—is required for a correct evaluation of the phase of any cycle at which a particular event occurs or situation arises. Are we today at the beginning of a new cycle, or near the middle, or somewhere before the end of one started centuries ago? We have first of all to determine the length and the character of the cycle we are considering. But a situation of extreme complexity confronts us, for we must realize that small cycles occur within larger ones, and these within still vaster cosmic periods, and any cycle includes subcycles. What makes the situation more confusing is the fact that Occultism (as presented by H.P. Blavatsky who, more than any other writer dealt with cycles) not only keeps the secret of the exact lengths and actual beginnings of cosmic and planetary cycles well guarded, but uses "blinds." This may be required in order to test the student's intuition and the purity of his motive, but it makes the determination of any date difficult, if not impossible. Not only do the dates, or even centuries, remain uncertain, as sometimes several dates are given for one event, but also *the level* at which the cycle being mentioned operates is often not clearly stated; and this of course is of capital importance.

For instance, one may apparently refer quite precisely to the time of "birth"; but it may not always mean physical birth out of the mother's womb. This problem occurs in astrology, and astrologers sometimes feel that the birth chart should be calculated from the moment at which the male sperm penetrates the female ovum; thus "conception charts" are erected which are deduced from the actual physical birth-moment according to rhythmic patterns which may not always be correctly applied or even applicable. Some occultist-astrologers even claim that they can calculate a "solar epoch" preceding actual conception.

For similar reasons it is indeed difficult to state *when* the Great Cycle of the precession of the equinoxes actually began, or when one of its twelve subcycles, the Aquarian Age, will begin; or perhaps it has already begun at some level. As we have already seen, the first half of a cycle refers to a descent of power, or, we might also say, to the gradual actualization of a set of spiritual potentialities released by the divine or cosmic creative Act—the Biblical "Let there be Light!" But the originating release occurs at a cosmic level and in terms of energies, vibrations, or qualities of being whose nature far transcends those we can experience at our physical or even mental level of awareness. Even if a man's consciousness could in some way become reflectively aware of the creative release, the inertia of Earth-matter and that of the collective mind of mankind would oppose an intense resistance to the new downflowing tide; and this means that *it takes time* for the new impulse to overcome the resistance and to become clearly manifest in mental, social, and physical changes. The time it takes represents the transition period between the old and the new (in Sanskrit, *sandhya*).

According to the Hindu tradition the transition between two cycles normally lasts one tenth of the length of the cycle at its close—I have called it the seed period—and a period of the same length after the start of the new cycle—the germinal period. If, then, a cycle lasts 2160 years, which is the average length of one of the twelve Ages (Arian, Piscean, Aquarian, etc.) dividing the Great Cycle of the precession of the equinoxes, the last 216 years of one of these Ages form its seed period, and the first 216 years of the next Age its germinal period. This means that one-fifth of the time, in a succession of cycles, is occupied by transitional activities.

It also means that the creative Impulse initiating a new precessional Age must have begun already to operate when, at the Earth-level to which these Ages apply, the upsetting effect of the seed-transition period can be felt. It is an upsetting effect because the new tide of energy is then exerting pressure upon all that the past has produced and that usually has become rigid and uncreative. Thus, when the last tenth of a cycle starts, the creative beginning of the next cycle has already occurred at a "high" spiritual-cosmic level. The two cycles, which can be said to succeed each other, if only one level of activity is considered, actually interpenetrate if several levels are considered. *The downward trend of the closing cycle calls forth and polarizes the descent of the creative Impulse of the succeeding cycle.* One may visualize such a process if one thinks of the way wind arises: as a region of low atmospheric pressure develops, air from surrounding regions of high pressure automatically flows, as wind, into it.

Wind, in Greek, is *pneuma,* which also means "spirit." When the spirituality of a society falls to a low level, a rush of a new spirit begins to be felt. This is an automatic action; yet because we live at the level of matter which displays both objectivity and solidity—and, in so far as human beings are concerned, *personality*—this automatic action of the creative Spirit *has to be focused in and to radiate through a human Personage, an Avatar,* and also through lesser avataric beings— as we shall see in the following chapter and Part Four of this book. It is for the same reason that we think of God as a person; "It" becomes "He" when in relation to a human person. Thus great philospher seers such as Sri Aurobindo state that Brahman has both a personal and an impersonal aspect, and the Christian mystic, Eckhart, differentiates between "God," the divine Person, and an utterly transcendent "Godhead."

The creative Power acts through human persons when the time for a new release of power has struck on the cosmic clock of evolution. It also starts into operation a multitude of less focalized transforming activities. The seed period of transition has then begun; but at the material and sociocultural level, the New Age has not really dawned. It is "conceived," yet not yet "born." The Avatar is the *Logos Spermatikos* known to the Greek philosophers. He impregnates the planetary ovum within the placental biosphere; and it is such an Act that the fecundation by the Holy Spirit of Mary, the immaculately conceived Virgin, symbolizes. Gautama's mother was also called Maya—a term which designates the personifying power of existence in the world of "name and form" (*nama* and *rupa*), a world which to the purely spiritual consciousness must appear as an illusion, an imaginative daydream.

These general remarks were necessary to establish what, to me, is a sound approach to the study of all cyclic processes. It is impossible here to deal with the many cycles considered significant by both the Occultist and the astrologer concerned with planetary changes, the growth of nations and the various periods marking the development of human civilizations. In my book *Astrological Timing: The Transition to a New Age* (Harper and Row, N.Y., paperback) the cycle of the precession of the equinoxes (with its twelve Ages) and the cycles of relationship established by the successive conjunctions of the larger planets (beginning with Jupiter and Saturn, and stressing more particularly the complex interplay between the revolutions of Uranus, Neptune, and Pluto) have been studied with their historical correlations. The interested reader has to be referred to this book, as the subject is much too vast to be discussed here.

It seems valuable nevertheless to point out that the precessional cycle (lasting around 25,900 years— a length that presumably varies slightly with each cycle) constitutes the third of the main cyclic motions of our globe—the two others being its daily rotation around the polar axis, and its yearly revolution around the Sun. This precessional cycle, as usually described in astrology, refers to the retrograde displacement of the equinoxes with reference to zodiacal constellations, which are supposed to be "fixed" (the fixed stars) but actually change shape very slowly. As the equinoxes represent the two moments during the year when the Sun sets exactly west and when days and nights are of equal length, this means that, *at the spring equinox,* the Sun today has moved away from a star with which it was in exact conjunction several centuries ago.

Actually, however, this movement of the equinoxes in relation to the fixed stars is only the secondary result of a cyclic motion of the polar axis of the Earth, a gyrating motion, because of which the North pole points successively to stars forming a cosmic circle. In other words, the *orientiation* of the polar axis slowly changes during a period approximating that of the cycle of precession of the equinoxes; it is also a cyclic change, and evidently a very significant one because it is along the line of a prolonged polar axis that *galactic forces* are said to enter the electromagnetic field of our planet's organism. This polar axis may be compared to the erect spine of man; and any student of esoteric philosophy and yoga has heard of the importance of this spinal axis in the occult process of development of consciousness, called in India *Kundalini Yoga.* The North and South poles of the Earth can thus be compared to the ends of the human spine, the Root Chakra in the region of the coccyx and the center at the top of the cranium, while the Earth's equator refers to the diaphragm and the region of the solar plexus.

Changes in the orientation of the polar axis bring this spinal column of our globe in direct alignment with a succession of "pole stars," and thus with a specific region of the galaxy—which, for man, represents at least symbolically the Spiritual World, the world of divine Hierarchies.[4] As I stated in my first book on astrology, *The Astrology of Personality* (first edition, 1936: *A Key to Astrological Symbolism* pp. 179 and 191 et seq.) it may be that the Great Polar cycle is most significantly divided into 7 periods of close to 3700 years each. Another possible division is also suggested in *The Secret Doctrine* (first edition, Vol. 2, page 505): a division of the Great Cycle (often referred to as "the great Tropical Year") into 370 "Days," each lasting seventy normal years. However, as astrology, at least in its popular aspect, deals primarily with the vital forces represented by the Sun, and as the zodiac—a creation of the apparent motion of the Sun—is the basis for most astrological measurements, the gyration of the polar axis has remained mostly unnoticed, even though it is the most basic movement. And not only has the whole attention of the people been focused on the precession of the equinoxes, but the peculiar idea that, as a new Age opens, the Sun successively "enters" Pisces, Aquarius, Capricorn, etc. has become popularized, though if stated in such a simplistic and inaccurate manner, it makes no sense whatever.

There are other less important or secondary motions of the globe; moreover the shape of the orbit of the Earth undergoes some very slow periodical alterations. But these periods are very large and are not used because it is not possible to experience them, or even their subdivisions. A celestial phenomenon which cannot be measured in terms of an easily available frame of reference, whose recurrence is too rare to be a collective human experience, cannot serve a useful purpose as a "word" in the symbolic "language" of astrology. Yet to the Occultist it could be a most meaningful indication of a cosmic or planetary process, if it has been so regarded in the accumulated group-wisdom of an occult Brotherhood existing for millennia.

As I see it, a Great Cycle for the precession of the

equinoxes began around 100 B.C., and as it lasts some 2160 years it will end in less than a century around 2060 A.D. Its seed period, being a tenth of the cycle, began around 1844. That was the year in which a young Persian Prophet announced the end of the Islamic era and the beginning of a New Age of which the Avatar (or "Divine Manifestation") was about to reveal himself—a revelation which came nineteen years later when one of his original followers proclaimed himself Baha'u'llah (meaning the Glory of God), the Expected One. In 1846 Neptune was discovered and in 1848 the Communist manifesto began the movement that has changed human history; American Spiritualism also began, and the Industrial Revolution, through the spread of the railroads and the invention of the telegraph, reached a more concrete and world transforming stage.

Thus the transition that at the existential level will eventually lead to the new Aquarian Age has begun. Yet, referring to what has already been stated, this means that *at the spiritual-archetypal level* the new cycle itself has already started with a release of cosmic power and archetypal Images. That release of power is slowly making its way "downward," producing a radical up-heaval in all institutions and cultural forms which had been developing during the Piscean Age, especially since the mid-point of that Age, around 980 A.D. and after the great crisis of the year 1000.[5]

We shall once more consider the character of this "descent" of creative, transforming power in the chapter concluding this book, but now we have briefly to discuss another kind of cycle, a cycle whose origin is no longer based on a motion of the Earth, but on a sociocultural-religious factor, the calendar: the Century Cycle.

It should be clear that when we speak of the nineteenth or twentieth century, we have reference to periods the beginning of which depends on the kind of calendar being used. These are solar and lunar calendars, and each calendar is made to begin on a certain date in the more or less distant past. That memorable date usually refers to some event of a religious nature or, in some cultures, to a specific cosmic event. However, the date is always selected after the event occurs. By selecting it, a particular religion and culture, as it were, returns to its actual or symbolical source, that is, to the original creative Impulse from which it claims to descend. The figure characterizing a particular century indicates therefore how distant from this point of origin a society and its culture find themselves—and perhaps how spiritually remote from the creative moment they are.

We are dealing here, in a sense at least, with the occult power of numbers. What is important is the number the century carries—whether it is the sixteenth or the nineteenth after the point of origin. The meaning of these numbers has also much to do with the expectable length of the total cycle, or life span, of the society. One hundred years for a cosmic entity lasting a million of years is a very short period; but for a civilization whose life span may be only two or three millennia, the century period may have a meaning similar to that which the year cycle has for the living organisms of the Earth's biosphere. The biospheric cycle of the year is a basic period for all that refers to the vegetable kingdom, and particularly for all that concerns the *cultivation* of living organisms. Similarly the century cycle appears to have much importance in the development of human *cultures* at the level of social institutions, styles of life and artistic creation, and collective psychological trends. What we call "culture" is the product of the "cultivation" of human traits and special values; both processes, biological and (collectively) psychological, aim at improving the type of organism they deal with—whether it be the production of beautiful roses and large chrysanthemums through breeding and the use of special chemicals, or the formation of a social aristocracy with refined manners, esthetic tastes, keener minds and, at the religious level, more spiritual aspirations and controlled instinctual urges.[6]

It is in this sense that we should think of the value of a century-long period of sociocultural development, and of the possibility of significantly subdividing it so that every decade of the century may be given some sort of general archetypal meaning— just as any year of the seven year cycle in an individual life acquires some basic significance from the mere fact of its being a first, fourth, or seventh year.

If we look back at the development of European culture we may readily see that each century can be broadly characterized by a few typical movements and features of the collective Euro-mind. The fifteenth century witnessed the growth of Humanism and the beginning of great voyages which established the global reality of mankind. The sixteenth century produced the Renaissance and the Reformation, the seventeenth century, Classicism and the rationalistic and mathematical foundations of modern science. The eighteenth century was the Age of Enlightenment, of Free Masonry and the Revolutionary Spirit; and the nineteenth century gave birth to Romanticism, Humanitarianism, and the Industrial Revolution. Our twentieth century is the epoch of the World Wars, of the Electronic Revolution and atomic power—an epoch now coming to a still uncertain seed culmination as the last quarter of the century begins.

Each century the basic attitude of our Western society has changed quite radically, and new concepts and social-cultural institutions have developed. The line of demarcation between successive centuries is certainly not clear-cut; yet if one tries to see through and beyond, and at the core of, the complexity of outer happenings and changes of fashion, one should be able to discover a seed reality (or archetype) underlying and undertoning the most characteristic developments in each century.

One really can speak here of a "seed" if one compares the development of a century culture to that of the yearly vegetation. A spiritual and (at least in our Euro-

American civilization) occult power is released that is to
the culture what the seed is to the annual plant. It is a
power, a keynote. A particular quality of "being-in-the-
world," a typical approach to interpersonal and social
relationships and to religion and morality, emerges out
of that key-vibration, as grains of sand spread uniformly
on a thin metal plate form into geometrical patterns
when the plate is made to vibrate under the impact of a
tone. A culture is the product of the collective mind of a
racial or national organism; and this mind is set in
vibration by a few creative individuals. These in turn often are the conscious, half-conscious, or unconscious
"agents" of higher Forces and Intelligences which are
set in operation *by the need of the time;* that is to say, by
the fact that a time has come in mankind's evolution for
certain qualities, faculties, and powers to come to the
fore. Such creative individuals are "seed men," releasing
"seed ideas" to fecundate the minds of their or succeeding generations—and we shall speak further of
them. These seed ideas, at the proper time, germinate
and manifest as cultural forms and institutions.

If we understand such a process in its essential structural time sequence, we can then relate it to the
statement made by H. P. Blavatsky that, at least since
the fourteenth century, the Occult Brotherhoods—or
some of them—have made a definite effort *during the
last quarter of each century* to fecundate the collective
consciousness of Western mankind with specific types of
transforming spiritual energy and with related seed
ideas. If H. P. B. is correct and the last quarter of each
century has been the time of sowing spiritual seeds at the
level of man's culture, then it follows that this last quarter corresponds to the Fall in the year cycle. We can
therefore divide the century cycle in four "seasons," each
lasting twenty-five years; and the century can be said to
begin at the moment when the new vibration, which its
main number indicates, takes hold of the collective mentality of our Western men and women. The century's

"winter" lasts from January 1, 1900 to January 1, 1925; then its "spring" extends from 1925 to 1950, its summer from 1950 to 1975, and its fall from 1975 to January 1, 2000. It was in 1900, and not as some would say 1901, that the twentieth century began because what counts is the focusing of the collective mind upon the number 19. Besides, there never was a Year 1, as the Christian Era was established long after that year would have occurred.

The correspondence between the seasons of the year and the four quarters of the century is logical so far as our Western world is concerned, for we begin the year after the winter solstice; thus we should also start our centuries with their winter period. It is also just before Christmas that a line drawn from the Earth to the Sun would point to the center of the galaxy—the astrological symbol of the divine Creative Power.[7]

H. P. B.'s claim that at the beginning of the last quarter of each century a "Messenger" from the Occult Lodge has appeared and sought to influence the mind of Europe is rather difficult to prove; yet if we look back to what happened at the corresponding time in preceding centuries we can perceive significant traces of such developments.

The Theosophical Society was formed in N.Y. in 1875 and marked the definite beginning of H.P.B.'s public work as an emissary of the trans-Himalayan Brotherhood. France's defeat in 1871 and the rise of a powerful Germany produced one of the most fundamental factors in the future development of the Western world during the twentieth century, as it led directly to our two World Wars. Before the nineteenth century ended, the discovery of X-Rays and radium, then Planck's Quantum Theory and, at the psychological level, Freud's revolutionary ideas, also set the stage for the two other most significant developments in our present century: (1) the Electronic Revolution and Atomic Power, and (2) the fantastic growth of concern with man's neuro-psychological problems and the development and/or transcendence of his ego.

In 1776 the Declaration of Independence and France's Revolution struck the keynotes of various attempts at transforming the social-political life. This fall period of the eighteenth century saw the earliest application of new discoveries on which the Industrial Revolution of the nineteenth century was based. According to H. P. B. and some of her later disciples, the mysterious Comte de Saint-Germain was the main guide in the occult operations which took place at that time; and he has been considered the head of the Hungarian Lodge of Adepts, whose earlier work was related to the original Rosicrucian Movement. Anton Mesmer, as we already saw, also started a movement of great importance that influenced a number of leaders during the nineteenth century.

What occurred at an occult level during the last quarter of the seventeenth century is not too clear, but Locke in England brought forth new ideas in political theory which greatly affected the attitude of the French Encyclopedists and American leaders. The Masonic Movement may have been planned in some secret groups, leading to its public emergence in 1717 as a powerful sociocultural force. And there were most important years in the earliest development of the American Colonies (King Philip's War, William Penn in Pennsylvania, etc.).

The last quarter of the sixteenth century was the last part of the Elizabethan Age, in which Francis Bacon and Shakespeare were reaching maturity, while France was torn by religious war between Catholics and Huguenots. The first unsuccessful English attempts to colonize the East coast of America failed, but soon afterward the Virginia Colony was a success (1607).

The last quarter of the fifteenth century saw the beginning of the Italian Renaissance and, at its close, the "discovery" of America and other "great voyages." And, according to the occult tradition, the Rosicrucian

Movement began at the end of the fourteenth century.

When we deal with the seed which falls into the ground at the theoretical fall equinox we refer, by definition, to a more or less hidden or occult process. The more materialistic a civilization and the more dominated it is by powerful and oppressive religious or political institutions, the more difficult it is for spiritual impulses to take public forms. They have to operate through the minds, and even the passions, of individual leaders or creative persons who are normally not conscious of the source of their inspiration; they also affect the collective mind of the society in a less focused manner.

As the new century begins, what has been started at the mental or occult level becomes affected by two types or trends: the seed ideas become popularized and often vulgarized and their consequences are being applied, at least in the more progressive circles; on the the other hand, the karmic momentum of the collective forces released during the now ended century relentlessly pursue their course. Thus, in our century we have the Russo-Japanese war, symbol of the rise of the non-European people, and World War I which resulted from the conflict between the great national entities who, during the nineteenth century, had been impelled by the results of the Industrial Revolution to expand in a competitive egocentric manner in search of raw materials and new markets for their industrial products.

A century earlier, the Napoleonic era marked an expansion of the forces that triumphed in the French Revolution under the leadership of a great military and managerial genius who became a model for what later became the powerful Executive type in politics or business—the Caesar type of national leader. Such a type replaced that of the "King of divine right" or the divinely appointed Emperor of the medieval tradition—religious authority having now become secular power, yet power linked, in the mind of the person wielding it, with a "star," a celestial or evolutionary

Destiny.

The spring quarter of the century seems to bring out a collective, emotional reaction to what has just occurred. After the fall of Napoleon Europe witnessed a regressive and conservative political movement; but the seed-ideas of the 18th century began to pierce this heavy reactionary trend, leading to an upsurge of Romantic and revolutionary fervor climaxing in the late forties. Romantic poets, novelists, musicians, artists flourished. And the frustrated revolutionary mass-movement of the popular aspect of the French Revolution, transformed eventually by the impact of the now spreading Industrial Revolution, was reborn into the Proletarian Movement of Marxist Communism just before the "summer" period of the 19th century began.

In our present century, 1925 saw the emotional revolt against Puritanism and the traditional position of women resulting in what is often called the Jazz Age. The power of American industry and finance soared to new heights. Soviet Russia began its amazing rise to power after nearly total devastation. China and India had begun to move toward a completely new future, and Japan dominated East Asia. The Theosophical Movement as such may seem to have no connection whatsoever with Asia's awakening; its founder had been discredited in the eyes of many, and the organization she inspired had split into several fragments. Yet the seed also splits as germination occurs. What is important is that in the last part of the nineteenth century, a spotlight of consciousness had been aimed at the occult wisdom and power of Asia, and that some of the seed concepts released at that time had begun to take root in the collective Euro-American mind. The second World War increasingly involved America's youth in Asia. At the same time the earlier revolutionary ideals of eighteenth century America and of the beginnings of Communist Russia became crystallized, and these two nations, armed with atomic power, faced each other in the cold war—somewhat as France under Napoleon III faced Prussia under Bismarck before 1870.

Ghastly as atomic power is in its destructive aspect, this very fact has, during recent crises, prevented a global repetition of the Franco-German war. Atomic power is an occult form of power, as it deals with normally invisible forces which, unnoticed, can destroy all life (radioactivity, fallout, genetic mutation, etc.). But it is not the only danger confronting the world, as we now are beginning to realize. More subtle, because more widespread and more difficult to control, are the effects of pollution at two levels: the pollution of the biosphere (air, water, soil), and that of the mind and feeling-responses of the masses of mankind under the deleterious pressures of masterful propaganda directed by intellectuals and technocrats without moral responsibilty and sense of spiritual values.

Polarizing this official type of thinking and the immense power of vested interests all over the world, we find the often confused and unsteady protest of youth, and the growth of a vast number of groups intensely (but usually not too discriminatingly) concerned with supernormal, parapsychological, occult and mystical phenomena. As this "summer" season of the twentieth century is ending, the most significant conflict is taking place in the field of consciousness. It is an occult conflict which can best be characterized and symbolized by the biological fact that, as the seed takes form within the fruit, the annual plant begins to crystallize and die. *The presence of the seed kills the plant.* The future destroys the rigidly institutionalized power-patterns of a past which refuses to realize its obsolescence.

This occurred in the eighteenth century when, just before the "fall" season of the century began in 1775, the old privileged classes were unable to face the impending revolutionary spirit. The American War of Independence was a special case in that it was officially—but, alas, not too realistically—waged in the name of an ideal new society. Freedom was won, but many of the old patterns of the past remained in great strength—not only slavery, but the aggressive drive to conquer and recklessly use the vast "real estate" of our continent, after destroying most of its nature-worshipping inhabitants. A new class everywhere was rising to power: the bourgeoisie of wealth fascinated by intellectual games and technique, and brutally materialistic in its desire for power, comfort, and glamor.

During the last quarter of the nineteenth century this growth of the industrial, commercial, and financial elements of our society reached a point at which counterbalancing forces had to increase in power—mainly the forces of Labor, but also subtler forces challenging the materialistic-scientific approach. These had actually begun to grow—as seeds do—around the "summer solstice" of the century, and mainly during the late forties. I am referring to Spiritualism (an inchoate attempt to break through the boundaries of bodily consciousness), Marxist Communism (a passionate and millenium-oriented attempt to force, through total antireligious despair, the violent rising of the working masses), and the Baha'i Movement (at least the first phase of it, begun by the Bab in 1844), a religious attempt to organize the whole of mankind on a global scale through the power of faith and all-inclusive love.

We probably lack the perspective required to understand what, in this century, began in the hidden seed around or just before 1950. But the generation of young men and women who became the new rebels, the hippies entranced with psychedelic visions and "flower power," were born after the end of World War II and Hiroshima. They were born in our affluent suburban culture, in an atmosphere of total permissiveness and spiritual emptiness and, during the cold war and under the menace of a nuclear holocaust, of insecurity. Under the inspiration of some of their elders, they developed a countercultural approach to life. They have represented the seed as yet surrounded by the fruit.

Now seeding time is at hand. A still very confused call for a new kind of *metanoia*—a going beyond the individual and rational soul *(nous)*—is being heard from many places. The greed and jockeying for power on a world scale, alarmingly revealed by the energy situation, as these pages are written, have explosive potentiality. Autumn begins in the harvesting and self-sowing of the seed, but ends in storms and the decaying of the leaves. 1789 saw the beginning of the United States as a strongly organized federal nation; but, a few months later, the French Revolution exploded. The two developments represented two ways of dealing with the past, neither of which led to *spiritual* success, in spite of America's tremendous material achievements—nay more, *because* of them—and of the highly significant Napoleonic vision of a united Europe, which, alas, personal ambition and insecurity vitiated and destroyed.

Soon 1989 will come; and with it a massing of planets in the zodiacal sign of political large-scale organization, Capricorn. We will consider various possibilities presented by this "autumnal" situation. But first of all we should discuss some of the characteristics associated with the capacity in men to act as transforming agents for the creative forces leading mankind along its evolutionary path toward a New Age.

References and Notes

1. The other two Fundamental Propositions are:
    (1) An Omnipresent, Eternal, boundless and Immutable PRINCIPLE on which all speculation is impossible, since it transcends the power of human conception and could only be dwarfed by any human expression or similitude . . . there is one absolute Reality which antedates all manifested, conditioned being . . . devoid of all attributes and essentially without any relation to manifested, finite Being. It is "Beness" rather than Being (in Sanskrit, *Sat*) . . . symbolized in the Secret Doctrine under two aspects . . . absolute Abstract Space representing

pure subjectivity, the one thing which no human mind can either exclude from any conception or conceive of by itself . . . (and) absolute Abstract Motion representing Unconditioned Consciousness . . .
(3) The Fundamental identity of all Souls with the Universal Oversoul . . . and the obligatory pilgrimage for every Soul—a spark of the former— through the Cycle of Incarnation, or Necessity, in accordance with cyclic and Karmic law, during the whole term.

(cf. p. 14 to 19: PROEM *The Secret Doctrine.)*

2. For a discussion of the astrological Houses, read my book *The Astrological Houses:* The Spectrum of Individual Experience (Doubleday, N.Y. 1972).

3. cf. my last book *The Astrology of America's Destiny* (Random House, N.Y. 1974).

4. According to some occult traditions the galaxy is the cosmic Womb of Souls, and each human Soul has its cosmic-divine counterpart in a particular star—its "Father in heaven."

5. As the cycle of precession of the equinoxes derives from the retrograde movement of not only the spring equinox but of both equinoctial points, the Piscean Age should actually be called the "Pisces-Virgo Age." The Pisces polarity dominates during approximately the first half of the cycle, but thereafter the Virgo polarity and the qualities it characterizes (particularly the faculty of intellectual analysis and critical objectivity) gain an increasing power. It dominates the sociocultural stage during the last fourth of the cycle, thus after 1520—the Renaissance period and, with Francis Bacon, the rise of the modern scientific spirit. Much that today is considered an expression of the Aquarian Age is rather the manifestation of a protest against this Virgo influence and a nostalgic return to the Piscean spirit of early Christianity—and also, in political Fascism, to the ideal of the Roman Empire and its Administrators who foreshadowed some of our modern "technocrats" at the centers of political power.

6. Aristocracy however, means "the rule of the best" and the term best may refer to diverse qualities, *those that are most needed in any particular phase of the development of a society.* Thus, there may be an aristocracy of physical strength and daring, one of knowledge and skill, one of spiritual dedication, etc.

7. The following should be of interest in this connection:
   "Babylon, in 2250 B.C., celebrated New Year at the Vernal Equinox, with an 11-day festival, Zagmuk, in honor of their patron deity, Marduk. The Egyptians, Phoenicians and Persians celebrated it at the time of the Autumnal Equinox. Until the fifth century B.C., the Greeks celebrated it at the Winter Solstice, as did the Romans with a festival dedicated to Saturn—the Saturnalia. To counteract this revelry the early Christians celebrated it in commemoration of the birth of Jesus with prayer and acts

of charity. When the year was made to begin on January 1st, Christmas was shifted to December 25th, the octave of New Year's Day, the while Pagan Rome made sacrifices to Janus, after whom January was named. Janus, guardian deity of gates, was represented with two faces, watching both entering and departing wayfarers: the going out of the old year and the coming in of the new."

Encyclopedia of Astrology. by Nicholas Devore, now in a paperback edition, (p. 44).

PART THREE

On Transpersonal Living

8. TWO POLARITIES OF THE SPIRITUAL LIFE
Toward the Spirit—From the Spirit

Within the last few years, especially since Anthony Sutich and his associates in Palo Alto, California, began the publication of the *Journal of Transpersonal Psychology* in 1969, the term "transpersonal" is frequently heard in psychological circles; and Carl Jung had used it occasionally, probably not for the first time. It now is mainly used with reference to what exists beyond, or to the process of reaching beyond and transcending the level of actions, drives, feelings, and realizations which are usually regarded as being personal. Moreover, in most instances, the word "personal" has rather pejorative connotations, even though Carl Jung used the term "personality" in a positive sense which contrasts with the meaning given to it in theosophy and related types of thinking.

Unfortunately the word "transpersonal" is ambiguous, and its use can be confusing unless one clearly states what meaning one gives to it. The ambiguity arises from the double meaning of the prefix "trans" in the formation of words derived from the Latin. *Trans* means both *through* and *beyond;* and the former is more basic and common than the latter. The words, transparent, transpierce, or transaction, imply a process of through or *across:* on the other hand, the terms, trans-Himalayan or trans-Alpine usually refer to what exists beyond or "the other side of" these mountains. Their opposites are "cis-Himalayan" and "cis-Alpine."

In the meaning of "beyond," the prefix *trans* duplicates the Greek root *meta;* but the psychologists who are using the word, transpersonal, apparently felt that "metapersonal" would constitute an awkward blend of Greek and Latin, and might establish an unwanted link with "metaphysical." In the fall 1929, I began to use the word transpersonal; but it was used to characterize the release of a power operating *through* the personal.[1] The source of that power, consciousness, or activity could certainly be considered as existing beyond the realm of personality, but the activity itself is transpersonal because its most significant feature is its using a person as an instrumentality or agent through which the activity is released in a focused condition. Because such a meaning of the word transpersonal implies the existence of a source of activity in a realm beyond, above, or even deep within that of the personal and normal consciousness of human beings as at present constituted, it evidently has suspicious and unwelcome implications for the typical scientist who refuses to deal with entities existing outside the fields of sense perception and strictly rational conceptualization. If, however, a transpersonal type of activity implies a *reaching beyond* the limitations and the concreteness or rationality of what is still considered by most people the normal state of consciousness and feeling-experiences, then it is much more acceptable to the scientific mentality. It refers to religious aspirations and to man's devotion to transcendent and either superhuman or collectively held superpersonal ideals. Evolution is seen as an "ascent" and the great individual is thought to be "superior" to the human average.

On the other hand, if one thinks of transpersonal activity as a *going through* a person who then becomes an agent for the exteriorization of a cosmic force or a spiritual entity, one has to accept the world-outlook characterizing true Occultism. One of the most essential principles of Occultism, as stated in H.P.B.'s *The Secret Doctrine* (vol. I p. 224), is that "the Universe is worked and *guided* from *within outward, controlled and animated by almost endless series of Hierarchies* of sentient Beings, each having a mission to perform, and who—whether we give to them one name or another, and call them Dhyan-Chohans or Angels—are 'messengers' in the sense only that they are the agents of Karmic and Cosmic Laws. None of these Beings, high or low, have either individuality or personality as separate Entities, i.e. they have no individuality in the sense in which a man says 'I am myself and no one else'; in other words, they are conscious of no such distinct separateness as men and things have on earth. Individuality is the characteristic of their respective Hierarchies, not of their units."

If at the cosmic-spiritual levels at which such Hierarchies operate, there is, strictly speaking, no individuality it seems logical to accept the idea that, in order to act in a precisely focused manner *at the level of human existence,* these superindividual Beings require an agent, emissary or messenger among men in order to produce a strongly focalized release of energy—just as sunlight requires a focusing lens to generate sufficient heat to set paper on fire. This focusing activity of energy or creative (that is, transforming and transfiguring) power is what I mean by the term, transpersonal, whenever I am using it. It refers to a descent of power—an action from the spirit (or God) through an individual person.

Some transpersonal psychologists would probably accept the possibility of such an action from some transcendental source, for their approach to the universe and man is broad enough; nevertheless they insist on taking an empirical attitude and on looking at what happens from an experiential standpoint; and as a result the main field of their research is the study of these phenomena which extend, elevate, intensify and transform or transfigure human consciousness along lines usually interpreted as mystical, or at least quasi-mystical and subliminal. What is perceived thus are the varied manifestations of an upreaching sense-transcending and perhaps ego-surrendering consciousness—the "peak-experiences" studied by Abraham Maslow, the bliss, the wonder, the ecstasy of the self-actualizing and self-transcending individual—the drop of water on its way to merging with the sea.[2]

The path of the true mystic has often been outlined and the several stations it crosses have been explained, symbolized, sung in inspiring poetry, whether in India or Medieval Europe, by Sufis, Christian Gnostics, or even more recently by various types of illumined minds which have reached from the darkness of human emotionality and egocentricity to the light of a state of supernal revelation. But there is another path, another kind of light-revealing consciousness that operates in another direction, because it is differently polarized. This is the path of the Avatar, the Divine Manifestation or In-carnation—and at a lesser level of operation, also the path of the creative genius and of the cultural hero. A spiritual, cosmic, or divine power acts *in and through* these men. Whether in total consciousness, half-consciously, or even unconsciously, they have become agents of forces of spiritual Beings or Occult Brotherhoods that use them as focalizing instrumental-ities—and in another sense, as "junior associates" or messengers—for the performance of actions de-manded at certain times by the state of evolution of humanity, or only of a culture and community of hu-man beings. These actions are "performed"—i.e. done through a form—and that form is the personality of the Avatar, the creative genius, or the hero whose deeds become symbols and examples for a whole culture or nation.

We shall return to this type of inspirited human beings, but before doing so a third type of persons should be mentioned, the great ascetics who, with intense and persistent will, *fight against* the biopsychic drives and passions of human nature in an attempt totally to con-trol, dominate, subjugate, and even "paralyze" them. India has witnessed and still witnesses the self-imposed disciplines and even tortures used by such individuals. In that land of often tropical exuberance these men seek to reach supernatural states of consciousness and power by the most violent forms of denial of all that, in their body, seeks gratification—all except perhaps the ego in its subtler aspects!

Asceticism undoubtedly is an integral component of the mystical life, especially in its first stages of "purification," and mysticism and asceticism can be characterized as *counterpersonal* modes of activity. They operate in counterpoint to all that feeds, satisfies, and expresses a "personal" way of life. One could use also the term "counternatural," because these men and women work in opposition to the natural functions and tendencies of their biological organism and also of its psychological overtones. The main difference between the true mystic and the typical ascetic is that the former seeks a state of union with the Divine through love and/or utter devotion, while the latter tends to consider the means for reaching a supernatural state as ends in themselves and, consciously or not, remains attached to his self-will and the manifestation of the supernormal powers he has attained.

In the lives of some of the Avatars there are also early periods of intense self-deprivation and self-disciplining, and they do reach at times moments of mystical consciousness and a fervent devotion to whatever they know or feel is acting through them; but the direction or orientation of the essential life-activity is opposed to that of the mystic, at least until the great mystic himself becomes a center of radiation for "That" with which he has become united in love and total ego-surrender. Thus in attempting to define the characteristics of these modes of activity—reaching beyond and fighting against the personal nature, or consciously allowing the personality to be used for supernatural purposes—I do not mean to set rigid categories of behavior and goals. If one can speak of categories then there certainly are nonexclusive ones; they interblend at many points. They represent basic attitudes and goals which should be differentiated if one is to understand and properly evaluate what each of them characteristically implies and outwardly projects.

The ambivalence and ambiguity of the prefix *trans* in the term, transpersonal, are an excellent index to the difference between the mystic and, not only the great Avatar or Divine Manifestation, but the lesser types of human personages represented by the creative genius and the cultural hero. In order to avoid this ambiguity I prefer therefore to use two terms, counterpersonal and transpersonal.

The mystic—generally speaking and as a characteristic type—deliberately leads a life and tries to reach a mode of consciousness which separate him from what the society in which he is born considers "normal." The mystic, just as the true Occultist, is a manifestation of a countercultural trend polarizing the basic vibration of the culture of his community and race. Even in old India, a land which we tend to associate with mystics and yogic feats of supernatural power, these manifestations, though generally accepted and revered as supremely valuable, stood in sharp contrast with the jungle-like character of the people's biological and psychic passions and the undisguised violence of the political life, at least during a great deal of India's history.[3]

The four-fold pattern of development of a human life which the ancient Laws of Manu established, or at least codified, had the great advantage of integrating the search for mystical realizations within the total lifespan. Each of the four age periods was given a definite task: the task of learning the tradition (*Brahmachara* stage); the task of perpetuating the race by producing a progeny and insuring its physical welfare by some productive work (*Grihastha* stage); the task of unremunerated service to the sociocultural community (*Vanaprasha* stage); and finally the task of preparing oneself for death, but death

considered as a transition toward a more spiritual form
of subjective existence leading eventually to a new birth—
the character of that new birth depending on "the last
thought in death" (*Sannyasa* stage).

This last stage, already to some extent prepared for by
the third, represented a complete reversal of consciousness, because while the first stages implied a fundamental attachment to and identification with the life-
energies of nature and the traditional culture of a rigidly
planned society, this fourth stage demanded of the individual total detachment from all that to which he had
been previously attached. The aging person in many instances withdrew from the village—the social unit of India's culture—and lived in the surrounding forest,
devoting most of his time to meditation. It seems to have
been out of such meditations on detachment and death
that the ancient "Forest Philosophers" derived the
teachings of the Upanishads proclaiming the possibility
of merging the individualized consciousness with the
universal "ocean of being," *even while retaining the
same physical body.* This meant the possibility of experiencing "death"— total detachment—and of re-
turning to the consciousness of personality in a transfigured state and with a transformed understanding of the
life-death-life cycle. Yoga most likely was at first a
technique ultimately leading to an experience of death
followed by the return to full consciousness, and we find
this death-experience an essential part of Judo and other
forms of training—not forgetting the Gospel episode of
Lazarus and his return from three days of the death-state.
The state of *Samadhi* is in a sense a death-condition as
far as the personal consciousness is concerned, and at
the last stage of the raising of the Kundalini force the
vital energy of every cell of the body is raised to a point in
the head, leaving the body itself in a death-like state
followed by a rebirth resulting from a descent of
spiritual energy.

The true mystic also comes to experience a death of

the natural person in him and a rebirth in a new state illumined by the memory—and ideally the possibility of reexperiencing at will—an ecstatic condition of being and/or consciousness. Ecstasy literally means a going out of oneself, thus a reaching out to and attaining not only an illumination of the individualized consciousness but a transcendent state of being in which separation, distinctions, and differences are absorbed in a feeling-experience of the unity underlying them.

Such an experience in many instances may be a reflection of the power and quality of the "field of consciousness" of a much greater Being upon the stilled and expectant mind of the mystic. It may come as the result of a temporary opening of doors of perception— the *letting in* of a supernal light—through the action of some personage who has become repolarized at that transcendental level. It may even be produced by psychedelic drugs tearing down for a few brief moments the protective membranes and safeguards built by the ego and by one's culture and religion—a dangerous way, for the protective agencies may remain permanently impaired and they are needed for the operation of the effective mind in our everyday world. In all these cases what is primarily affected and revolutionized is the feeling-aspect of consciousness. And this is why most of the great mystics, trying to transfer to others something of the quality of their experience, had to use experiences of human love and physical union as symbols.

Because of its rationalistic and dogmatically theological approach to human experience, European culture could not truly integrate the mystical state in its regular patterns of human development. Monasteries and convents became the only acceptable forms of counterpersonal activity; but that activity was totally contained within the collective boundaries of the religious spirit, and it operated through intense devotion to and worship of a divine Person, be it Christ or Mary, the Virgin-mother. A similar, yet more fragmented and pluralistic approach to transcendent realization developed also in medieval India in the great *bhakti* movement and the Radhakrishna cults, and persisted in the typically Hindu relationship linking chela and guru.

I apply the term counterpersonal to such manifestations of the apparently deeply human urge for self-transcendence expressing itself as intense devotion, and (at our individualistic state of evolution) as a longing to return to a primordial condition of unity and "spirituality," because for some twenty-five centuries the mainstream of human development has been flowing in the opposite direction. Mankind on the whole has sought to develop the individualizing and atomizing mind; and that mind operates best with almost infinitely divisible and strictly measurable matter. Man's consciousness has therefore been unfolding its latent capacities in a matter-ward direction. It has been concerned with an ever increasing multiplicity of data, always more complex and refined sensations, and a myriad of intellectual variations on the basic themes of sexual enjoyment, bodily comfort, and nervous excitement. These are the foundations on which our Western civilization has been built, especially during the last 500 years, and before that time the same trends operated in varied forms in other cultures, though not with the same character of near-exclusiveness. Thus every movement working against this evolutionary mainstream can rightly be called, at least to some extent, countercultural and, particularly in our American society, counterpersonal.

The path of the Avatar, the hero and the creative genius leads those who tread it in a direction which actually is that of the evolutionary mainstream; but in most cases these men act against the *inertia of this mainstream*—an inertia which manifests in the institutions, the unquestioned paradigms, the standardized patterns of feeling and behavior and the intellectual stereotypes of a particular society built at a particular time, in a particular locality, and for a particular evolutionary purpose. These men are transformers and, if not destroyers, at least relentless critics and reformers of sclerotic social organisms. Yet, though they are considered "movers and shakers" of self-complacent and overritualized societies, they nevertheless are themselves moved by cosmic Powers and perhaps superpersonal Beings who not only inspire but "in-spirit" them. They are *agents of destiny*. Around them and through them everything begins to move and to change, seemingly perhaps of its own accord, yet impelled by a contagion of change, a will whose fire burns until the physical organism itself is totally consumed by the energy that flows through it and often leaves the personality shaken and empty. These men essentially belong to the line of the Promethean spirits. They are the manifestations of those great *karma yogins* who had to assume much of the almost unavoidable consequences of their gift of fire to human beings who were not ready, not willing, and therefore not able to act as co-creators with these divine "Flames."

The Avatars come to a race, a country, or a nation in which a poignant need has arisen for the experience of death-rebirth, because the old structures have become empty of vital and compelling meaning, and a combination of inertia at one level and chaos at the other dominates everything. They come when the time is ready. They are creatures of time (*Kala* in Sanskrit), because time is the structural aspect of change, and these men are haunted by the will to change and the urge to transform all they touch.

This will, this unquenchable, relentless urge is not "theirs" as individual persons. The will to destiny is the only will they really know—the will to perform the acts that must be done, regardless of consequences to their earthly personal vehicles. That Will to Destiny is the very power that moves them, often toward a tragic consummation. It essentially operates beyond what ordinary men name good and evil, because death polarizes rebirth, and tragedy is the dark brother of every release of new potentiality.

These Promethean beings should not be considered mystics, though the source of their activity is in a realm that transcends the personal and the merely human. The source is in that realm, and to that source we may give a more or less glamorous name: higher Self, Master, Lord of Karma, God—and in some cases their negative counterparts on the path of total disintegration beyond the possibility of rebirth in this world-scheme, for there are also avatars of Evil. The source may be personified and the avataric personage may feel himself identified with it and those who follow him may proclaim him as a "divine Incarnation"; yet a more accurate term would be a *transcarnation.* The fire of transformation burns through the flesh (*carne)* until its work is done—or at least until the disciples attracted to the flame have exhausted their capacity to respond to the fire and the light it radiates.

The mystic characteristically is an individual who has reached a phase in his Soul-unfoldment permitting him to experience, in the light of an intense desire for union with the Divine and of a love that accepts no limits, the unitive state. The Soul of a being manifesting as an avataric personage may have reached such a unitive state in a past existence or he may be on the way to reach it in a future life, but *his life as an avatar* (or a creative genius and a cultural hero) is polarized by a totally different purpose. This life is, I repeat, a performance, a ritual of transforming activity—and creativity implies the power to transform that upon which one concentrates one's attention. This activity is *an answer to a collective need.* It is a particular answer conditioned by a particular need, a particular place and time.

In a sense, therefore, the deeds being performed, or the creative work being produced, when considered in themselves, can be called "personal." They are determined by what occurs in the realm of human personalities, even though the occurrence follows a cosmic cyclic rhythm far beyond merely human personalities, *as such*. Because the results of the avatar's work refer to the transformation of a collective group of persons, and (in the case of great Avatars) of humanity and the planet as a whole, they inevitably are conditioned by the type of consciousness and the possibility of feeling-responses relevant to the basic level at which, at the time, mankind or a community is operating. The avatar accepts what is at the time of his appearance; he uses it in order to be able to transform it. One can transform only that to which one either belongs or has belonged—that is, from the inside. One has therefore to have experienced this inside and to some extent to act as if one belongs to it—thus as if one were merely a human personality.

The avataric being can be considered as the earth-terminal of a line of transmission of power. He is a magical instrumentality, a mask used in a collective ritual. This metamorphic ritual may deal only with a narrowly defined racial-cultural situation at the very close of a small cycle of which the avataric being is the mutating seed; or it may refer to a large evolutionary cycle. Thus there are avataric beings of several levels. The difficulty in determining the level of any one of them is that the beginning of even a small cycle may coincide with that of one or several larger ones. The line of transmission of power may reach much farther toward the galactic center, symbol of our cosmic God or Logos, than would seem to be in the case considering the character of the mask—the personal instrumentality, the ritualistic officiant.

What it is essential to understand is that the true character of the avataric being resides *not* in himself as an individual person, but in the *quality* of his acts or his creations. He actually *is* the enactment of a qualiity. He lives in the act he performs, in the message he reveals. He was born for that purpose, and in many cases his life is a sacrifice, simply because it is not really "his" life. This does not mean that he should be considered a medium in the usual sense of the term. One could perhaps speak of him as a "mediator." He performs "trans-actions" between a cosmic or divine Source of power and those who need the release of that power to be able to become more than they are. He is as much conscious of the purpose of the performance as his personal biopsychic organism is capable of clearly responding to the consciousness and intent of the source and the nature of the power released through him; and the higher the evolved condition of his biological ancestry and of the collectivity to which he has to address himself according to the pattern of his destiny, the greater and more precise his consciousness of the purpose he is fulfilling. Yet if there is consciousness it is consciousness revealed *in the act and through the performance.*

The terms clairvoyance and clairaudience today are commonly used. One should also speak of "clair-thinking" and "clairacting" when one refers to a quality of thinking and acting which implies far more than what is usually meant by thinking and acting. In clairthinking there is very little, if any, cogitative activity; and therefore an occultist like Sri Aurobindo, or an inspired philosopher-scientist like Teilhard de Chardin, have stressed the superiority of a certain kind of internal "seeing" over the rationalizing processes of analytical and conceptual brain-thinking. What appears to be a "seeing" is rather an immediate identification of the mind with an idea of a cosmic principle upon which a spotlight of certainty is focused. Likewise "clairacting" refers to a performance the inevitability of which is evident as the will-to-act mobilizes the required organs of action. What we call instinct in the animal kingdom is clairacting at the level of a generic, nonself-conscious consciousness. But in the avataric personage consciousness pervades the act; even if it does not precede it. A truly avataric action is not deliberative. It is spontaneous; but the source of the act is beyond the personality and its ego-consciousness. The act is trans-personal because the power it releases uses the person as a lens to focus the release.

The creative artist, who does not merely imitate and, with a relatively few superficial and personal modifications, reproduce the patterns which his culture and his teachers in school have impressed upon his mind, can be considered an avataric being at the sociocultural level. He is one insofar as a power transcending the ego-controlled field of his personality inspires or truly in-spirits him; and this means insofar as he exteriorizes in concrete forms—musical, plastic, or literary—what is actually needed at that particular time and place. These forms have to be acceptable at least to the most open minds and feeling-natures of his contemporaries or their progeny; and they are acceptable if they truly answer such a need, and when at least a few persons have become, or can be made to become, aware of what the need is. Nothing can be poured into a vessel totally full. Unless a group of individuals in a community have experienced some degree of inner emptiness, their collective consciousness cannot be filled with the power of a new aspect of the spirit. They must have been ploughed and harrowed by anxiety, loneliness, alienation, and deep suffering—even if such suffering has no apparent cause—in order to be able to receive the new seed.

There are creative artists whose mission it is to make concrete and give public form to a style of living, feeling, and thinking that through them, rather than in them, finds its perfect flowering. They indeed represent the flowering of a culture. They *essentialize* its fundamental character. They abstract its purest quality out of the perhaps heavily obscured or confused patterns of their society's way of life; they extract its meaning by selecting and emphasizing its most revealing features. They may be able to evoke the "soul" of the culture; and great art is always evocative rather than descriptive. Johann Sebastian Bach is an outstanding example of such a type of creative personality.

Only men of a lesser stature are content merely to faithfully depict in a quasi-photographic manner what is; they may be outstanding craftsmen, but they cannot be considered avataric beings, even though—or perhaps just because—they receive great and immediate applause. They may be outstanding personalities, but not transpersonal beings. In the same manner, a religious personage at the head or within the rank of an organized religious institution can be a great personality, a perfect exemplar of the ideal promoted by the religion, an excellent organizer; but this would not make him an avatar, unless he came in the midst of a widespread crisis, as one needed to restate the perverted ideal in its purity and to purify and reorganize a drastically shaken institution, whose cycle of validity is not yet exhausted. This would imply a transformation, but one that would specifically come under the category of "reform."

It is usually stated that the great Avatar is entirely self-taught and is born with an innate knowledge of his function and destiny; but a good deal of glamor and incomplete understanding may be involved in such a claim. The Avatar's mind, being widely open to the collective consciousness of the race of society which, at his birth, has reached the end of its cycle, is able to use whatever is required by the actions he is meant to perform. He does not know and learn simply for the sake of knowing of or achieving a social position. *His actions "know"* what they need to know in order to proceed according to the intrinsic rhythm of the Avatar's destiny. As an "emissary" of Man—or of some cosmic spiritual Power beyond the field of the Earth, or even of the solar system—all that he needs is available, but not to him as a personal possession. It is available to the power that expresses itself through him. That knowledge may not be repeatable. It really does not involve memory, any more than does an animal's instinctual knowledge of how to build a nest or paralyze an insect which its progeny will require as food.

The believer in a personal kind of reincarnation process will say that any obviously inborn knowledge "proves" that the avataric person—including the child prodigy who is a born composer, mathematician, or chess player—had acquired in a past incarnation that knowledge and the ability effectively to use it. This is undoubtedly a way of explaining the phenomenon. Yet is it the only and the deeper way? It is a way which individualizes a process that most likely has its root in a special relationship between the abnormally knowledgeable youth and the one Mind of Man. In the life of any avataric being it is Man—or rather one of the many aspects of Man's multidimensional potentials of being—that acts, speaks or intones the keynote of a new cycle of the planetary evolution of humanity-as-a-whole.

It is also Man—or the particular aspect of Man that a particular race or emerging community of human beings needs for survival or expansion—that acts through the performer of great deeds, making of him a "hero" for generations yet to come. In the most general sense of the term, a hero is a man (or a woman) who, in a totally consistent and significant "style," performs the acts of destiny which, at the deepest level of his being (though most often not in his ego-consciousness) he has accepted and assumed. A heroic performance is at least relatively a "per-fect" (i.e. achieved through and through) act or series of acts. It is the performance of a role which releases the creative potentiality inherent in a specific moment in the great play of man's evolution. In this performance the performer, having totally identified himself with the roles, is pouring his life-substance into the action. He is the action as well as the actor; and he is also, in a sense, that which is acted upon, because spiritually speaking the three are one. The need, the perfected adapted answer, and the answering constitute but one moment in the cyclic drama of existence, however large or small this cycle is conceived or realized to be.

Often the hero displays not only great courage, in-

domitable persistence in the face of ever renewed obstacles, and strength of character and magnanimity in
victory, but also intense passions and what, in lesser
men, would be called pride. Yet these seemingly negative
or personal characteristics should be seen in somewhat
different light than when present in ordinary human
beings who are not open, as the true hero is, to relatively
boundless horizons of power and, in some cases,
knowledge. If there is pride in the performance that
produced results of major collective significance, this
pride may hide a profound humility before the inner
Source whence flowed the energy that not only powered
the deed, but steeled the stubborn resistance and loyalty
to the envisioned goal. It is only in the more banal type of
actors that the proud evaluation of the value of the performance spills upon the ego of the person playing the
role. In any performer who realizes that he himself and
his entire life are but a form or ritual mask through
which a "god" (or focusing center for the universal Life-
force) operates, there can only be an exalted sense of
vicarious glory—a feeling of participation in a sacred
drama or rite, before whose greatness the small quasi-
organic pride of work well done reverently bows.

Reverence is the very soul of true heroism; reverence
before the supreme and always mysterious Source of the
power and the intensity that makes the actor vibrate often seemingly far beyond any conceivable natural
strength. The true hero, either at the moment of doing or
in a deep, unexplainable but constant manner, is aware
of a mystery within. He may not want to acknowledge
before others what to him is the quintessence and sacred
center of his whole being; but without such a deep
awareness of that which, in him, is divine rootstrength,
he would not be able to go on acting in a world which he
knows he must transform and, to this end, in which he
must ceaselessly fight the institutionalized inertia, so
that a new life may surge on the ruins of prejudices and
tradition-worshipping fears.

After his death, the hero's deeds, his life and his appearance may become immortalized into a style of behavior. He may remain an ever-inspiring example of revelatory thinking filled with the contagious fervor of living consecrated to an ideal or divine Presence. As this occurs the avataric being has become himself a Word of power, a mantram which millions of others may intone in moments of crisis, anguish, or uncontrollable despair. But while ordinary men glorify and perhaps worship the hero as a person, he himself has always known, by a kind of uncontrovertible knowing, that he is only a ritual mask, a personage, in the great *lila* of the universe, and a servant of cyclic purpose, an answer to a collective human need.

Avatars, heroes, creative geniuses, cannot be regarded as saints, even less as mystics; nor are they occultists or Masters in the usual sense of these much abused terms. They do not claim impersonality or the kind of purity that obeys the laws established for the sake of structuring a particular society or perpetuating institutions. They are not "fallen Angels" or gods in disguise. They are links between the divine and the human. They are channels of communication and transmission, and as such they are like the words of any language, the great symbols of any culture. They are utterances of destiny through human bodies and individual minds that—genetically as well as the end-result of a long line of incarnation—have the capacity to respond to a divine will and to form means of communication through which the human masses may be reached.

Theirs is the transpersonal way, the way through, the way of sacramental deeds and power-condensing utterances. It is also the way of compassion; for only the love of mankind can give them the warmth that fascinates others—unless they have fallen into the tragic and essentially desperate way of those magnificently dark egos whose cosmic destiny it is to destroy those that resist even the fascination radiated by the avatars and, unable to love, bind themselves to the divine by the power of absolute hatred.

Hate too is relatedness. Every release of potentiality has its dark aspect. But he that is rooted in love fulfills time and destiny, while time crushes whoever has repudiated love and refuses to acknowledge and revere the divine Source whence flow all noble deeds and beautiful loves.

References and Notes

1. This use appeared in the magazine THE GLASS GIVE, edited by the then well-known writer, Will Levington Comfort, and in a series of articles, entitled *Mountain Talks with Rudhyar:*

   . . . Instead of impersonal, let us use another word more telling—transpersonal. A personal type of behavior (or feeling or thought) is one rooted in the substance and conditioned form of the personality. A transpersonal type of behavior is one starting from the universal unconditioned self in Man and using merely the personality as an instrument. Such a type of behavior will be colored obviously by the personality—but not so much the personality of the actor as of the one toward whom the act is directed. It will be conditioned by the race, time and locality.

   The keynote of the spiritual life is transpersonal adaptability. Transpersonal love is protean. It shines upon all; but is concentrated upon each according to each need. In some cases it may seem to all most personal, most like ordinary human love. And what of it? Who can recognize what is or is not super- personal, save one whose level of being is established beyond the realm of substantial form; who is free from clinging to form and name, from vanity; whose consciousness deals fundamentally with tides of Energy, the same through multitudes of forms? (from the article "On Personal and Impersonal")

2. In the first issue of *The Journal of Transpersonal Psychology* (spring 1969) we find the following under the subheading "Transpersonal Definitions" (p. 15-16):

   The emerging Transpersonal Psychology is concerned specifically with the *empirical*, scientific study of, and responsible implementation of the findings relevant to, becoming, individual and species-wide, meta-needs, ultimate values, unitive consciousness, peak experience, B-values, ecstasy, mystical experience, awe, being, self-actualization, essence, bliss, wonder, ultimate meaning, transcendence of the self, spirit, oneness, cosmic awareness, individual and species-wide synergy, maximal interpersonal encounter, sacralization of everyday life, transcendental phenomena, cosmic self-humor and playfulness; maximal sensory awareness, responsiveness and expression; and related concepts, experiences and activities. As a definition, this formulation is to be understood as subject to *optional* individual or group interpretations, either wholly or in part, with regard to the acceptance of its contents as essentially naturalistic, theistic, supernaturalistic, or any other designated classification.

This evidently covers a vast variety of possible data and interpretations; but the italicized word *empirical,* gives the general direction. In order to be acceptable to the vast majority of the college-trained, *science-oriented* psychologists and medical men—such an empiricism is required; and this fact already conditioned Carl Jung's basic attitude, at least in his public works.

3.   cf. Heinrich Zimmer *The Philosophies of India* (paperback, Meridian Books, N.Y.) Part Two: The Philosophy of Success, and the Philosophy of Pleasure. Particularly interesting is his reference to Kautilya's *Arthashastra,* the treatise on government written by the super-Machiavelli of India.

)

9. THE GREATER FAITH

As far as records of human thinking and human society reach into the past we find mentions of the concept of law. At least, we find words which we translate today in that term, and we note social practices which resemble outwardly what we now refer to as law and its enforcement. However, words and records of behavior can be very deceiving. The men of thousands of years ago may have acted outwardly in ways which we assume were quite similar to ours; the actions may be similar, but the feeling-quality back of those actions and their essential meaning in terms of inner values may have been very different from those which we usually encounter in our time and society.

Such a possibility has interest not only for the historian; for today philosophies and religions of the past are being revived, and quite a few of their unfamiliar concepts and ideas are being absorbed by our minds. As ancient hieroglyphs, Oriental scriptures and alchemical manuscripts are being translated, we cannot be certain that our modern words carry for us the same meaning that apparently similiar terms did for the people of the past. Do the words we use today have the same meaning and convey the same "feelingtone" to *all* people who now read them? Obviously they do not.

All systems of philosophy, theology, metaphysics and even science at the abstract level, are essentially attempts at defining, in different ways, words such as: reality, God, matter, spirit, force, space, time, ego, soul, self-surrender. If it is true that humanity is entering a new cycle of civilization—a "New Age"—a fundamental change of values is inevitable. The meaning of the words we use is changing, slowly but steadily. The meaning may not be essentially new, for in past centuries a few men or groups here and there may have already thought and felt in this, to most of us, new manner; but what was an exception in the past may become a fairly common fact in the future of man's thinking and man's experience of value. Thus, the occultism of yesterday may be gradually becoming the science of tomorrow; and what but a few mystics have realized is probably touching the consciousness of an increasing number of sincere seekers after ultimates.

Here again we should beware lest we use glibly such words as occult, mystic, scientific, religious. Not really understanding what we are talking about, or with an understanding biased by set traditional use or personal complexes, we may produce more confusion than ever. Because most of those who have sought for years to overcome their narrow and dogmatic religious or moral traditions and to reach a new and higher or broader experience of "reality" *are* confused, one of the most important tasks today for the true philosopher is to seek to clear up as much of this confusion as is possible. Thus as this little word "law" is a fertile field for confusion, emotionally colored prejudices and superficial, all-too-easy (because nicely memorizable) statements, let us try to enquire into its various meanings.

Law is primarily defined (Funk and Wagnell's College Dictionary) as: "A rule of action established by recognized authority to enforce justice and prescribe duty and obligation," and as "a system of rules and regulations recognized by men or nations." This definition applies mainly at the social and political level. Later, another one follows according to which the "rule of action, as for governing human conduct" is understood to be "emanating from, or attributed to the Deity"; thus, "the commandments or revelations of God taken collectively."

The main concepts in such definitions imply or presuppose that there are "estabished rules"of action. What is the "recognized authority" establishing them? At one level we would normally say that it is the State and its ruler or the Legislature and the common or majority will of the people (or at least of the voters). At another level it is the Deity conceived as operating through, or in the person of, a Law-giver—for instance, the fabled Manu in India and Moses for the Hebraic people.

However, the word "authority" is a very interesting and little understood term. What it literally means is simply the status of being an author. An author has authority over what he is producing or creating; he can alter what comes out of him. A novelist has authority over the personages of his novel; an architect has authority over the building, the blueprints of which he is drafting. Once the blueprints are accepted and the foundations are laid down, *basic* alterations become nearly impossible unless the whole process is stopped and begun again from the beginning. Yet the owner or future tenants of the building may ask the architect to make many detailed changes—the more so the longer the building process lasts, making it possible for new emergencies and needs, or improved concepts of space-utilization, to arise. Other contingencies—labor strikes, sabotage, waste or sudden scarcity of rare materials—may also demand numerous modifications of the initial plan. Translating all this at the cosmic level may help us to understand many factors of a cosmological and social nature.

A number of religions, and today esoteric groups, are stressing the concept of *plan,* following a similar emphasis in politics, economics, even home economics (the famous "family budget" required every month to meet all installment payments—our karma!). Christian fundamentalists speak of "God's Plan of Salvation" in a way which probably would have startled and saddened

Jesus; and some modern prophets are disclosing what "God's Plan" is, according to some "revelation" from some great Personage who is said to be close enough to divine Headquarters to know about the blueprints of the Great Architect of the Universe. The symbolism of Architect and Plan is taken bodily from Masonry, as is also the concept of the "Lodge." A related concept, that of the Hierarchy, is obviously influenced by the Catholic Church's organization and perhaps by experiences with the Army. It should not be confused with the references to "Celestial Hierarchies of Builders of the Cosmos" (*Cosmocratores*) which H.P. Blavatsky and others have made, following archaic traditions.

The important point in any discussion of the concept of "law" is whether or not the "system of rules and regulations" is *external* to that which is being ruled, or *inherent in* whatever follows the rules. Unfortunately, in our misuse of words—which in turn has largely been produced by a deviation or perversion of the principle of conduct expressed by the earliest archaic words—we make no difference between a rule imposed from the outside and *an inherent or instinctive compulsion to act according to a structural order.* Neither do we most of the time clearly distinguish between "ruling power" and "authority"; and the results of such confusion are far-reaching.

Whenever one speaks of law one should have in mind a ruling power—but *not* an authority. The author does not make the law for the personages he imagines and creates in his novel; they are his creatures and therefore they obviously act acording to the way he has imagined them to act. The romantic idea dear to many a novelist that the characters of his stories acquire an entity of their own and *make him* develop the story in their own way, is simply an instance of inaccurate thinking; the novelist who makes such a statement may be correct insofar as his conscious ego is concerned, but the fact that this conscious ego is forced by the *inherent logic of development of a situation and a character* to make things happen in a way he at first had not thought of simply means that the real author-creator is not the novelist's ego, but a super-conscious power in him beyond the ego.

That creative power is the real author. This author "sees" rather than rationally thinks or plans. He emanates seed-ideas which are both ideas and forces *(idée-forces* in French). They are archetypes, i.e. definite sets of organized potentialities, which contain inherently *the energy necessary for their spontaneous actualization.*

After having had a more or less clear mental picture (or flash of inspiration), the novelist's ego writes down, or engineers, the story. Usually the mental picture is imprecise and full of holes; therefore, as the story proceeds, the writer is often surprised by the way it appears to unfold with a will of its own. It is not that the story has a will of its own, but that what the true "author" has *emanated* into the seed ideas of the story and the characters must unfold with an inherent logic of growth, just as an oak tree unfolds out of an acorn. The seed ideas must unfold; there is compulsion—but an inherent compulsion. There is nothing that, from the outside and through the use of some ruling power, forces anything to happen.

Compulsion does not mean coercion, but rather a state of "being driven together," a pulsing together. The cells of a body are compelled to act following a *principle of organic order* unless and until destructive and anarchistic forces break down the integrational power of "com-pulsing." Any forcible pressure from the outside cannot accurately be called a compulsion. If it could, that would mean that the seemingly compelled individual has ceased to be an individual entity and has become a unit within a larger whole, permanent or impermanent. For instance, it is impermanent in the case of a mob moved by a single violent passion, a mob of which the component persons cease for a time to feel, think and act as individuals; then they pulse-together;

compelled by the mob spirit.

In other words, the law is a system of rules and regulations which must be established *just because* the real sense of authority is lost. Laws are necessary when and where the inherent principle of structural order fails to operate adequately.

Seen from this point of view, to speak of a cosmic law or of natural law is to show that one has actually lost the immediate feeling-intuition of the immanent presence of the Author of the cosmos and of nature. One thinks as an ego fallen from a state of grace; one has so lost the sense of the divine order operating in and through the World-Process (the building of the cosmos) that one must interpret the evident regularity and amazing intelligence displayed in natural phenomena (including one's own bodies) as a law established by some ruler *outside of the World-Process*. A Big Boss is ruling the whole show. A Big Ego is setting down the law policing the world and human souls by the use of rigid decrees, sanctions, and all the paraphernalia of earthly states transposed to an imagined cosmic level.

Modern science speaks of laws; and the dictionary defines the term at the level of scientific inquiry as "the uniform occurrence of natural phenomena in the same way or order under the same conditions so far as human knowledge goes; a rule of the universe"—rule meaning here a "common or regular course of procedure." Scientifically speaking, what is meant therefore by natural or cosmic law is simply the fact that, as far as we know, natural phenomena occur in ways that are dependable and predictable; thus they can be foreseen and controlled for our use. Nothing is said or implied as to *why* they are so dependable.

But why the word, law? Why take this word from a certain field of human experience where it applies—the king or the legislature making "systems of rules and regulations"—to a field where we have no reason to believe it makes sense in the same manner?

Of course the theologian says it makes sense, for God is the King of the world and He establishes the laws of the universe. Does He? Does the Architect establish laws as he draws the blueprints of the temple he has visualized in imagination? He does not! He projects a form, *a system of relationships* between the many component parts of a whole which will gradually unfold and actualize the original vision of the architect; but relationship does not mean laws. To establish a form is not to set down a "system of rules and regulations"; such a system becomes necessary only when the form is no longer perceived by the builders—when spiritually blind, "stiff-necked and proud" egos (cf. Jehovah's estimation of His people in the Bible) are the only type of workers available. Let every worker be a true builder able to see or feel *as an immanent compulsion* the whole image of the building and particularly *his place and his job* in the building process—and there would be no need of rules and regulations by a managing boss. Each worker would identify himself with his work of destiny, whatever it be, and perform it to the best of his ability. He would fulfill his dharma—but not obey a law imposed upon him by a thundering Boss, such as we see pictured as Yahweh in much of the Bible.

Some of the students will exclaim that dharma means law in Sanskrit. Yes, it does for the modern mind (whether of 100 B.C. in India or of our day); but it also means "truth" and its primary, essential meaning was and remains the *fundamental nature of anything*. When the Hindu says that it is the dharma of the fire to burn, he certainly does not imply that some personal God has decreed that Mr. Fire will have to burn whether he likes it or not! It is the fundamental nature of fire to burn, and (in the *Bhagavad Gita)* that of Arjuna, a member of the Warrior Caste, to fight and kill enemies. These are their respective functions or places in the World-Process. The fire cannot help burning; but on the eve of the battle, Arjuna, as an ego, can feel dejected and ready to give up his natural function—thus to betray his fundamental nature, the very quality and form of his being in that particular incarnation.

It is Arjuna's congenital temperament to fight; he is made for that. He does not *obey* anything when he does fight; but he *betrays* his fundamental nature (thus, his destiny and his individuality) when, as an ego, he is overcome by weakness, confusion, and doubt. Krishna (the incarnate God) does not actually command him to fight, as a policeman would order someone to move on, or a fiscal agent demand income tax. He simply reawakens in him the realization of his dharma and presents to him a picture of the universal Whole. The gods who command or dictate messages are not the higher gods.

Modern science is actually coming at times very close to such an attitude toward the concept of law. Some years ago it was written in an article that Einstein, in his effort to formulate mathematically a single law that would unify all laws of nature, had come to realize that it might be most simply expressed by stating that everything tends to follow the path of least effort. But, such a law is no "law" at all any more than the *all-inclusive precept* which Jesus gave to his disciples: "Love ye one another as I have loved you" can be called a law. In the small book, *The Voice of the Silence,* which H.P. Blavatsky transcribed from old Buddhistic texts, is written: "Compassion, the LAW of Laws." But this "LAW" (the capitals are H.P.B.'s) is not *a* law either!

All such statements present a concept of universal order which utterly transcends all normal meanings to be given to the term law. They simply show that as the statements are made to human beings who are predominantly egos, jealous of their prerogatives and of their peculiar ability to do the wrong thing (our so-called precious freedom!), these egos have to be led out of the level of existence at which the idea of law operates and to a sense of reality and truth where systems of rules and regulations are no longer necessary, because the consciousness is irrevocably attuned to and one with the essential Quality of its being—its dharma, its fundamental nature.

Nevertheless, this identification of the ego with the dharma and essential truth-of-self cannot be accomplished by evading or escaping from laws. Gautama the Buddha sought perhaps more than anything else to free man's consciousness from the sense of obedience to the rules and regulations (castes, rituals, etc.) supposed to have been given by Manu, the Law Giver, who received them from this God. Yet Gautama did insist on a strict observance of his "dharma"; he made of this dharma a kind of substitute for the personal God idea, in much the same sense in which Thomas Paine, the "Father of Democracy," said: "In America the Law is king."

Men must be led on step by step; and for this reason the discipline in Buddhist monasteries, including Zen monasteries, is most rigid. But it is rigid discipline aimed at "compelling" the monks to overcome in group unison all sense of external laws, as well as eradicate the urges and appetites that feed the ego. One overcomes the need for obedience only through *implicit readiness* to obey. Then, when there is no longer any ego-block against utter obedience—and against humility or even humiliation—what was ego within the mind becomes a *clear lens* focusing the quality of the Soul into acts of destiny in which the dharma-individuality radiates as a transforming and illumining power.

Then the state of illusory freedom of the ego is superseded by a state in which right action becomes inevitable—right because exteriorizing the adequate solution to the need of every conceivable situation. This state of being is one of absolute wakefulness and lucidity; the necessary act is done consciously. In this respect it is the polar opposite of the typical instinctual act of the "natural" creature who also does the right thing in any of the emergencies belonging to a *particular* epoch and locality, but does it unconsciously. The animal is inwardly compelled to act rightfully, but does not know why; the Sage is also inwardly compelled to exteriorize in acts the spiritual quality he focuses into earthly existence, but he knows why he does so—and up to a certain stage of unfoldment, until all traces of ego-desire have vanished, there is still a possibility he may fail and fall.

At the tribal state of society in its original purity (the Edenic state), man, as a passive reflection of the inherent harmony of a divinely emanated nature, is compelled to act righteously, but he cannot help doing so. Even in later-day tribal societies the tribesman *cannot* break the taboos; they are inherent structures within his generic Unconscious, his utterly unfree psychic depths. *Taboos are not laws* any more than the stomach, liver, and intestines can be said to obey laws of metabolism! It is the nature of the tribesman to act in a traditional way because he is *psychically structured* so to act. Only when the ego gains power and can challenge the root-tradition of his tribal nature is man free—free to act regardless of what his fundamental nature is.

From the tribal point of view such an ego is a cancer-like cell in the body of the tribe; and it has to be ruthlessly cast away or destroyed. Yet with this act of independence a new stage of human evolution begins. The "gods" are confronted by the great "rebels." Zeus faces Prometheus who steals the divine fire to ensoul men with the god-seed of freedom and will; and the god's reaction is terrible.

Zeus-Jupiter "rules" the liver, the alchemical crucible in the human body; thus the Karma of Prometheus is to have his liver periodically devoured by a vulture. What he stole, he must surrender in sacrifice; but his gift gave to men the potential of self-consciousness, and self-consciousness requires for its growth the state of freedom to will and act as an independent self—*spiritually blind, yes, but independent!* Eventually the spiritual blindness which the Buddha called Ignorance or Maya, will be healed by the compassion of those who, in another way, sacrifice their peace so that men may consciously see and, seeing, realize their dharma and become identified with it in essence and in act.

Until this occurs, it is evident that society cannot endure without laws; and men's minds, hypnotized by their own need for laws, project that need upon the universe. They picture a universe of material atoms which look as solid and rigid as egos feel. These atoms therefore also require laws to keep them in order. This concept of rigid laws and determinism is now breaking down. Atoms are neither irreducible bits of solid stuff nor do they act individually in absolutely predictable ways. The rigid causal laws of nineteenth century science have become this century's statistical averages. No God or cosmic Law is there to force the atoms to obey their dictates; yet in some as yet unclear way, things even themselves up. The average results are dependable and predictable, at least within the limits of human sense-perception. What makes them predictable, however, should no longer be called a law.

"In the beginning" a solution is emanated out of the Infinite Potential (which is the ultimate reality of what we call SPACE) to answer the need of a closing cycle. This solution balances and harmonizes the need, as the need of a family for a home is satisfied or neutralized by the architect's blueprints of the house they will be able to live in. Every need is always and forever balanced by a solution, and the power of this *potential* solution is "spirit." Spirit is the energy of the infinite potential of SPACE . We live within an infinite ocean of potentiality. The protean *activity* of this ocean of potentiality is spirit in manifestation. To experience this ever-present potential is to know Reality; it is to sense infinite "Love." But being blind, we can only think of "laws"!

There is only one Supreme Law: *Everything is as the need for harmony requires. Everything acts in order to satisfy what, at the time and to the best of its knowledge, it feels it needs. Everything seeks to act according to its fundamental nature.* Any other path of action increases the need, because it intensifies the resistance to the action and this calls for a greater effort and exertion.

Man's nature, however, is to be conscious of the *meaning* of the infinite and cyclic interaction of need and solution; for only thus can he be what he essentially is: a focalizing agent for the power of the metacosmic Principle of Individual Existence which I have called simply (in capital letters) ONE. This Principle or Essence (the words are most inadequate, alas!) is what is at the root of eternal, cyclic MOTION. Always and everywhere harmonic MOTION animates SPACE—and the results are an infinity of universes in which individualization produces basic needs and these draw out of the infinite potential of SPACE wave upon wave of spirit.

To feel, sense and experience this immediate response of spirit to individual need; to become oneself the channel or instrumentality for the release of such a response of spirit, is to realize the superficiality of the concept of law. *Everything is possible that an essential need requires.*

However, as long as men behave, feel and think as egos who have no sense of infinite potentiality, no realization of the cyclic picture as a whole, no awareness of the Great Architect's vision and of his divine formative Mind (whence emanates the archetypal form of the cycle of which He is origin, source and guiding Intelligence), and no impulse toward absolute harmony, save as the latter is dimly reflected on the agitated surface of their passion for what they call love—to such egos laws must appear necessary.

They will indeed be necessary in societies forever disrupted by the chaotic desires and the free will of our egos. It is the ego which calls for kings; and its karma requires tyrants and dictators, generals and atom bombs, to be worked out up to some *Götterdämmerung* finale.

It is the ego which places its faith in laws, because its shaky faith must be bolstered by something rigid, unchangeable, rational, and never upset by passion or caprice: the law. It is the ego which worships law-givers, human or divine, because the shadow of such a faith, fear, must cling desperately to some awesome but magnificent Countenance that seems to the ego "authority," but in sober fact is only "ruling power."

The creation of the universe by "authority" is that creation of which the first chapter of *Genesis* speaks. The Author is ELOHIM and He Creates with "Light" the essential Ideas of the universe of which He is the multiune Seed. It is a creation in Harmony; the harmonizing solution to the need of "the Deep," of Chaos. By contrast, the second chapter of *Genesis* tells of a "secondary creation" by *one aspect* of the ELOHIM—"JH-VH Elohim" (Jehovah or Yahweh) who fashions man from earth and water, then animates the statue which He produced with the "breath of life." This divine producer of natural man is the manager and ruler of the realm of life (the biosphere); and it is from this realm of foundations and of unconscious shapes that man must emerge. He is faced with a command: "Thou shalt not eat of the fruit"; but where there is *command,* man must break the order. The command and the breaking are two sides of the same coin; law and anarchy are *inseparable polar opposites.*

Let me state once more that the realm of law and law-breaking is the realm of egos. A Big Ego rules over it. That He must so rule is His ordeal and His karma; for He performs there the cosmic task of forcing individual men to rebel against His will in order that, through the tragedy and trials which He must, as Lawgiver, focus upon those who break the law, these rebels may *in time* rise above this tragic realm of laws and of the possibility to be free to break laws.

As human beings so rise, they emerge eventually into the realm of the "primary creation" by ELOHIM; they have the vision of the Temple-to-be as emanated by the Mind of ELOHIM, the Great Architect. In full wakefulness they *know*, through total attunement and identification with the clear mind that reveals to them their destiny, their dharma, their truth-of-self. This perfectly clear, egoless, unobstructed state of dharma-fulfillment is nirvana-in-action; it is exemplified by the Buddha who, having experienced nirvana, *returned* to teach and work among men for forty years of a perfect and illumined life.

Having reached this state man no longer needs to place his faith in the laws of nature or of the cosmos. He experiences a "greater Faith"—the faith in the inexhaustible potentiality of SPACE and in the omnipresence and all-harmonizing potency of spirit.

The lesser faith in laws belongs to the ego always seeking to *use* something to its own advantage, for self-assurance or self-aggrandizement. The ego is like the corporation lawyer whose job it is to be so conversant with all the systems of rules and regulations imposed by the State to coerce people into the superficialities of a well ordered society that he may find ways and means safely to circumvent the law.

Our modern engineers are merely lawyers! They find out what natural laws allow within a more or less safe margin of risk; then they proudly use their knowledge of laws to gain their ends. But anyone who thinks of gaining his end is still an ego. Anyone who "uses the law" is bound to the concept of law; he is self-imprisoned in the realm of legality—social or cosmic. His allegiance is to the realm of the ego, of separativeness and of fear—the fear that is masquerading under boastful arrogance, cocksure optimism, and human pride, or under a feigned humility before the Big Brother or the "jealous God" that rules the world of laws.

This faith in laws is indeed the "lesser faith" because it is faith in some power that is, in the last analysis, always outside of the self. It is the child's faith, once his

faith ceases to be an absolutely unconscious and instinctive reliance upon the mother and has turned into a
conditional faith in his ability to get the parents to give
him what he wants if he obeys enough of the parents'
laws to be able to break them safely by cajoling, prayer,
or ruse. The child accepts punishment as part of the
bargain. One must risk, must one not, when one is an
ego bent upon achieving success and pleasure? Some im-
petuous egos go in for foolish and daring risks—whether
or not karmic spanking is more or less inevitable.
Others, grown wiser and more calculating, plan carefully
in terms of what military men and our State Department
call calculated risks. But there is no essential difference
between the foolish and the wise when they act in terms
of this lesser faith.

Yet, such a faith is certainly not to be belittled, as it
represents a necessary phase of development just as the
ego does. But beyond the narrowly focused consciousness
of the ego, and reaching toward a condition of essential
openness to whatever may stream forth out of the ocean
of Infinite Potentiality, a higher stage of human development should appear to the ego-weary mind. A greater
faith, a faith in the spirit which, in a kind of sublime
"automatism," provides all existences with the answer to
all essential needs, can dawn at the horizon of man's
consciousness. Such a faith is crucially needed as man
strives toward a transcendent state of being and consciousness in which he becomes his living truth-of-self.

"Openness" here does not mean passivity or mediumship, or the unconscious inevitabilty of animal instinct.
It means first of all total wakefulness and utter lucidity.
It means an unglamored evaluation of the past, a
profound historical sense of cyclic processes, a
disciplined mind that can form itself into a translucent
lens through which the Light-energy of spirit can be
focused in a perfectly formed revelation of *meaning*.

What will be revealed is the essential meaning. The
precise formulation and the action which the individual

will produce will be "his", but not his in terms of ego-desire or ability to use the law cleverly. It will be his in terms of the particular destiny, individuality, or dharma that he essentially is—in terms of his fundamental nature. Spirit does not *dictate;* it reveals; it makes the deeper, higher consciousness *see.* Then the flash of vision is given form by the mind of the perceiver in terms of what is needed—needed by the individual, or by those he or she may serve by sharing with them what can be made understandable of the vision.

Alas! Something often occurs to a person who has had but fleeting experiences of the greater faith. He finds himself confronted with needs that seem crucial and immediate, the solution of the spirit does not appear; the vision is clouded; the lens of the mind is barren of forms, symbols, or meaning. Then the panicky individual falls back on his old lesser faith, as Moses did when he struck the rock several times in his impatience for seemingly so badly needed water. Fear reawakens the ego-will. The eagerness for a solution—for a sign from God, the Christian mystic would say—is so desperate, so emotional, that the individual's consciousness slips into the old realm of laws and regulations. There *someone* is always available to answer the need in the way of the legalistic mind. In the realm of ego there is always some Big Ego to tell you, the little confused ego, exactly what to do or say . . . "for better or worse."

This may be necessary; the individual's failure of faith will have made it necessary. When the greater faith fails, it is probably good to depend upon the lesser faith. Yet in an ultimate sense a thorough crisis, even a break-down, may at times be better than a comfortable solution, or another kind of orthodoxy to confuse a little more, even while it helps, for a while, the mind and the will.

This is where the difficult discrimination concerning when and how to help others comes in. The eagerness to "save," whether oneself or others, may be a sign that the

would-be savior knows only of the lesser faith. It may be
a lovely glamor with which the ego masks its real desire
for being a Big Brother to some little ego, an "old soul"
well ready to take care of "just a beginner"; and how often this is the case in so-called occult or religious
organizations! Yet, even a sincere reliance upon the
greater faith may also turn into a "spiritual" excuse for
not helping those who ask for needed assistance; it may
become a kind of soul-weariness, or rapturous selfishness.

No one can tell another what his faith should be.
Indeed there is no question of what it *should be,* but
only of what it *can* be. There is no ideal or path
absolutely valid for all people. All that one can do
is to exteriorize whatever way has been revealed
by an experience—or is known through a basic inner
awareness—of one's fundamental nature. There is no
law greater than one's fundamental nature. There is
no religion or system of laws greater than dharma.

10. LOVE ON THE TRANSPERSONAL WAY

Everybody speaks of love; but how few are consciously aware of the higher possibilities of the love between man and woman! There are many kinds of love; but we should at least distinguish two basic levels at which today love can operate. It may operate as an unconscious biological, social, and psychological compulsion, or else as a consciously acknowledged, polarized, and trans-figured power, used by mature personalities, in the service of a freely accepted superpersonal purpose. As man and woman come to see and to evaluate one another in the light of new ideals of manhood and womanhood, as their sense of purposeful and productive participation in the social and universal Whole increases intensity and inclusiveness, the love which gives substance and fire to their togetherness must necessarily assume a new character, a new quality. This quality should be understood and defined today as clearly and vitally, as inclusively and convincingly as possible, for upon its cultivation and generalized expression in the New Age will depend the fundamental quality of all basic human relationships, of marriages and social interchanges, of culture and manners. *The essential quality of any human society is derived from the quality of the love which unites its men and women.*

When the tribal law operates with unchallenged instinctual compulsion because there is no individuality as yet developed in the tribesman to challenge it—the union of man and woman is completely conditioned by biocultural purposes. The man tills the soil and is happy in the feeling of muscular release of energy and of fruitful work. The man likewise "husbands" the woman's earth-nature, and is happy in sexual release and in his progeny. He is deeply attached to the productive substance he fecundates with seed—be it the dark soil or the vibrant body. This attachment is functional and instinctual; it has deep roots in the collective unconscious of all human beings. It is a compulsive force operating at a level where there is no freedom of decision or choice, no personality. It is, nevertheless, a productive force. Its one goal is the fullest possible increase of seed and substance; and, at a later stage of social evolution, of usable wares and cultured products.

When transcendent ideals begin to superimpose themselves upon the goals of biological and cultural productivity, and eventually seek to reduce the latter to a low valuation—when the devotional intensity of the mystic or the saint feeds on asceticism and subliminal ecstasies or martyrdom—then a new type of love emerges which is given a "spiritual" valuation. Yet such a love remains essentially a compulsive type of emotion, even though it be the love of God, or some deified person or image. The passion for the beyond can be as tyrannical a force as the hunger for sex; its roots as deeply submerged in unconsciousness and fate. The green leaves of a plant are drawn irresistibly to the light of the sun ("heliotropism"—from *helios*, sun and *trope*, turning) in order that they may perform their vital function of photosynthesis (the conversion under their impact of lightrays of the carbon dioxide of the air and water into sugars and starches). In a similar manner, the devotee turns his emotional nature toward a transcendent image in the "theotropism" of a love which aspires to capture the effulgence of divinity and to fix it in the "leaf-substance" of a humanity still far away collectively, from the condition of mature "seed-personality."

When, in a later period, the trend toward individualism

asserts itself; when the rational intellect and its analytical outlook atomizes society and isolates every ego from every other ego; when, as a result, personal complexes, fears, and passionate yearnings toward some experience of union with, and self-loss in, others harrow the distracted soul, a new type of compulsive love develops. It is love based on psychological emptiness and need. It is the love of the romanticist; the love of adolescent egos frightened with the responsibility of conscious and productive selfhood. It is the "erotropism" of insecure personalities seeking to warm themselves at, or be consumed by, the fire of universalized and unpersonalized Eros. The inital purpose of this type of love is to stir the soul-substance into activity, to release emotional fire, to transpierce—as with lightning—the inertia of the flesh and of the unconscious earth-bound psyche. To vibrate, to feel alive and in a state of inner motion, in a flaming state: these are the needs of the adolescent type of personality, just as it is the need of the virginal soul of the devotee and mystic to experience the ecstasy of divine love, the glowing state of self-surrender to the inrush of universal light-substance.

In both cases, the purpose of the love is lost in the thrill or rapture of the experience of love. The participants are inwardly forced into the tormenting fire or the blinding light of such a love. Of conscious choice, there is practically none. The individual is *in* love with love. He does not consciously perform acts of love for, and together with, another being—be the being human or divine. He does not *share*, deliberately and purposefully, his fullness with another, simply because he is not yet a mature personality, because his love is conditioned by scarcity and bondage. It is a passionate and irrational attempt to compensate for a youthful, or later crystallized, egocentricity, to burn the binding structures of the individual ego, to become free from self and one with all life and, first of all, with the beloved. In some cases, it is a vehement rebellion of human beings seeking to assert their individual egos against the tabus of tribal life or the traditions, allegiances, and shams of society.

In any case, this love, which is the nature of fire, seeks liberation and emergence into a wider realm of power and activity. It consumes limits and boundaries; it is a revolutionary force, an emotional fervor which yearns for transcendent beyonds. It stands thus in sharp contrast against the tribal love of men and women which is the glow surrounding work well done in common, the natural perfume of common accomplishment in an instinctual-cultural sense, the happy feeling of joint participation in a collective organism, whose structural law is unquestioned and never felt as bondage. This biological-social love is an expression of the will to increased productivity. It serves and glorifies the seed. The love of the Christian mystic, or of Tristan and Isolde, or of Dante for Beatrice, is a consuming fire which stirs, uproots, liberates, and transfigures—or maddens—men and women craving for freedom from ego and from social rules, yearning for the infinite sea of "cosmic consciousness."

The fire of this love surges, in most cases, from sex; but sex, here, must be understood not in terms of seed-producing functions as much as in terms of the release of a basic power, electromagnetic in essence and with very strong psychic overtones. It is not sex for the purpose of producing a progeny (procreative sex), but sexual union as a means to overcome differentiation and the polarized state, to stir in the soul the will to merge with another in a conquest of individual separativeness, personal isolation, and loneliness. Under the burning psychic "heat" produced by this sexual but nonprocreative love, the molecular and atomic patterns of individual selfhood become deeply altered. The personality can become "ionized," stripped of unessentials, free to unite in ecstasy with other individuals under the compulsive power of the energies which surge from the common root in which all men are one in *unconscious* unity.

This ego-transcending and difference-obliterating love, when finally disassociated with the last thought of sex, can be interpreted and experienced as the urge for *union* with the One or, through a one, with the Whole. The transcendent lover may seek inward union with God, or an outwardly expressed communion with humanity. But whenever the former quest reaches its goal, it always must lead to the type of life exemplified by a Buddha or Christ. He who has become one with God must assume the spiritual burdens of a distracted and earth-bound humanity. He must forever strive to transform unconsciousness and the dark compulsions of instinct into conscious illumination. He must demonstrate the radiant charity which transfigures the service of the poor or the wounded into an act of love for all mankind.

Such a compassionate love is not productive of seed; but it gradually releases humanity as a whole from bondage to the thought of separateness and to the seeming inevitability of conflict and war. It is a unifying power. It integrates the essential realities of individuals, groups, and nations by consuming in its fire the nonessentials which produce division and hatred. It seeks to reconstitute at the conscious level of mature personalities the primordial unconscious unity of the tribe state, and to reconstitute it in total inclusiveness. Tribal unanimity was exclusive of all other tribes; but transcendent love is boundary-transcending, culture-transcending, creed-transcending. Its goal is the "One World" of a truly organized, global humanity. In this goal it finds itself a partner of modern science and technology, thanks to which world unity has become an actual, concretely experienceable fact that no honest and intelligent man can ignore.

Science, in its multipersonal and cooperative attempts to establish a body of truths acceptable to all men because self-evident, like transcendent love overcomes the rigid barriers with which traditional cultures, organized religions, and racial pride have hemmed in the differentiated human collectivities. Science's techniques could build generalized means required for mutual understanding and personal interchange on a very large scale, if they were spiritually handled. Science too is a releaser of fire; the fire within the atom which could establish the foundation necessary for the integration of all peoples. And if atomic energy potentially is destructive of antiquated structures and regressive nationalism, so is the love that is a consuming fire, an iconoclastic force burning away personal crystallizations and goals made obsolete by the pull of creative tomorrows. Until man is established individually and collectively on the plane of conscious intelligence and mature responsiveness to universal creative principles; until man has reached the spiritual status possible only to a truly individualized person, there must be destruction by fire; there must be transcendence and overcoming.

The day comes however, when, at long last, love once more operates as the servant of productivity: productivity no longer conditioned by instinctual and unconscious compulsion, no longer biological and tribal in character—but instead, the co-productivity of mature persons in and through whom God, as the Universal Creative, *acts*. The type of "seed" which this co-productivity seeks to increase by an earth-transcending kind of cultivation is an ideospiritual or, symbolically speaking, "celestial" type of seed: the seed of man's personal immortality, as well as the seed of a new culture established in the fullness of conscious human interchange.

The co-productivity of mature personalities in and through whom God acts—God the Universal Creative: these two phrases establish the only foundation upon which a new image of love may develop, which our modern humanity so poignantly needs to see exteriorized in the fabric of its marriages and of all the social activities bringing together men and women as co-participants and, potentially, as "companions." These phrases may have a mystical ring which makes them sound strange and elusive, or meaningless, to the modern intellectual of either sex. Yet they refer to the deepest realities of human consciousness and love. Any one can fathom the meaning of these realities who has relinquished his or her reliance upon the superficialities or the transcendent idealism of a society yearning for fullness of life while, at the same time, opposing incessant obstacles to the inrush of power and vision which alone can give man fulfillment, peace, and the sense of paricipation in immortal values.

There is co-productivity of mature personalities when man and woman come together as individual persons in order deliberately to perform, in fully conscious cooperation and love, productive activities. This is production *from* personality; whereas the instinctual, unconscious production of man and woman bound to biopsychic patterns of behavior and feeling—or helplessly driven by their yearning to transcend and deny these patterns—is production *toward* the eventual attainment of mature personality. The state of truly mature personality, however, is never realized until the individualized person is able to relax what C. G. Jung called graphically "the cramp in the conscious," and to accept a transpersonal way of life; until the individual person, whether man or woman, overcomes the tightness of an ego haunted by the preoccupation of keeping its structure so rigidly what it is, that it finds itself completely shut to any influx of power.

A truly mature personality operates within the structural framework of a relaxed ego. The center of this relaxed ego is able and eager to open to the downpour of universal energy and ideospiritual realizations. In another sense, it is like a lens through which the vast tides of the universal mind are brought to sharp focus and given *operative form* as ideas and words, as emotionally stirring images and symbols. The first alternative—*the open centrum*—if not taken too literally, pictures what the transpersonal way archetypally means for a woman who is a conscious individualized person. The second alternative—the crystal-clear lens—gives a basic clue to the inner nature of the man who has reached a similar level of development. In both cases the essential fact is that the universal spirit is able to act *through* the individual ego, to permeate the total organism of personality with the purpose and the power of God.

Through the "crystal-clear lens" at the core of the man's ego, God's purpose is focused as a formulated idea, an operative structure (blueprints and schedule of work). Through the "open centrum" at the core of the woman's conscious and individualized personality the potent tide of the Holy Spirit flows. As the man and woman unite their beings in the ritual of a consciously all-inclusive, transpersonal love, the bipolar emanation of the Divine becomes a concretely creative and transforming act of power. This is accomplished *through* the love of man and woman. This love is consciously co-productive—not compulsive and unconscious. It is not rooted in biopsychic instinct. It is instead a deliberate answer to the need of humanity, *whatever this need might be.*

At the biopsychic level, male and female are brought together, under the compulsive thrust of instinct, to provide a bipolar agency through which life can operate. In such a type of union man and woman act as *carriers of ovum and sperm*—not as individual persons. Even when the purely instinctual act develops potent overtones of feelings, of personalized emotions and ideals; even when passionate love surges as an all-consuming flame from the furnace of aroused sex and seeks to deny its biological source; even then, unless artifically blocked, the meeting of sperm and ovum occurs under the control of the impersonal generic life that animates the human species and assures its perpetuation in spite of personal human wishes or superficial plans. Life is the Actor through men and women unaware of its plans.

When men and women are able to operate at the ideospiritual level, life is superseded by the divine creative Spirit. In and through the consecrated man and woman who consciously and purposefully unite their beings in order that the need of humanity might be answered, and their voluntarily assumed shares in the great planetary purpose might be completely fulfilled, this divine Spirit acts. In that creative act of the Spirit, *through* the man and the woman, love reaches its most perfect expression. It is, then, divinity in act. God *is* love—love, not as a vaguely idealistic sentiment or feeling of unity, or a poignant burning passion that yearns for unattainable ecstasy of self-forgetfulness and transcendent bliss, but love as a clear creative answer to the need of the world.

Spirit, I repeat, is always a creative answer to the need of the world. Creation is not a "play"—as Hindu philosophers who sought to react against the functionalism and totalitarianism of the Brahminical society would have us believe. Creation is God's answer to a world in chaos, to the need of that which has come to experience total disintegration and the atomizing of matter utterly unillumined by spirit. Creation is a perpetual reestablishment of universal Harmony. It is an act of integrative Ideation by the divine Intelligence that is absolute Harmony.

Man and woman can partake in this ever renewed act of divine Creation consciously and in the full productiveness of their total humanity. They can do so, in an incomplete manner, as single personalities, because in every individual person the whole of the universe and the full essence of divinity is latent. Yet, in order to bring that which is latent and only potential to a condition of total actuality and complete efficiency, the individual person must reach beyond the boundaries of his ego, to those with whom, in interdependence and joint consecration, he can perform the ritual of the Spirit. Man reaches toward woman; woman reaches toward man. And both man and woman can know themselves as participants in a vast Company of consecrated persons who, together, are building out of the root of man's common humanity the ultimate and global Seed, Man. In that Man, God's creative purpose is fulfilled, insofar as humanity on this earth is concerned. In that bipolar Man, the divine Word that was "in the beginning" is made fully concrete, and the power of divine Nature is condensed; as in the seed, archetypal structure and potency of life are combined.

11. REPOTENTIALIZATION AND THE VIRGIN STATE

In physics two states of energy are considered: potential and kinetic energy. Energy is defined as "the capacity to perform work." More generally, it is the capacity to act. There can be no activity without a release of energy, but this release can occur at several levels of existence. To exist is to use energy. Energy being used is kinetic energy, whether it be at a cosmic or a biological level. Any cycle of existence begins in a release of energy. Such a release occurs when potential energy becomes kinetic energy.

A wound up spring, a stone balanced on top of a high wall, have potential energy. They have a *latent* capacity to generate activity, the spring by unwinding, the stone by falling. A seed during winter months has potential energy. When spring comes, it is stirred into activity; the latent potentiality of growth as a plant manifests as a release of biological energy. The emergence of the rootlet and the germ begins the yearly cycle of existence for that plant.

If we try to imagine the beginning of a universe in the most metaphysical way possible to the human mind, we can say that this universe emerges into existential being when the cosmic energy that moves the very first type of material later to manifest as stars and galaxies passes from the state of *metacosmic potentiality* to that of *cosmic actuality*. How such a passage operates is the great enigma. The religious mind solves for itself this enigma by speaking of God's Creative Act: "Let there be Light!" But the problem is merely shifted to the need to elucidate what is meant by "God."

However God, the Creator, may be pictured by the human mind, this picture has to include a tremendous reservoir of potential energy. God, as the Prime Mover —if he be "the One without a Second"—has to be, or to contain, potential energy on a metacosmic scale. This being so, one might simply say that the beginning of any universe constitutes the emergence of a cosmogonic tide of kinetic energy out of a vast reservoir of metacosmic potential energy. This metacosmic reservoir of potential energy may be significantly symbolized as an *infinite Ocean of potentiality.*

We have, however, to be very careful of how—consciously or unconsciously—our mind pictures the state of potentiality at the metacosmic level. When one speaks of the potential energy within a seed deep in wintry soil, one has something concrete and tangible: a seed, serving as the container of, or basis for, the potential energy. The seed objectively exists, even though in a condition of biological latency. But when we try to think of a metacosmic ocean of potentiality, we have to somehow transcend what we call existence (ex-istence). Potentiality does not "exist"; latency is not existence—nor should it be called nonexistence. It is the possibility of existence; and we may well postulate that whatever is possible *will* exist at some time or *does* exist in some dimension or region of infinite space. In an acorn a very limited and clearly definable possibility of existence—existence as an oak tree—inheres. But "inhering" is not the same as "existing." We should say that the potentiality of existence as an oak *in-ists* in the acorn. The state of potentiality is one of "inistence," not of either existence or nonexistence.

Hindu cosmology speaks of periods during which Brahman manifests as the cosmos, and periods of non-manifestation—*manvantara and pralaya.* In a more popular and anthropomorphic sense, mention is made of the "outbreathing and inbreathing" of Brahma, the Creative God. But the concept of nonmanifestation (pralaya) is usually formulated in terms of negative statement. It is conceived as the negation of everything and every value we associate with existence in our dualistic world. "Not this, not that"—a void *(Sunya),* utter darkness. Because we live in a world filled with a multiplicity of entities in a state of constant change and transformation, we must postulate nonmultiplicity in the state of nonmanifestation; in this state unity prevails. All is one in a timeless condition, and space is reduced to the nondimensional point— a condition of mere subjectivity.

But if the state of nonmanifestation implies unity, we should not speak of absolute unity, for the concept of absolute unity precludes the possibility of multiplicity or even duality. And the very fact that I am thinking and writing implies duality. Everything may be withdrawn into the unmanifested Brahman in the pralaya state, but the desire for eventual manifestation must remain in the One, at least as a possibility; otherwise there could be no universe.

The confusion comes from the ambiguous meaning of the term, unity. When one speaks of "unity in diversity" one actually means by unity integration or wholeness: diverse entities realize that they are parts or at least that they have emerged from an original One in whom they can and eventually must be reabsorbed or reintegrated. When Sri Sankaracharya, the great Hindu philospher whom his disciples have considered a major Avatar, long ago originated his Adwaita system, he spoke of the nondual character of the supreme Reality *(a-dwaita).* In so doing he was following the old tradition which had as its essential purpose to impel human beings to free themselves from the dualistic oscillations between pleasure and pain, and from dependence upon the external powers of life (instincts, desires for expansion, passions) which compulsively operate in a polar (thus, dualistic) rhythm. Hindu philosophy, even at its seemingly most metaphysical level, is eminently purposeful. It intends above all to show people how to take *the next step* in the development of their consciousness, thus to *trans-cend* the existential state in which they live.

Nondualism is a conceptual means to transcend the attachment to the life-force and the processes of the mind which serve as a foundation for ego-structures. It seeks to achieve this very practical result by devaluating all that belongs to the world of existence and its myriad of attractions—thus, by presenting them as mere illusions, the products of ignorance. What really is absolute is the character of this devaluation or repudiation of all aspects of existence; and it has led millions of Hindus to seek an escape from existence—escape into a condition of pure subjectivity from which they believed there would be no return.

Yet there always is return, as Gautama the Buddha clearly showed in his own life—a return moved by *compassion*. There is return in time, but what returns may be a being whose consciousness has become transfigured and who no longer is only a part of the cosmic whole, but is the Whole focused through him in order to perform deeds of wholeness and compassionate love.

To put it differently, potentiality and actuality are the two poles of "That" which includes them both—somewhat as, in Chinese philosophy, Tao includes the two principles Yang and Yin. These principles wax and wane in turn. If we think of them in terms of objective existential realities, we associate them with the polarities of life, male and female, light and darkness, expansion and contraction. But we also can think of these two principles in terms of actuality and potentiality. If we do so, a different world-picture emerges, presenting us with two fundamental *trends:* the trend toward ever more objective and concrete actualization, and the trend toward repotentialization. This latter trend represents an attempt so to transform any particularized or individualized form of existence that it becomes more inclusive, ever more open to a flow of new possibilities, and more able to begin again through fresh creative, that is, originating and/or transforming, acts.

From this point of view, the "illusion" which the Hindu philosophies associate with existence itself should be related only to the inertial character of most of its forms. *There must be forms,* at whatever level we may think of them—be they physical bodies, psychic structures, of habitual feeling-responses, mental concepts, or cosmic existences. Existence is a state in which kinetic energy operates within some kind of field, each existential field having more or less definite boundaries and a characteristic rhythm of operation (or "tone"). Every release of energy occurs in "quanta", and that "package of energy" manifests concretely as a form or structure—as an entity (ideas and the structured products of mental activity are also entities at the mind level). Every entity occupies some kind of dimensional space and the energy which flows through it will wear out according to a more or less definite time schedule. It has a specific or individual character and some kind of consciousness, diffuse as it may be. It has a cosmic purpose or function, a dharma or "destiny."

Most forms of existence pass through a set schedule of concrete transformation, and the schedule is quite rigid. It resists *radical* change which would alter its natural character and its function within a well defined environment. When this function reaches its normal operative capacity—that is, when the process of actualization of this very limited aspect of the total potentiality released at the beginning of the universe has reached its apex—degeneration and sclerosis set in, leading to death.

Death simply marks the triumph of the trend toward potentiality, because the death of the formed organism releases the energy potential in the substance of its body into the immense ocean of potentiality. It is released toward some more or less distant rebeginning, as some future "springtime" occurs. In the vegetable kingdom it is released both as seed and as decaying leaves which will be humus to seed the future germ.

As the human kingdom is reached in the world-process a new situation slowly develops. Man acquires reflective consciousness, a consciousness centered around an "I" subjectively aware of being both center and consciousness. Any living organism is a whole, a limited field of activity; but while it has a life-center this is not an individualized center of consciousness, a Self. The form of the entity characterizes a *species* of life, not an individual center of I-consciousness.

This is a tremendous difference. It implies that in man the trend toward actualization and objectivity has reached a point at which it is increasingly pervaded with the opposite trend toward repotentialization and subjectivity. Man's presence announces the nearness of a symbolical equinox point, as at the equinoxes, day and night are of equal duration. In man, actuality and potentiality are coming close to a condition of equilibrium. Because of this, man has the at least latent capacity to repotentialize his consciousness, and to some extent his physical organism. Even when this organism can no longer be renewed, death can be a conscious and deliberate act of repotentialization. It can be a conscious entrance into a realm of relative nonmanifestation and subjectivity in which potentiality has won over actuality. It can mark the beginning of a seed state at the level of mind-consciousness. In that state an equally conscious mutation can be subjectively experienced, polarized toward a new birth, a new beginning.

It can be, but it need not be and perhaps rarely is. Most human beings are still operating mainly at the level of biological energies and their psychic overtones. Because the I-consciousness in them is most of the time identified with one or another body function, encased in sociocultural forms, and focused in the ego, (a social-biological compound which people usually think of as "I-myself,") this consciousness is no longer able to envision totally new beginnings. It has lost what may be called "originability"—the ability to envision, and then to perform acts which can be origins of new developments—acts which release new potentialities not strictly implied in a person's birth, and especially which were not defined by the limitations of physical ancestry and social-geographical environment.

In order to envision such new possibilities, a man does not have to think of existence itself as illusion; and while the Hindu term, *maya,* is usually translated "illusion," Maya was also the name of Gautama the Buddha's mother. Existence at the human level implies the possibility to be born out of it and to transcend its fate as the Buddha did. And the word "fate" simply refers to the inertia of existential forms and the entropy of energies that operate through all biological-emotional, social-cultural and ego-controlled forms of living. The human condition so tragically depicted by self-defeated men of a civilization stifled by inertial institutions and fears, actually is a condition of allowing *conscious and deliberate self-renewal through the creation of always new forms,* or at least through the radical alteration, expansion, and recharging of the form of an individual selfhood refusing to bend to the pressure of the past and accept defeat.

How can such a recharging, repotentialization or creative rebeginning be accomplished? The first condition is to believe in the possibility of it; then to dare be open to new images that may well up from the deepest center of being. Through that center a new influx of potentiality may surface into the consciousness of the existential mind.

The belief in the possibility of rebeginning or rebirth has evidently to take a form consonant with the individual's metaphysical or religious beliefs. The way the process of repotentialization is described and the names and symbols used in this description vary, but essentially what is experienced is an attunement of the consciousness to "That" which to the mind represents an infinite potentiality of as yet unknown modes of existence—cosmic, spiritual, psychic, human, cellular, or molecular as these modes may be according to the level at which the consciousness operates.

If one believes totally in the validity of the great images of the Christian tradition, one undoubtedly tends to picture to oneself a personal all-loving and all-powerful God. One will believe that, as the Gospel states, "With God all things are possible." One also believes in the infinite power of God's "Grace." We have to believe without any shadow of a doubt that in our life, God is a constant Presence aware of all our needs and ready to assist our disenthrallment or redemption from the dualistic oscillations, the fears and passions of our biological and egocentric existence. We must be willing to let Him point to us the new goal, the vibrant way of life, which follows our rebirth.

This divine Grace gives us the potency to neutralize the karmic tendencies of our past—the residue of the unfinished business of past cycles and the negative cosmic imprints of ancient unremembered acts. We have first of all to empty our consciousness of all ghostly presences and unconsicous tendencies before we can be radically repotentialized. To the disciples of Sri Aurobindo this divine Grace is presented as the Mother-Force—and even to Christians Mary the Mother appears as the Mediatrix who channels down to weary and distraught humans the "living water" of Christ's immense love. According to ancient Hindu traditions the guru who has experienced his divine state is able to assume the karma of his disciples' past lives—a karma operating at the unconscious level—just as the Christ was born to wipe away the stigma of an Original Sin deeply rooted in man's collective unconscious. But the disciple has always to take care by himself of *all that he is conscious of*—thus, of the karma of his present life.

An individual person may have developed his mind

and his courage to the point where he can assume without fear the totality of his own karma, and deliberately seek to attune his whole being and his boundless imagination to the rhythms of the infinite ocean of potentiality. Yet this would be a lonely way if constantly pursued without the help and love of other human beings, and also without the realization that there are presences that, invisibly in most cases though often not without voice, surround the wayfarer and guide his or her confused steps in the darkness of a materialistic, competitive, and lustful society. Christianity speaks of "Guardian Angels"; other religions refer to them under other names.

In many cultures, since patriarchal times, and even more since the great movement of chivalry and particularly in Southern France during the twelfth and thirteenth centuries, the capacity to be attuned in feelings and intuition to a vast reservoir of spiritual inspiration and/or healing love has been considered a natural role for a woman, provided she is true to the highest and purest potentiality of her nature; for woman may also be pictured as the Temptress, *la femme fatale,* who embodies the entropy of material energies and leads to passionate disintegration. Today, the modern woman is confused and in her demand for equality and liberation—such ambiguous and deceptive ideals!—she tries hard to identify herself often unreservedly with the great gods of Productivity and social success, while relying increasingly upon an asexualized intellect able to memorize data, handle computers, and manage systems. By so doing she almost inevitably becomes, like most men, a mere mechanism in the production lines of factories and managerial offices. Just because she demands to be fully "actualized," she tends to lose her contact with the great ocean of potentiality.

To use Jungian terms, she loses the capacity to act as an anima figure, as a mediatrix between the vast realm of the unconscious (or superconscious) and the actively exteriorizing and systematizing mind characteristic of the male sex, at least during the last millennia of human evolution. As this happens, the men she tries to emulate and socially compete with may tend to develop the contrasexual aspect of their nature. Theoretically this may be a valid trend and it may be related to the emergence of a new kind of humanity—the sixth sub-race of which H. P. Blavatsky announces the gradual but slow development. Nevertheless <u>the immediate result is very often emotional confusion and mental instability</u>—all of which is caused by a disturbing feeling of lack of functional purpose and by the ambiguity of unclearly defined roles in interpersonal relationships.

A LOT OF THAT IS SHOWING UP

One may refuse to accept traditional roles, but one should also be able to understand that these roles, especially if based upon biological imperatives and functional differentiation, are the reflections of great archetypes. New archetypes may be brought to act on the stage of human evolution, but until they are truly understood and actualized, they may remain a deeply disturbing potentiality within the unconscious of individuals who are not yet free enough of the past—or,—just as important!—of an emotional rebellion against this past, to envision new modes of relationships, and have not yet the strength and courage required to compel society to accept them.

In the preceding chapter the possibility of raising the level of productivity of an interpersonal relationship dynamized by love from the biological to the ideo-spiritual level of creativity was evoked. I should now like to speak of an archetypal image of womanhood that is closely associated to the concept and ideal of repotentialization, the image of the Eternal Virgin—an image that is also embodied in a still more life-transcending manner in the great examples of the Kumaras, the Virgin-ascetics.

To the Occultist, SPACE, abstractly considered as the infinite ocean of potentiality, takes the idealized and mythic character of the Eternal Virgin, for the virginal state symbolizes the possibility of any future manifestation. The woman virgin, traditionally speaking, can be whatever the beloved who will dynamize and fecundate her field of creative possibilities demands of her; for the archetypal Woman is the sacred vessel ready to receive the *Logos spermatikos*, the creative Word that fecundates, and that fecundative act transforms potentiality into emergent actuality. Before fecundation she is SPACE, the infinite possibility of any and all cosmic modes of existence. Once fecundation has occurred, woman becomes the mother; and the mother's existence, symbolically speaking, is utterly oriented toward her progency. The mother's rhythm of existence has been set. She is no longer free; that is, un-conditioned. Actuality, in her, has absorbed—for a time at least—potentiality.

The Virgin and the Mother represent therefore two fundamental images or archetypes of womanhood. They are two basic aspects of the Eternal Feminine—symbols of potentiality and actuality. At this present stage of human evolution, the Mother represents productive energy and the capacity to guide and manage the early biological and even sociocultural, stages of her children's life. Without children there is no state of motherhood. When the religious devotee worships the Great Mother, or the Mother Force, he or she acknowledges being a child. On the other hand, the man who bows before the image of "the Virgin of the World" accepts the power and responsibility to become a "father"—a creative origin, a "logos." He comes to the virgin, as a mind and will yearning for a new field for his activity. His capacity to fecundate may be only latent; he too may be poten-tiality far more than actuality. Yet this potentiality is polarized toward the creative act.

For him, the virgin girl may still be represented by a sister because the time—biologically or socially—has not yet come to actualize his creative potential. Yet a polarization already exists. If that polarization is too strong, the brother may keep seeing in every woman he later meets, a sister; and this may interfere with his normal love-relationships. Yet at a higher level of consciousness, the woman may appear to him as the *Soror Mystica*, the Sister participating in the Great Work of true, spiritual alchemy. She is then the Holy Virgin who, like him, has been self-consecrated to the service of the Divine in man—and therefore to the service of those who are building Man's future state of existence, the "Brothers" of the essentially hidden, yet at times *revealed* Great Lodge—the Seed-Pleroma of Humanity.

An entire society may be characterized by whether it emphasizes the mother aspect of women, rather than the Virgin of Light. In America today the cult of the mother has achieved world recognition, and often world notoriety. The Mom who "knows best" and makes a nondescript Daddy work hard for boudoirized Cadillacs and pastel Frigidaires has been the subject of endless discussions, psychological analyses, and comic strips. Often frustrated in her life or love with a business-engrossed husband whom she takes for granted, fascinated by her newly won intellectual and social independence from home and husband, self-consciously assuming an important place in the daily patterns of our economic, cultural and political life, the American Mom is most often torn by psychological conflicts. Caught as she is in a fever of self-exteriorization, she tends to ignore and deny her deeper feminity, and to live, tensely and relentlessly, and with much intellecutal pride (a mask for insecurity!), at the very surface of the exteriorized portion of her nature.

Yet the very dependence of the typical American male on his mother and the quasi-matriarchal character of some aspects of our society have engendered in men and women a more or less conscious yearning for youthfulness. Just because our society has become mechanized and automated, and we officially worship the formalistic intellect of the technician hemmed in by written formulas and of the lawyer hypnotized by the need for success through cleverness, there is a nearly poignant longing once more to be unconditioned, as-yet-non-automated—once more to be young and at least in a deep spiritual sense virginal.

Thus the mature man and woman of Suburbia dress young, try to act young, and to make believe they are not the slaves of a system which, rigidly even if subtly, determines their manner of thinking, feeling, and behavior so that they will be "liked," accepted by everybody who counts, and successful in an indistinct and nonindividualized way. When the young generation rebelled and desperately tried to actualize their inner repudiation and protest by different clothes, hair-styles and loose way of relationships, the older people—upset as they were—quickly tried to imitate the countercultural fashions.

Alas, the process of "revirgination" or true repotentialization cannot be real if it means only the imitation of what is chaos rather than true virginity. In the deepest sense of the term, chaos is also a state of potentiality. The cosmos condition has broken down in the year cycle; the plant has lost its leaves which now are disintegrating into mere chemicals. These chemicals may be used in any new process of germination; but they will be used in a condition of unconscious absorption into the new germ. Today our society has not yet produced pure chaos, even (most often and exceptions notwithstanding) among younger generations who are still very much attached to their Western civilization even if only by their emotional rebellion against it. Chaos no longer rebels against anything; it is a passive condition.

The virginal state of which I am speaking here is totally oriented toward the future, but a future which as yet might have any form. In contrast to it the state of motherhood is completely determined by the need of what it has produced. Yet in some way the two states can be integrated within the life and the consciousness of women; and it presumably is what, at the deepest level, constitutes the new possibility toward the actualization of which many modern women more or less unconsciously and emotionally are striving.

Actually this possibility can be seen symbolized in the Catholic symbol of Mary, *the Virgin Mother*. What is implied in the symbol is the possibility for a woman who has a child to function as a mother without being exclusively committed to that function and to the man who fecundated her. The Virgin Mother knows in her deeper consciousness that it is the universal and impersonal power of Life (or God) that impregnated her virginal field of existence, and that regardless of what her future relationships to any man might be, she remains the servant of the creative Spirit, and thus a channel through which a fresh spring of potentiality may always emerge through her. Even in relation to her child she knows herself as a focus of love and intelligence guiding the child toward self-fulfillment, but what is concentrated by and passes through the focus of her body and her whole person is Spirit—not the will, love, or intelligence of a particular man who was merely the carrier of sperm to impregnate her ovum, or even whose ego and personal character sought to make her in his own image and possess her.

In this sense, virginity does not refer strictly to the fact of not having been "deflorated" by a male; it does not actually exclude sexual experience. It simply refers to a state of being in which the natural condition of productivity for exclusivistic goals implying possessiveness is transcended. Whether there is biological productivity in terms of child-bearing or none, the woman's consciousness is not fundamentally affected. Her body, for a time, may be caught in a current of biological procreation; yet even as this happens, her consciousness and life-purpose remain unattached to that current, because they do not expect anything personal from this

life-process. The process passes through the woman who
neither desires nor will claim rewards of any kind from
her role as progenitor. She gives love to the baby, as she
gave her body to the man—in the Name of the Divine
that equally dwells in him, her and the child.

What has just been said in terms of the procreation of
a new body can as well apply to creative processes at the
ideological-mental-cultural level. Every creative person
is, or rather should be, a Virgin Mother in relation to his
or her creations, be they works of art and literature,
scientific theories or the organization of sociocultural institutions. In such a creative activity there should be no
personal-emotional possessiveness or the type of intellectual pride which binds the creator to his work. The
creator "pro-duces" (brings forth) that which is the
result of the fecundation of his mind by a power that, in
its noblest form, transcends the mind acting only as a
womb. A creative process occurs *through* him, rather
than *from* him. If he does not remain attached to, and
possessive of it, he remains virginal. New flows of potentiality again and again will occur through him.

At the social level, money is a profound and vital symbol of potentiality. A dollar bill is ever-virgin, for it can
be used for a multitude of purposes. With money (nearly)
all things are possible—it would seem today. A modern
bank should be a vast field of social possibilities, but a
field exacting no price for the flow of its credit—a symbol of trust, which is "social love." The whole social
process is vitiated and turns destructive of human values
when exclusive possession is attached to money; and a
constant increase of productivity in terms of material
goods, on an Earth swarming with ever more bodies, is
the one overriding goal of society.

The goal of productivity can be transferred to an
ideospiritual level at which the needs of minds and souls
is of far greater importance than the need of bodies. Yet
even there the patterns of productivity will always tend to
become rigid and resist transformation. Therefore to the

inertia of every form that at any cost seeks to maintain itself and to expand, a new surge of potentiality must answer. No cyclic process must be allowed to turn into
exact circles. Creativity alone can inject into the process
a new spirit of creativity, and where creativity and spontaneity have been defeated by habit, technical routine
and automatism, then repotentialization is the only way
to spiritual transformation—even though it mean con-
frontation with the past and crisis.

It has often been remarked that women tend to be
conservative in social matters and politics, because they
are basically concerned with their offsprings' security;
and crises of social transformation inevitably challenge
what has until then appeared as security. Let me repeat
that the mother-type of woman is geared to *what has
been*. Her natural function at the biological level is to
transfer to her progeny the patterns of instinctual
behavior required for physical survival. In the same
manner the natural function of woman at the
sociocultural level is to teach her children the behavior,
the traditional types of emotional (and later ethical)
beliefs and responses, and the simple basic skills that
will insure the child's acceptance in society.

Thus, for a man who, after growing up, seeks refuge in
the past, is afraid of changes and the big wide world, and
whose mother has been psychically possessive and over-
protective, the desired woman, be she wife or mistress,
will be asked to carry the image and function of a
mother. It may be a mother function at the sexual and
emotional and home level; it may also be that function
raised to the spiritual level of divine Motherhood.

On the other hand, men who are servants of the future
and are consecrated to the ever-renewed possibility of
creating unrepetitive tomorrows, will seek women who,
to them at least—and they may be misled by temporary
stirrings of sexual desires—can be embodiments of the
virgin spirit; women who will seem to hold the ever-
glowing promise of the actualization of as-yet-unknown

possibilities, even possibilities beyond this earth, beyond the natural realm of loving and begetting progeny.

To such men, woman as the ever-Virgin can be the romantic "Muse," the inspirer, the Beatrice of Dante in search of the center of ever higher perfection rooted in the experience of ever deeper abysses of human tragedy. She can also be the companion of the true alchemist, traveling with him as a Holy Sister upon the mystical Path. Such a dedicated companionship may not necessarily exclude sex; if sex can be consciously ritualized and attuned to the interplay of the great cosmic Powers, that is the foundation of all existence. But it should not be, except in rare occasions, sex based on unconscious instinct, thus on compulsive biological and mere organic satisfaction. It should be a purposeful sexual togetherness freed of animal excitement. In this togetherness, the fire surging from the depths of the two harmonized human fields of forces may be transmuted into a light glowing within the field of the united vessels of life, united but open to the beyond that is also the ". . . within; open and free, free of each other as well as of the all-too-human patterns of our present humanity."

Such an alchemical, deeply quiet and unemotional process is, however, most difficult to accept or even to understand for vitally exuberant persons avid for orgastic release, or for individuals tense with frustrations, tragic hurts, and perhaps guilt complexes. It is not only difficult; it is often quite dangerous—thus the usual emphasis upon absolute chastity in the relationships between the brothers and sisters who have become consecrated to the Divine within themselves and within humanity, the "Great Orphan" (a traditional occult designation.) And there may be such a consecration outside of official religious orders!

Chastity is actually only an exaggerated emphasis upon the principle of proper "spacing" in all relationships that do not seek to reconstitute the original Egg (the male-female whole) and thus to close a cycle. The

French speak of "l'egoisme a deux," a phrase difficult to translate tersely, but which refers to the fact that the male and female in productive union (or in a short circuited state of involved bliss, lost in each other) actually build jointly a larger and more final ego. All egos long for finality, for the closed cycle within which all is perfect, finished—the successful person, the happy home!

Such an ideal can produce beautiful and wholesome results, as far as they go; but it can only bring to a conclusion what has been released in the beginning of the relationship. Then the cycle closes and a new one, of the same kind and at the same level, must begin. This is *Samsara,* the ever-resurgent urge to repeat the past, whether individually as a separate individual self, or collectively as a generation compelling the following generation by unconscious pressures and semihypnotic example to repeat its patterns or to rush rebelliously to the exact opposite, which is as compulsive and binding a procedure as unconscious imitation.

The only other solution—besides some form or other of self-destruction (and there are so many of these forms!)—begins with a refusal to close the cycle in exhaustion of vital energy and inner weariness; it is a breakthrough into the realm of those who, as brothers and sisters, exist in a state of ever-renewed potentiality and essential virginity—which is indeed Nirvana, the condition of infinite latency from which all is possible and nothing is ever final or finished.

This does not mean leaving this world or reaching the timeless and unconditioned. Gautama the Buddha accepted the time, the place, and the conditions of India's society, culture, and climate in the sixth century B.C. After having become liberated from the desire to bring his cycle of existence to a final close through yoga practices and starvation, and having been revitalized by the milk given him by a simple milkmaid, he understood ("stood under") the World-Process. For forty more years of radiant peaceful living he presented to his society an infinitely noble, beautiful, and self-contained example of freedom and of peace. He transformed his society and the whole of Asia.

We are not Buddhas, of course. Yet we can rise beyond the compulsive living which must end in exhausted power and pattern-frozen consciousness; we can awaken in us the Virgin-potency that is exhaustless and unbound by repetitive actions. This is perhaps what mystics try to say when they speak of living in the Now, unconditioned by precedents and unburdened by expectations. But to call this state timeless is just as fictitious and glamorous a statement as to speak of, and to desire the end of time (as in Biblical eschatology).

There are forever cycles. This moment is within one of them. Each man exists at this moment, in this cycle. Even denying time must necessarily take time, must occur in time. We should live this moment, because it is what we are essentially. We are not different from it in the living of it. We have to live it, to love it; because indeed it alone exists for us now, because we are its fulfillment. We are time. Consciousness is time, cyclic, rhythmic, harmonic, whole in its divine condition, as an Eon; partial, biased, tormented by conflicts in the human mind. The real fallacy is to think that we are only a small part of a cycle of existence and that this now-fulfillment is all there is of us. We potentially are the whole cycle; more still, we have in us the potentiality of always breaking through the fulfillment of any cycle into the vast measureless Movement which unceasingly calls forth new potential out of the infinite expanse of Virgin SPACE, within and from which all is possible.

Yet one should not think of *escaping* into this ineffable, nameless ocean of possibilities, this ever-Virgin Nirvana. The gates to Nirvana are seen only within the fulfillment of now, but in a fulfillment which does not *close* anything, which leaves the quest, the movement, the ascent unresolved. Nothing is ever resolved. No cycle ends in total perfection, for the very search for perfection rises by stepping upon one's own and mankind's rejected imperfections. The rejected must again be met, absorbed in love, integrated; this forever and ever.

Why? Because there are always greater possibilities; always the Virgin—*Alaya*, Soul of unbounded Space—calls, with new dreams, with her infinite latency, her inexhaustible potency of form-releases, of time and cycles. Possibilities are exhaustless; Cosmic Motion is unceasing. If we aspire toward a final condition, an end-of-process and the absorption of time into a timeless ecstasy, we merely create illusion for ourselves. Our passion for a formless state is as binding a form of desire as any narrow dogma freezing the Virgin within us into a set pattern of consciousness. Every existence has form; and it is powered by the as-yet-unformed Virgin-potency, ever ready for any and all possibilities of formation and transformation. It is all here, now; yet this "here and now" are but one moment in the infinite Movement that releases forever new potentialities into eventually inevitable actualities, in whose fulfillment lies the seed of future cycles. Cling to the moment, and you have lost it. Escape into the Movement, and you are lost, only to be found again and institutionalized in a future, more rigid framework of karma.

It really is all so simple! One should not have to talk about it, which is like trying to catch atoms with a butterfly net, or painting the irridescent ever-moving panoply of northern lights with thick oil paint and coarse brush. All that one can do is to call, to stir, to awaken to the ever new possible, to evoke and to move on before the vision sets and the ever-Virgin becomes impregnated, patterned-out by the male "fact," caught into the mesh of productivity, compelled to repeat words which repetition makes meaningless because familiar.

Familiarity is the negation of spirituality. Promiscuity, lack of bearing, sloppiness, are insults to the Virgin. There should always be distance, proportion, form, effective focusing of attention, self-discipline and a vast, deep quietness of emotional vibrancy. And yet all this *not* definitive, *not* final, *not* binding.

Acts do not need to bind the actors. The Avatar is both Eon and man; Krishna is the lover of the Gopis as well as the "beginning, middle and end" of the universal cycle. The now, lived in full concentration on the potentiality it is called upon to release as one phase of a vast cycle, is one with the cycle—IF the wholeness of the cycle is evoked and focused in the act here and now. This is avatarhood, divine manifestation. This is the trans-personal way.

All living is a "per-formance." What is essential is not to be bound by the form. Use this form. Pour yourself unreservedly, utterly, into that form and into the releasing act. Then, pass on; walk on. Now is always with us, always demanding to be lived as if it alone existed; but also to be lived in the consciousness that it is but one among the infinitude of drops in the ocean of potentiality, but one of the many smiles of the Virgin of all possible worlds.

12. THROUGH CRISES, NEW BEGINNINGS

One of the little understood and advertised aspects of
the relationship between a real guru and his disciple is
that through such a relationship the disciple is made to
face a deep crisis. His entire future depends on how he
(or she) meets the crisis, on the quality of the emotional
attitude, the depth of understanding, and the character
of the will he brings to it.

A crisis is almost unavoidable, because as the disciple
meets his spiritual Guide he brings to the meeting not
only an eagerness for inner growth, or perhaps only an
intense and fascinated devotion to the guru, but also the
karmic residual of his past—and not only the past of his
present life. In his aspiration for a more spiritual life and
consciousness, the disciple has forgotten this past. In
fact he probably has never realized the heaviness of this
karmic past, and unconsciously he is quite eager not to
meet it at this time when all he aspires to is light and
divinity. The ego of any individual either is not aware of
the ancient past, or he half-consciously finds ways of get-
ting around it and to evade harsh confrontations with his
old sins of commission and even more omission. He is
like a lawyer trying to circumvent the law, even though
he would be amazed if he were told that he was doing so
deliberately. By meeting his guru and earnestly asking
for spiritual guidance, the disciple, unbeknown to himself, sets in motion an equally spiritual reaction.

The presence of the guru, even more than what he actually may do, say, or suggest, focuses upon the disciple
the karmic harvest of the latter's past. Impersonally, and
perhaps with some deep sadness and compassion, the

guru brings about situations which force the disciple, who probably is eagerly waiting for revelations and illumination, to squarely or frontally face the darkness of a perhaps long-forgotten past of indolence, selfishness, or spiritual bankruptcy. The disciple comes face to face with what, in the most extreme instances, has been pictured (in Bulwer Lytton's famous novel, *Zanoni)* as the monstrous Dweller on the Threshold. In any case he faces a crisis; and the word, crisis, from a Greek root which means "to decide." This root can be traced to the still more universal radical *Kri* which we find in the names of the great Avatar of India's tradition, Krishna, and of our Western divine Manifestation, the Christos. In Javanese the so often used dagger or specially shaped small sword is called "kris."

Christ brought to men, *not* peace—as he himself stated—but the "sword of severance." Krishna originally was known in India as a great statesman who, through his consummate diplomacy, brought face to face and with equal strength the two great clans of the Warrior caste who had made of the land a constant battlefield. On the plain of Kurukshetra, the two clans met and destroyed each other. This ended the power of the Warrior caste and marked the rise of India's great Age of Philosophy, dominated by the power of the Brahmin caste.

Whether this be fact or myth it should bring to us the realization that the divine Guru, in whatever form and according to whatever circumstances it may be, brings to the people among whom he is born, a some time fearsome crisis, forcing men to "decide." In the *Bhagavad Gita,* on the eve of the great battle of Kurukshetera, Krishna faces his pupil, Arjuna who, seeing friends and relatives in both camps, is ready to evade the issue and refuse to fight. Krishna confronts him with his dharma as a warrior and Arjuna makes his great decision, and the battle is "won." But who wins it? Not the victorious army that is also decimated; not the victorious ego of Arjuna the warrior. *Spirit alone wins*—within Arjuna's Soul and inner consciousness, and within an India relatively freed for a time at least from the conflicts and passions of the Warrior caste.

The divine Spirit—the Christos—also won through the courage and endurance of Jesus, Son of Man. But it was victory as yet only in the realm of Archetypes: the Great War has been raging ever since in the planetary consciousness of mankind and in the innermost heart of all men, who swear by the name of Christ, yet remain asleep and betray the Christ spirit, as the apostle, Peter, and the Church founded on his symbolic name, betrayed the master they pretended to worship. The Great War may still wait for its climactic Kurukshetra. The *radical* decision is not yet made, except by a few individuals here and there.

Assuredly many small and valid decisions are made by individuals and groups at one time or another; but unless the issue is truly *focal* the decision may not be "radical" enough; it may not reach the very root of the individual person. It may not demand as yet the irreversible crucifixion of the individual as an ego and lord of whatever comes under the sway of its autocratic power.

The strong individual whose mind is open and wise may not need a guru to force him to meet his karma. To the strong, life itself answers with compelling and ineluctable circumstances. The disciple who relies on his inner center and his *potential* divinity may himself precipitate the confrontations generating one crisis after another. The ever-present danger is that, under strain and stress, he may make what appears to be the wrong decision or that, unable to make any decision at all, out of sheer inner exhaustion, he may slide into insanity or premature dying. Yet there are perhaps no wrong decisions, if they are sincere and open to whatever may come; if the results are placed on the inner altar of one's dedication to the Divine, for God to accept or reject.

The guru is nevertheless always present behind the

scene, even though in the awesome abysses of the "Dark Night of the Soul," of which many mystics have spoken his presence is not felt, his voice not heard. The disciple is left with only one weapon: the sword of his pure, unadulterated will. He alone can wield this sword, not to cut a mythical Gordian Knot, as the youthful Alexander, the conqueror, is said to have done with his sword, but to cut the rope his own ego had made to tie the ship of his consciousness to some safe, secure, and comfortable haven. As the ship is left loose to brace the currents and storms of the immense sea of an astral realm that one can only reach *through* as well as *beyond* the solid physicality of our everyday world, the life of the self-consecrated individual produces radical crises.

Crises are thresholds which one must pass through; what counts is the essential quality of *the movement-through*. That we may stumble, fall and get badly hurt, or make tragic mistakes or blunders and hurt others—this is in most cases unavoidable. The main difference between victory and at least temporary defeat resides in the quality of our being. This quality of being goes deeper than mere conscious motive—for is it not said "Hell is paved with good intentions"? By quality of being I mean what we cannot help doing, feeling, or thinking, because *we are that.* Victory comes, ultimately, because everything in us and beyond us—the whole balance-of-power within the field of actualization of the Soul in which our personal self participates— everything *comes to a focus* in some essential "Yes" or "No" saying.

The ransom of spiritual victories almost unavoidably is suffering; but here again all depends on the quality of the suffering or, one might say, on what suffering is geared to. It may be geared to a will to victory over the domination of the ego or to a stubborn decision by the ego to gain control over whatever challenges its power, or even to a feeling of defeat and impotency which in some instances may turn into a semiconscious will for self-annihilation.

Suffering should be differentiated from pain. Any living organism experiences pain when some of its vital functions or the integrity of the body is interfered with. Nature inflicts pain upon all living organisms caught in its more or less violent processes, its storms, its droughts or flood, its fires, its extremes of heat or cold. The implacable law of the biosphere, "Eat or be eaten," produces everywhere pain; a pain which under certain conditions, even in the vegetable kingdom—as recent experiments by Cleve Baxter have shown—can be shared by other organisms vibrating in sympathy.

Human beings also experience physical pain in natural circumstances affecting the nervous system. But with suffering we reach another level of feeling, because suffering implies a more or less individualized consciousness of pain—not only physically felt, but pain referred to the personal desires, the goals, the expectations, and the potentiality of self-unfoldment and spiritual growth of the individual person. As an individual severs his bondage to his society and to the instinctual rhythm of his participation in nature; as he places a priority on the development of mind and of social power, prestige, fame, and wealth in a competitive society, regardless of what this will do to the natural harmony and smooth-workings of his biological functions and emotional drives, he invites suffering. He who is following the transpersonal Way and is definitely ready and intent upon entering the Path—the path of total transformation—can expect to travel with suffering as his companion. He has deliberately entered a process of transition. He has placed himself "out of gears" in order to be able to change to a higher gear; and the change is very rarely smooth, because, unlike a well-engineered car, each position of the gears resists change; instead of some kind of lubricant to facilitate the displacement, each gear is surrounded with a mass of particles opposing the shifting. The result is an often harsh and potentially destructive grinding noise, especially if there is no experienced driver to teach the novice.

Every transition between two states results in suffering; and the suffering is greatest when fear, a clinging to the past, or an exuberant eagerness to race ahead introduces tensions, inner conflicts, or false expectations into the process; and this is by far the most common state of affairs in our modern world. The individual in our Western society is caught into a *collective* process of transition, the historical transition between the archaic tribal state of natural living in tune with the rhythms of the biosphere—a state in which the whole tribe has a common psyche and a common will as it faces basic issues—and the state of at least relative individualization of each theoretically independent person, responsible for his or her own growth toward some kind of transcendent ideal. Individualization leads to conflicts between supposedly self-sufficient individuals proud of their difference and eager to expand and to conquer all obstacles; and conflicts produce the type of suffering based on inferiority, fear, deprivation, and a humiliating sense of failure—or the disappointment and emptiness which often follow success and fame.

The individual moving ahead on the transpersonal Way may not only experience all the suffering which these feelings at one time or another are bound to cause at the psychic and psychosomatic levels, but he has stepped out at least partially from the wheel of social success and failure into another kind of transition which is just as radical. In the depth of his consciousness he has left both the biological and the social levels at which his will can no longer *exclusively and naturally* function; yet he still operates as a biological organism and, try as he may to deny the fact, he is still conditioned by the culture that has provided him with a specific language and patterns of thinking-feeling, and even of behavior if he still lives among men. Three levels of consciousness, of activity and will speak their own language in the disciple on the Path. How can he fail to experience inner discords and suffering until he has, as the Buddhists say "reached the other shore." A difficult crossing!

It most likely is impossible to achieve this crossing unless in one way or another the aspirant has been prepared for it by those who have already passed to the other shore and who, after having left instructions to the novice, watch and are ready to proffer guidance and perhaps assistance, even if unnoticed by and unknown to the traveler. Yet, helped as he undoubtedly is, he alone must do the crossing; he alone must fight against the powerful current of material entropy, against overwhelming weariness, loneliness, and an insidious sense of futility. He has to accept pain and overcome its thrust against nerves taut and ready to break.

Any individual person can follow the wide road of planetary evolution caught in the swaying slow movement of the masses of mankind. This movement displays a cyclic but eminently *repetitive* character. There must be repetition because the person advancing—or it could be regressing—on this road too often is passively swayed by the up and down motions of the evolutionary tide. At best he uses his will in order to try to remain at the crest of the waves when there are waves that crest. Cycles come and cycles go. One person succeeds another person; and though the Soul to which they are linked by magnetic threads watches and tries to establish a closer intimacy, these successive personalities respond but feebly. The fire of the divine will burns low within their tepid, ever so normal emotions; or else it rages but for a moment and is gone, overwhelmed by the pressure of surrounding mediocrity, unable to carry through a half-hearted and fleeting commitment.

Then it must all begin again, alas, so often repeating the past that left so much unfinished business. It is so difficult at times for circles to turn into spirals! They can do so only if a centrifugal force steadily acts to overcome the inertia of circular motion; that force is the Promethean will. It is the will that every rebeginning should be a *new* beginning, a fresh, original, spontaneous release of new potentiality. There is no worse defeat than defeat by sameness and repetitiveness; no more monstrous concept than that of the "Eternal Return" imagined by the tragic mind of Nietzsche. The Ocean of Potentiality of which I have spoken is *infinite*. When the Christian repeats: "With God all things are possible," what he does is to personalize this infinite Ocean of Spirit, for spirit is the possibility to meet every need with a fresh, ever renascent will *through which* a new potentiality of answer is being *mobilized and focused*. The new possibility is always present; but the individual has to be ready with his unsheathed will. His hand does hold the sword, but the spirit, God, will move the hand if the man's consciousness is ready and willing to let go. Then the goal will be struck.

We must ever be ready to accept the totally unexpected, the miraculous. We never have to feel totally defeated. A new dawn can always occur, in some way unlike any previous dawn; but we must have faith. Faith is the intuitive, unchallengeable, even if intellectually unexplainable feeling-realization that the Ocean of Infinite Potentiality surrounds us; we live, move and have our being in it, but most of us refuse to feel, refuse to see, so wrapt are we in our frantic agitation, our fear, our masochistic concentration on how much we suffer. Such a suffering is in vain and calls for endless repetition.

We must become still, and "feel" the soundless sound of the vast tides of spirit lapping at the shores of our consciousness, or perhaps beating at the jagged rocks of our pride and our greed. We must turn our consciousness toward this inner sea and try to sense the end of a cycle of experience peacefully moving into the yet imprecise and unfocused beginning of a new cycle. We must *dare* to summon the potentiality of an essentially new and, for us, unprecedented beginning. We should become the altar and the sacrifice; and the perfume of the burnt offering of our past, and even of the most fragrant memories, will rise to the gods; and the gods will answer, for they are the glowing forms which new potentialities take when they appear to our open eyes. They are our luminous tomorrows, should they accept the descent and take birth within our inmost being.

These words may sound oversymbolic, mystical, and remote to the reader whose consciousness is caught in the seemingly hopeless entanglements of modern city living; yet everyone should find it possible to translate their generality into the particular language of his or her personal circumstances. It should not be difficult to think of people we have met who, in early or mid-life, or as old age comes near, are being or have been confronted with a crisis altering radically the pattern of their lives—the sudden or painful death of the marriage partner, a divorce, a crippling illness or accident, the loss of home, children leaving for marriage, or simply retirement after a life of intense business activity. Of crises there is no end. To every person they come in different circumstances. All have this in common: they challenge in us the desire, the power of imagination, and the will *to make a fresh start*.

We may refuse the challenge and, in the acute feeling that now life has become empty and meaningless, settle to die more or less comfortably, perhaps at somebody else's expense of money or happiness, perhaps taking an unconscious revenge on others for our own failure of faith. Or we may move to some kind of California or Riviera and enjoy sunshine, play bridge, sip drinks while gossiping at some fashionable hotel. If we do, what of the energy, or talent, or wealth and influence we have? Will we let these go to waste? Will we stop actualizing our inherent potentialities of consciousness and personality-unfoldment, defeated by circumstances? But these circumstances have called upon us simply and solely to offer us rebirth!

Anyone who is not born anew with a new faith and a new sense of potentiality after a basic crisis has accepted defeat. To return to the *status quo,* to "pre-war boundaries" or "the good old days," is defeat, even if celebrated with pomp as a victory. The Prodigal Son has returned home—with what? for what? I am not referring to goods and treasures, but to how transformed—how radically and permanently transformed—he is as he returns.

Yes, defeat is the only word for these revivals of ghosts, these political and international compromises fostered by the legalistic minds, the unimaginative "old men," the frightened holders of privileges. How many such defeats have we not seen after the tragic crises of our World Wars, in our debacle of policy in the Near East and the Far East. It is the same kind of defeat our modern psychiatrists perpetrate by way of brain-surgery (lobotomy), or less irrevocably, yet essentially with the same attitude, when pushing back the energies of an aroused, exploding mind into the subtle straightjacket of conformism: "You go home now, and you will be very good and blandly smile; it may not be very pleasant, but, you know, that's what living in society means." And so, one more crisis will have been *in vain;* one more war fought to no purpose . . . or was it perhaps to pave the way to a more total conflict between more exactly matched forces, as it occured on the battlefield of Kurukshetra some 5,000 years ago!

Why is it so hard to summon the new potentialities of existence, to begin again with faith in "tomorrows that sing," to *be* once more virginal under the dawn that calls for expansive newness?

We don't know how to offer the New—ritualistically, in sacrifice—the fruits of our past to which we remain so attached; or we do not dare, because the ghosts of the closing cycle crowd upon us, oppress us, and block the door to the new possibility. How we love the dear old ghosts! We could never say a really good thing about our husband, but now that poor old John is gone, why, we are lost: "He was such a wonderful person, you know!" We weep, and John reappears as Paul, in whom the ghost comfortably settles. And the wheel whirls on—birth, decay, death, birth, decay, death, forever and ever the same. O Conformism, the religion of ghosts! . . . with the greatest ghost of all, the "Almighty God" of our Churches, enthroned in the ever more inclusive *Past,* whose servants refuse to even consider the possibility of an unprecedented Future.

Yet, I repeat, Jesus came to bring us the sword of severance! The Heaven within us of which he spoke is the field of infinite potentiality and creative abundance. He came "to baptize with fire." His apparent peacefulness was a scourge for all ghosts. He told us to leave behind and hate all that the conformism of his day and race taught to worship, to take our Cross and follow him. His way led to the most total crisis; thus potentially, to the most complete victory. How stubbornly has the Church that enthroned his name been recrucifying him throughout three long cycles of hell on earth, so perhaps to be terminated, as a New Age dawns! It is "religion," most of all, that has made us afraid, as it pictured God as a tremendous Personage far away; as it fed us forcibly with passionate emotions of guilt, sinfulness, and spiritual impotency. And the modernized rationalistic and social Churches that make Jesus safely human replace one kind of impotency with another, one type of conformism with another!

Courage is the need: the courage to have faith in man's inalienable right and responsibility to make new and unprecedented beginnings; the courage to dismiss and forget the ghosts; the courage to face the awesome darkness of the Night of the Soul in certainty of dawn; the courage to allow one's consciousness and ego to be ground like a lens to the perfect form that will enable the creative light of the new potentiality to become precisely, effectively, and accurately *focused* upon one's innermost center of being, and thence released in love for all. Courage, faith, and throughout the whole way, love, and clarity of mind: these are the essential requirements for whoever dares to enter the Path, the path of ever-renewed transformation.

PART FOUR

The Impending Transformation

13. AVATARS AND SEED MEN
For a New Civilization

If we are to make sense out of the chaotic situation in which, in this year 1975, mankind is blindly and emotionally struggling, we need to obtain a broad perspective unclouded by momentary local issues and partisanship. We need above all an awareness of the rhythmic processes undertoning historical events, thus of planetary as well as sociocultural patterns of change. We need to realize that any process of transformation challenging the validity of the long taken-for-granted symbols and myths that have ensouled and intergrated an entire society, and its religious and cultural institutions, necessarily implies a "descent" from a region of cosmic-spiritual being and activity to the level of sociocultural events. It is a progressive descent which touches one level after another, inducing in each field of collective and planet-wide human activity potentially radical changes. The nature and outcome of these changes depend upon the state of affairs and the character of man's collective consciousness and the nature of the personalities through which such potentialities for transformation become focused, actualized in mental images, and released into society.

The future possibility and ideal image becomes the present fact in terms of inherent ability to overcome the inertia of the past. The features of the present moment inevitably are the results of the meeting of the future and the past, of what *should be* because the time for its actualization in a cyclic process has come, and what *has been*. In this meeting the possibility that has come to maturity not only encounters, but has to accept and interact with the human situation which it has radically to transform. This interaction of the future with the past is what is meant by the term karma. Karma basically means action; and no action operates in a vacuum. No creation is *ex nihilo* (out of nothing)—the creation of a universe as well as that of a work of art. The results of a release of kinetic energy at any point of space and time depend as much on what the situation and evolutionary state of affairs was at that place and at that moment as on the power and character of the power being released.

Everything in the universe is what it has been able to become when a new evolutionary potentiality which has reached the state of spiritual maturity struck with fecund energy at structures that, at that very moment, had proved to be fundamentally obsolete. The reactions or responses of these structures—personal ego-structures or social institutions—reveal the karma of the individual or the collective person, of a man or a nation. What is popularly called "bad karma" simply means a strong inertial resistance of the past to the transforming action of the future possibility. A set of negative images based on past actions or refusals to act either tries to block the descending power of the transformative spirit, or to deviate and pervert it so that it can be made to operate along the old grooves of some past institution or personal complex.

An Avatar appears as a divine transformative answer to a human collectivity which has reached in its cycle a crisis of growth. Crisis etymologically means "decision." A decision has to be made; a definite expansion or a basic repolarization of consciousness is needed, perhaps in order to break the stranglehold of institutions and sociocultural habits and traditions which, useful as they may have been in the past, are now obstacles to essential growth. The Avatar answers the need by bringing to at least a few human beings whose consciousness has become dissatisfied and expectant the fascinating embodiment and radiation of a future for which they have

yearned, dimly perhaps or without real hope of its actualization. Now, for them, the ideal, the new way of life,
the revolutionary quality of feeling and/or thinking, have
become man—the inner vision, concrete and adorable
reality. But ready as these few may be to *resonate* to the
divine, because transformative, manifestation, their
readiness is nevertheless still conditioned by the culture
and religion in which they were born, or (and this can be
as determinant and binding a factor) by their revulsion
against the Old, now that they have beheld the New. In
any case, these few are a very small minority. The masses
still respond to the old emotional slogans; they still worship the ancient images though they have become empty
of real spiritual vitality and meaning. The Avatar must
speak their language. He must be human. He must have
experienced the need of the human collectivity, personally, in himself; he may have been tempted and overcome the then expectable human ego-responses. He may
then *radiate his own victory* upon the people around
him; he becomes an exemplar of victory.

All spiritual living is a constant victory over the inertia
of the past. The racial or group karma must be accepted,
faced and absorbed into the dharma's victory. The divine
destiny is fulfilled, but it can only be fulfilled in relation
to all that in man represents the past up to that point. It
is fulfilled *through* the past which, sensing it is being
challenged, always tends to renew its vigor and increase
its hold upon the masses. The Avatar meets his
"shadow"—which is the shadow of the human race, or
of a particular culture—in men who fanatically, because
fearfully, persecute him, or twist his message so as to
make it sound ridiculous.

These things have been said before, but how few
realize their importance and their implications! It is
because the fighting clans of ancient India were ravaging
the country in their perpetual wars that the Avatar,
Krishna, became a statesman of consummate skill who
managed to induce the rival armies to meet with equal

strength at the Battle of Kurukshetra so that they would destroy each other, a destruction which marked the end of the rule of the Warrior caste. Then, and only then, could the rise of the Brahmins produce the great Age of Philosophy which lasted until after Gautama the Buddha. An old way of life had to be superseded by a new one; or perhaps the perverted forms of a once pure system had to be eradicated, at least for a time. Krishna, as often great gurus do, set the stage so that the antagonistic passions of mankind could destroy each other. But, according to the tradition, at the eve of the great battle, he gave to his disciple, Arjuna, the great discourses of the *Bhagavad Gita,* establishing what presumably was the first complete statement of an all-inclusive theistic and devotional religious philosophy which foreshadowed the spiritual needs of a humanity about to experience a gradual process of individualization and egocentralization.

It was also the past failure of mankind—or at least of what H.P.B. called the Fifth Root-Race—which gave form and a tragic character to the manifestation of the Christ-spirit of universal Love in the person of an at least partly Jewish man; this because the Jewish people, *as a sociocultural whole,* embodied the most specific need that many inadequate and perverting responses or actual failures had produced in mankind.

Western mankind was pathetically unready to accept or even understand what the transformation of man's feeling-responses and essential being implied. But are we any more ready to accept, or even to recognize, the new Avataric descent whose time has now come? It is this descent of spiritual planetary power that, acting at first at high spiritual levels, precipitated or induced the present-day crisis of a world-wide transformation of human society. This crisis has taken and is still taking the form required to meet the many failures and perversions of Western civilization. "God" creates *through* the Avatar, but man's past is the material available for the creation. Because of this, the creative process takes a long time. The present crisis of transformation has not yet reached its climax at the level of human collectivities. It is a process which involves more than one great divine manifestation, more than one avataric being.

Some fifty-five years ago, in a book long ago discarded, I wrote about what I called "the Avataric Cycle," suggesting that such a transformation had to include many phases, each affecting a particular level of human activity. Each level has a basic rhythm of its own, and corresponds to a specific type of event or manifestation. As this is a time in which several cycles are interacting, the human situation is particularly complex. I have already spoken of these cycles (cf. the chapter "Planetary and Social Cycles"), but we may now discuss the relation of great avataric events to them, century after century. It is nevertheless essential for us to hold clearly in mind the idea that we are dealing with *one* great planetary movement which constitutes the gradual process of actualization in various forms—each responding to the essential nature of one level of Man's activity—of a new quality of consciousness, and a potentially new way of collective living for a regenerated humanity.

The Avatar essentially is a process. It is a "rite of passage" for mankind. It announces the coming of a new vibration, the beginning of a new way of life. One may wish to think by comparison of human biosocial periods of transition such as puberty, coming of age, change of life; but correspondences usually are dangerous, or at least confusing, if literally applied. If a very general analogy were to be established it probably would be best to compare mankind's present situation to the change of life during the "dangerous forties"; yet this would tell only part of the story. Whatever it be compared with, the planetary crisis mankind is now experiencing, if seen from an occult-spiritual point of view, is truly a vast ritual. In this planetary ritual, great personages, some visible but many more invisible, are performing their acts of destiny according to cyclic rhythms. Unfortunately to most human beings these rhythms are unknown or unclear and the performances are ambiguous or ambivalent. *They have to be,* because they take place on a human stage nearly totally obscured by either the doctrinarian or the intellectual concepts of our tragic European-American civilization whose gods are the ego and the rationalistic mind, though in name we may worship God as a superego and His Biblical revelation as a supermind.

The Age is dark with blatant pride, violence and greed. Passions are wild, after a period of artificial containment. We worship success, comfort, material possessions. Confusion is in every soul and mind. How could the great "rite of passage" to a new humanity, or at least a new consciousness of the meaning of *being human,* be anything but a mysterious performance in the crypt of the human temple, while on the floor above nations as well as individuals indulge in mock trials, and devastating and absurd wars? Yet the ritual unfolds its potentialities of human renewal as ineluctably cosmic time moves on toward its fulfillment.

Something will be fulfilled. At least the multifarious seeds of future collective developments will have been sown upon the Earth. Some individuals will perform their roles of destiny, even though they falter and stumble in the darkness and against the powers of darkness. What mankind as a whole will accomplish, how the crisis will reach its apex and what will follow, who can really tell? One should go on, regardless; for man's essential duty in such a time of crisis is to walk on, in faith and patience, with a mind open to the future and uncluttered by ghosts or memories, and, in one's deepest being, with love to illumine, however faintly, the roughness of the path.

As we saw in the chapter, "Planetary and Social Cycles," three clearly defined cycles are operating at this time; and undoubtedly there are larger ones of which we have no working knowledge. The widely publicized transition between the so-called Piscean and Aquarian Ages began with the spread of the Industrial Revolution in the forties of last century; it is a phase of the nearly 26,000-year-long cycle of the precession of the equinoxes. Because that cycle refers to one of the slow rhythms of our planet, Earth, it affects the entire biosphere; and within this biosphere, mankind as a whole. As we have already seen at the close of the chapter, "A Planetary Frame of Reference" the fundamental vibration or tone of the Earth in our present evolutionary period can be symbolized by number 4. We are in a fourth Round, or a "fourth world." This number gives the key to all *natural* processes on this planet. It defines the characteristic quality of Earth nature. Inasmuch as mankind operates within the Earth's biosphere, it too *generically* is responding *en masse* to this vibration 4. But Man as cosmic archetype represents on this planet the potentiality as it were, to fecundate the 4-controlled biosphere with the vibration 5 which refers to the transformative Mind. It is therefore man's Great Work, in the alchemical sense of these words, to transform Earth nature by pervading it with the type of consciousness vibrating to the 5. It is to raise his biological and psychic nature to the level of the creative Mind. Man's archetypal image is the five-pointed star, the pentagram.

When this star points upward, the human mind is reaching toward the realm where the vibration 6 operates—the realm of spiritual being and of a holistic and unanimous consciousness which includes all in a realization of divine Unity, or one should rather say of all-encompassing wholeness and synthesis. When, on the other hand, the five-pointed star of Man points downward, the great reversal has occurred and SANAT has become SATAN. The mind, instead of being illumined by the light of the unitive spirit (*manas tajasi*), is overcome by the entropy of all natural processes within the biosphere; it is being quartered on the cross of matter, and the spiritually fecund power latent in the highest chakras is supplanted by the generative, then degenerative, passions rooted in the lowest centers.

The vibration 5 pervades what should be strictly called "civilization," in contrast to "culture" which refers to the natural process of cultivation (biological and psychological) operating under the vibration 4. The word civilization comes from the Latin, *civitas,* which means "a city." It may be related, at least symbolically, to the Sanskrit, Shiva, the god of transformative processes, which may mean spiritual rebirth, or merely death. The German historian, Oswald Spengler, opposed civilization to culture (*Kultur*), praising the latter and presenting the former in its most degenerative aspect, the modern metropolis, symbolized in the Gospel by Babylon. But civilization is as ambivalent as the human mind. It can lead to the Holy City, the New Jerusalem, which desends from the spiritual-archetypal realm, or to Babylon. To the true "Fifth-Rounder" the "black magician" answers in the darkness of the netherworld.

The realm of mind apparently unfolds its inherent potentialities in cycles whose common denominator is a 500-year period. A large cycle of 10,000 years is mentioned in *The Mahatma Letters* (p. 117) which is said to refer to the reappearance of the Buddha. As Buddha essentially symbolizes the power and wisdom of vibration 6, this 10,000 year cycle may refer to periodical attempts by him or by great beings related to him to focus a strong spiritual "Light" upon those whose work is attuned to the higher aspect of the Mind.

We have seen that conjunctions of Neptune and Pluto occur close to every five hundred years. I believe that these conjunctions, and the periods during which Pluto moves within Neptune's orbit, are very important indicators, clocking, as it were, the process of civilization in a global sense. There was such a conjunction in 1891-92 and in a very few years and until the end of the century, Pluto will be closer to the Sun, and thus move a little faster than Neptune. Fifty years—a tenth of the whole cycle—had elapsed since the Neptune-Pluto conjunction when the U.S. entered World War II and the atom bomb project was started; and the idea of atomic fission can be traced to the discovery by Roentgen of X-rays, a discovery soon followed by that of radium by the Curies. We can refer to these fifty years as the germinal period of transition of the 500-year cycle; the seed period of the cycle began fifty years before in the early forties of the nineteenth century. And this was also the time (1844 to 1848) when the seed-period of the Piscean Age began.

According to Hindu chronology, the Kali Yuga (or Iron Age) began in 3102 B.C. If we add five thousand years (ten 500-year periods) we come to the last years of last century. H.P. Blavatsky died in May 1891, and Baha'u'llah on May 29, 1892. William Q. Judge, who worked devotedly and in close spiritual contact with H.P.B. and was instrumental in starting the Esoteric Section of the Theosophical Society, died in 1896. A new phase in Western occultism seems to have begun with the new century.

This leads us to a consideration of the century which, by its very nature, refers to sociocultural processes, inasmuch as it depends for its start on the calendar adopted by a particular society and religion. A century constitutes one-fifth of the 500-year cycle of civilization and of the development of the mind as a principle of activity at least relatively independent (or susceptible of becoming independent) from the vibration of nature in the Earth's biosphere. As a new 500-year cycle began in the 1890's, the preceding one started at the close of the fourteenth century. And a number of theosophists believe that this was the time when the trans-Himalayan Brotherhood (and perhaps other Brotherhoods as well) planned to attempt during the last quarter of every century to bring to the Western world as much of the ancient planetary and "Kumaric" knowledge as Western people could respond to and assimilate. It is said that the true Rosicrucian Movement began with Christian Rosenkrantz in the last quarter of the fourteenth century. This period was also the beginning of the Humanistic Movement which led to the Renaissance and the development of the modern mentality.

A very interesting fact is that, if we consider the five centuries which, broadly speaking, began in 1400, we can establish a very suggestive relation between the specific character of these centuries —at least at the level of the transformative Mind of Man—and the sequence of planets in the solar system.

We will start with the Earth, as the foundation of civilization, and relate it to the fourteenth century (1300 to 1400), when the need for a new vision and new social concepts was arising, leading to the formation of modern nations. Mars then corresponds to the fifteenth century which ended with the start of the great voyages that enabled at least a few men to circumnavigate the globe and thus to experience the fundamental nature and shape of the Earth. The sixteenth century can be symbolized by Jupiter. It witnessed the Renaissance and the creative activities of visionaries and many-sided men who sought to expand man's cosmic vision and to build a new Europe. It also saw the birth of Protestantism.

Saturn solidifies what Jupiter has expanded; and with that planet we come to the seventeenth century, with its cruel religious wars, solidifying a division in the Western mind, and the triumph of Classical formalism and rigorous ritualism (the French king, Louis XIV and his Versailles Court). The seventeenth century also began with Francis Bacon's *Novum Organum* which established the principles of the scientific method and of objective, rationalistic thinking—principles which gained full control of the official Western mind after Descartes, Newton, and in sociopolitical matters, Locke.

The eighteenth century is the Uranian century, the century of the Enlightenment, of Free Masonry and of the Revolutionary Era. What had begun in the Mars century with Humanism, the birth of a national consciousness, the discovery of America and the first attempts at breaking the stranglehold of the "one and indivisible Medieval Catholic Order," reached a powerful new stage of manifestation after 1700, partly in opposition to the formalism and autocratic rigor of the Saturn century. The transformative operation of the vibration 5 associated with Uranus nevertheless was confined to the level of intellectual abstractions. Democracy, freedom, equality, fraternity were mainly ideals embodied in great slogans and declarations of individual or collective independence. They had to face the crucial test of how to meet and respond to the availability of the vast new powers released by the Industrial Revolution and by the need for the world expansion in order to obtain raw materials for industry.

The European and American nations failed quite miserably to meet that difficult test; and the nineteenth century is largely the story of that failure. It was the Neptune century; and as Neptune is the universal solvent of alchemical lore, so that century witnessed the dissolution of the old aristocratic and feudal traditions and the rise of both a mercantile materialistic bourgeoisie and an increasingly desperate proletariat, progeny of the new industrial order. But this was also the century of Romanticism and Christian socialism and humanitarianism, of Utopian communities and the Red Cross.

During the forties of the century, as Neptune was discovered, two great religious movements—one of which was atheistic—were started which envisioned a totally new and global society: the Baha'i Faith in its initial form, and the Communist Movement as introduced by Karl Marx and Frederick Engles. Because these two movements have not been seen in a truly significant, not only historical but planetary perspective, and their very special polar relationship—spiritual and material—has never been understood or even less referred to the seed period between the Piscean and

Aquarian Ages—I feel it is important for me here to discuss them at some length.

The Baha'i Movement began in Persia in 1844 with the proclamation by an inspired and soon martyred youth (the Bab, a descendant of Mohammed), that the Islamic era had ended and that a new age was beginning, whose source would be a great "divine Manifestation." In 1863 one of the Bab's main disciples (the son of one of the ministers of the Shah of Persia), after experiencing harsh persecution and exile, proclaimed himself "He who was to come," taking the name of Baha'u'llah (the Glory of Allah). Soon after, while a prisoner in the pestilential Turkish town of Akka (in what is now Israel), in his "Letters to Kings" and in many Tablets, he set down basic principles for a new World-Order and a detailed body of directives for its practical social and political organization. The concept of unity (or integration) is basic in such an organization. Twelve basic principles are formulated: (1) the oneness of mankind, (2) the independent investigation of truth, (3) the foundation of all religions are one (4) religion must be a cause of unity, (5) religion must be in accord with science and reason, (7) prejudices of all kinds must be forgotten, (8) universal peace is the goal, (9) universal education must prevail, (10) a spiritual solution of the economic problem must be found, (11) a universal language, and (12) a universal tribunal must be established.[1]

These principles—let us not forget—were proclaimed by a prisoner of the Turkish government just after 1863 without any contact with Western society. Some of them are very idealistic, as was the Uranian slogan of the French revolution: liberty, equality, fraternity. But the Baha'i's were first in Asia to demand and to practice the full liberation of women, their equal participation with men in all social and religious matters, a complete lack of race and color discrimination, and their Faith has no room for any kind of priesthood.

Marxian world-communism also aimed at

establishing a planetary society free from conflicts and from what Marx and Engels considered to be the fundamental cause of international, interclass, and interpersonal warfare: but it believed in achieving ends by violent and (whenever necessary) deceitful and utterly ruthless means. It has sought to foster hatred between social classes and to induce in the proletariat and the oppressed people of the world total despair by denying them even the consolation of religious other-world beliefs, so that *being desperate* they would risk everything to achieve physical and materialistic social victory over the privileged and oppressing classes —an important point often forgotten.

In these two movements, the Baha'i Faith and at least original Communism, the ideal end in view is a world-society in which all human beings would live in peace—thus one might say, Millennium, a New Age global world. But for the Baha'i's this new world is seen as the outer manifestation on Earth, at a time dictated by the vast cyclic processes of a God-created universe, of a divinely appointed World-Order embodying the perfection of justice and moved by all-encompassing Love. In contrast, Communism thinks of human freedom and social equality only in terms of material power, wealth, and opportunity; and its philosophical and evolutionary philosophy was and still is determined by the concepts of a materialistic and godless nineteenth century science.

For the Baha'i's, the means to actualize the ideal vision and the Divine Plan can only be love and utter faith in the Divine Manifestation, Baha'u'llah, which implies total surrender to the will of God and social unanimity achieved through such a surrender. For the materialistic Communist, the only surrender is to a Cause that forces upon its adherents obedience and the use of violence and deceit in a prolonged ruthless conflict aiming at unanimity only through the brutal suppression of opponents and dissent in all its forms.

Communism has achieved great political victories during the twentieth century, dominating vast countries and populations. The Baha'i Faith has spread to nearly all countries of the Earth with its small "local assemblies" and, since 1963, its international "House of Justice" in Haifa, Israel where its headquarters are located, close to the tombs where the bodies of the Bab and Baha'u'llah rest, protected from still violent Mohammedan fanaticism by the Israeli state.

In view of the expansion of the Baha'i Faith, of its most remarkable history and its possible future, it may seem strange that so few people concerned with "spiritual" values and believing in a divine Plan pay any real attention to and study all that is implied in the Baha'i phenomenon—certainly the most significant, dramatic and compelling religious event since the birth and spread of Islam in the seventeenth century; but there are several reasons for this. The most obvious one is the manner in which Baha'u'llah expressed himself, using the involved, metaphoric, and apocalyptic language of Persian and Sufi mysticism, and even now the way his followers present his teachings to a humanity conditioned by scientific rationalism and the practical down-to-earth demands and problems of our present society. People today, either are still very much depending upon the Western Christian tradition and its basic symbols and concepts, or else they seek to avoid any absolute commitment to any doctrine based on suprarational claims, unless these claims are made by living persons who can provide them with *directly experienceable manifestations* of their supernatural wisdom and power. Most Baha'is today, passionately certain as they are of the divine character of Baha'u'llah's mission, can only radiate their often dogmatic fervor and the absoluteness of their beliefs. Moreover, the Baha'i way of life makes certain demands on the individualistic men and women of our time which are not too easy to accept, for individual opinions not based on the revealed "Truth" are usually not favored in Baha'i communities. Such opinions have been and are even less acceptable in doctrinarian Communist cells.

With the Baha'i Faith (in a spiritual God-enthralled sense) as with the strict Communist Movement, (in a materialistic and destruction-oriented way), we deal with forms of totalitarianism—subtle yet powerful in the first case, and harsh and deadly in the second—because the compulsive pressure of the need to achieve unanimity requires monolithic features and policies. Mankind has been subjected to such pressures throughout the centuries and millennia, but the Uranian revolution of the eighteenth century, stressing the value of the individual and of "free" scientific inquiry, has brought to a focus in our society the individualizing process, and therefore also the inevitability of strong centrifugal forces. Even then, how free is scientific inquiry, and how devoid of compulsive pressures, financial or psychological, is our democracy? While democratic individualism is an attempt to give free expression to the character of the vibration 5 which has now great power, this power very often lacks a truly spiritual foundation, simply because the fundamental character of the stage of evolution at which the masses of mankind and Earth nature as a whole operate remains, as I have already stressed, the vibration 4. And both the Baha'i Faith and World-Communism essentially are *mass movements,* as are all organized and institutionalized religions.

Nevertheless, there are many levels at which this vibration can and does operate. It is at least possible, and even probable, that at this time in human evolution the Baha'i Faith represents the highest possibility of organizing mankind as a whole on a divinely inspired basis. On the other hand, Marxian communism, even in its most idealistic and "religious" (even if atheistic) form, represents a matter-bound, spirit-denying response to this mass vibration of the Earth and mankind. To the individualistic mind eager for freedom and self-determination, both movements are difficult to accept, at least in their entirety. Other paths are therefore provided for such minds to follow.

To get a deeper, more "occult" grasp of what is involved at this present critical time of history, I shall once more refer to the dynamic relationship between the numbers involved in a septenary system of evolution. The fourth stage (Round or "world") constitutes the bottom section of the cycle. As we begin with number 1 on the top, we see the evolutionary process "descending" through stages 2 and 3, reaching bottom with 4, ascending through 5 and 6, and with number 7 reaching again the top—or rather reaching above the original starting point when we deal with a spiral and not merely an abstract circle. Number 7 symbolizes in this septenary formula the Seed which is both a cycle's culmination and the potential beginning of a new one.

There is, therefore, a definite vertical connection between the numbers 1 and 4. What was "the First" *can* reflect itself into the fourth stage of the cycle. It can, in a very real sense, do more than reflect itself; it can *project its power* (shakti, Holy Ghost) *through a fourth stage person,* who becomes not only illumined by it, but transfigured and even transsubstantiated—that is, who becomes an Avatar of· the Creative God, *the Root of the entire cycle.*[2]

What this means is that we may see in Baha'u'llah the Avatar for the new cycle in his manifestation *in the very depth of Earth nature* and as an embodiment of the Root-power of our present Fourth Round humanity —the power that was in the beginning of that particular phase of the evolution of the whole planet, Earth. We may give to that Root-power any name we wish; it represents the God of Nature in this particular aspect of the Earth's total evolution. And, significantly, the Baha'i calendar begins with the spring equinox, the time of the rebirth of nature. This calendar divides the year into nineteen months of nineteen days, plus four days of festivities just before the spring equinox.[3]

On the other hand, Karl Marx and world communism represent the process of "chaotization" of the past, thus, a culture-destroying return to the state of non-differentiation in matter. And we must not forget that the humus of the soil represents "virgin potentiality" as it exists in the Earth's biosphere. Thus many men having given up hope of seeing their ideal vision triumph over the stubborn inertia and conservatism of an obsolete social system can conceive no other way but that of bringing about total chaos, in the hope that mankind may thus become revirginized and repotentialized, and a new world may emerge. However, this is not the way of seed men; for seed-men have faith in (and Avatars fully realize) their ability to serve as focusing agents for a new descent of the creative and transforming power of the spirit.

Allow me to repeat that this spiritual descent of power does not operate only at the level of Earth's nature, even if it may find there its most *complete personal formulation and human incorporation.* Because the vibration 5 of the mind has been strongly stressed, especially in the European races, a large number of human beings have succeeded in developing an at least minimal response to the opportunity to experience directly and manipulate creative forces at the level of archetypal principles. Our Western civilization as a whole since the sixth century B.C. is oriented toward mental activities beyond the realm of biopsychic urges and needs. Therefore the Avataric Descent of our seed-period of history had also to take form at that level of the transformative Mind.

It is at that level that the great Occult Brotherhoods *make contact with humanity as a whole,* because the "more-than-men" who form these Brotherhoods are "Fifth Rounders," though they are also illumined and empowered by the vibrations of a still higher level, the level at which vibration 6 operates. Their point of public contact with mankind last century was essentially the person whom we know as Helena Petrovna Blavatsky—a lens through which the Brotherhood poured some of its *mind-transforming knowledge.*

Baha'u'llah did not claim to be an "incarnation" of God whom his followers revere as El Abha. He said only that in one of his two "stations"—the station of divine unity—he was an Image of, and a mouthpiece for the Divine.[4] In a similar though probably different manner, H. P. B. also was a dual manifestation—the vehicle for the Brothers, and a human body. In that sense, she can also be considered an Avataric personage *in terms of the level at which her mission was to operate.* The heavy karma of the collective mentality of the Western civilization was also a part of her being, defining its limitations and special character. The Avataric descent and the circumstances surrounding the release of the Mind-power had to be conditioned by the at times unbearable pressure of the vibrations of the perverted and obtuse mentality of the West and by the satanic impact of institutions bent on preserving their privileges at all costs. The "revelation" expressed in *The Mahatma Letters* was not only the manifestation of the Trans-Himalayan Brotherhood's mind and the formulation of its knowledge; it was rather the outcome of the relationship between the Mahatma K. H. and Mr. A. P. Sinnett. Always the Avatar is God-man; but actually *he takes the form that the relationship between man and God makes possible at the time.*

Tragic misunderstandings and often violent partisanship result from most people's inability to accept this as a fact. God speaks to every kind or group of human beings in the way this kind or group is able to understand the words spoken. Thus, I repeat that every divine revelation is partly divine and partly human; it is a "revelation"—the One cosmic Truth is "veiled again" so that it may not blind the consciousness receiving the

message. It is only in the Seventh Race, "a race of
Buddhas and Christs" (H.P.B. wrote in *The Secret
Doctrine*) that men's minds, having become totally
clear and pure, will be able to "see God face to face,"
to use a traditional expression. Yet the more the
consciousness becomes open and clear, the more it
may *hold and understand* the illumination, formulating it
in the increasingly adequate words of a gradually
more flexible, multidimensional and spirit-oriented
language.

Every race or nation has its culture and language,
and the language reveals the character of the culture.
What we are witnessing in our Plutonian twentieth
century—and to a lesser extent this occurred also
toward the close of last century—is the coming of
human beings who incorporate within themselves the
seed harvest of the culture of the race or nation in
which they have been born, and in some creative
manner who release this harvest to those who, by
dharmic connection, will become attracted to, or fascinated by it. They are seed men, and in nations like
India where the identity of *atman* and *brahman* has
been for so many centuries a powerful belief—and in
a sense, an experience—these men are prone to say
"I am God" and not only call themselves avatars, but
claim to be *the* Avatar.

A number of men are living today who make or have
recently made this claim—in India, in Korea, in France,
and in other lands. Lesser claims of a similar nature
are also heard; and they all may *to some extent* be
based on real experience and on the existence of a
more or less direct, pure, and effectual *line of descent*
whose origin is in the realm of the transformative Mind
of Man. In different ways, the individuals making such
claims attempt to convey to others who are attuned to
them at least the quality of their responses to the
planetary Avataric descent which is still moving along
its path of destiny marked by the combination of

culminating or starting cycles.

The nineteenth century was, I believe, the century during which the spiritual (or shall we say "monadic"?) release of Avataric power occurred in terms of the *planet as a whole*. Power was released, the fundamental Tone of the future Age. But power is not consciousness, any more than spirit is the same as mind! It was only in the last quarter of the century that the seeds of a new Mind and a new civilization were released, and these seeds still pertained mostly to what had inevitably to assume an "occult" character because of the collective mentality of our leading and ruthlessly dominating Western world. The nineteenth century constituted a period during which the divine Fatherhood was at work; but the fecundative act does not mean birth. It even takes time for an awareness of pregnancy to rise in the mother-to-be. Because of this, the twentieth century spiritually is the era of divine Sonship—or at least that of the intimation and revelation of a new progeny, a New Age. There might also be a miscarriage; but in terms of planetary evolution, I do not believe that a total miscarriage of what the divine Power initiated can take place. What may happen is the birth of a deformed child, perhaps a spastic one—and certainly our Christian European Piscean Age culture had features and behavior suggesting spasticity!

It seems that we are approaching a moment of crisis; and perhaps the coming of Pluto closer to the Sun than Neptune may soon signal the beginning of the crisis. The last quarter of the century is now beginning. A century ago the Theosophical Movement was started in New York. Two centuries ago the Declaration of Independence proclaimed to the world of nations the birth of a collective person, the United States of America, whose destiny it was to demonstrate a new type of society and political operation. Did these two departures, so different in character and importance, yet based on similar principles, achieve what it was their archetypal destiny to achieve? Hardly so. From the very first, both have groaned under the burden of the heavy karma of Western society and of an early perversion and dogmatization of the great Christ-Impulse that was the source of the Avataric descent of nearly two thousand years ago.

Then, the Fathers of the Church persecuted the different groups of Gnostics who sought to fecundate with the Christ spirit the seed harvest of by then disintegrating societies and religions. Unfortunately the Gnostics were too pervaded with the intellectualism of the Greek tradition, and their integrative synthesizing endeavors were defeated by ambitious men who knew how to play with the emotions of the masses and were not averse to resorting to deceit and destruction. In our present time, Occultists, (or esotericists) are in a very real sense the Gnostics of this cycle. Will the Second Coming of the Christ that so many hope for or expect, illumine the spiritual and intellectual confusion of our humanity and stabilize the minds of so many seekers and devotees? Are we to expect, after 1975, only a century-cycle manifestation in and through a new agent and mouthpiece of Occult Brotherhoods, or can we hope for the culmination of the entire Piscean Age in a truly divine Personage? Has this culmination already occurred, as Baha'is believe, in the person of Baha'u'llah—or did he, as some have said, belong to some sitll larger cycle, as probably Krishna did?

A number of esotericists seem to believe that the Christ is not to reappear in a physical body, but that of human beings who will channel forth his power as the new sixth subrace begins to manifest, so that the energy of the vibration 6 may be strengthened and brought to focus in and through a number of "germinal" personages. The development of a strong interest in

Buddhism, especially since Tibetan monks fled from Tibet and found refuge mainly in America, may be a significant part of the strengthening of the vibration. Moreover, we must not forget that the spiritual power of evolutionary currents may also take seemingly destructive forms, and especially that whoever may now function as a public agent for the Brotherhood may be found in places where the typical student of esoteric knowledge does not expect him or her. He might operate in any country, even in or behind the political scene.

If the celestial symbol for this twentieth century is Pluto, it is a rather mysterious and ambiguous one. In my book *New Mansions for New Men* (written in 1935-36) I spoke of this remote planet as a cosmic symbol of the Seed. It undoubtedly may be related to various kinds of underground manifestations and to decay; but above all it represents the power that destroys all superficial glamor and all illusions. It leaves whatever it touches stark naked, void of all external attributes, but also strictly and purely *what it essentially is*. The whole life-species and its power of persistence and also mutation are condensed in the seed. But only what is essential is there; no superfluity can exist within the hard shell of the seed. In this sense the Plutonian century, now in its autumnal season, is a period during which many seedmen are living in whom an immense potency of futurity operates, in whatever field of activity they may perform their perhaps hidden (occult) task. One might say that, in the nineteenth century a great planetary mutation occurred in the occult world of the seed of Man, and that in this present century the transformation-in-depth has reached the level of the conscious mind in those human beings who were born ready for the focalization and formulation of the new vision and the new hope. In many people, and especially in today's young people this is still only an intuitive and difficult to express *feeling-realization;* but before the year 2000 something should occur to give a more tangible and evident character to the expectation of a fundamental change in human affairs, both at the level of consciousness and psychology and in terms of at least a preliminary start in social organization at a global level.[5]

In 1891-92 a new 500-year cycle began. I related symbolically the preceding five centuries to Mars, Jupiter, Saturn, Uranus, and Neptune. The new 500-year series of five century units could then be said to start under the rulership of Pluto. Perhaps new and distant planets may be discovered; the existence of at least one more seems certain. What this may mean is that, with Pluto, we definitely enter a realm that is the foundation of a definite relationship with the cosmic forces and principles operating in a truly "galactic" manner. The fact that mankind's collective attention has recently been strongly focused on space-travel and unmanned investigations of the planets of the solar system now provides us with a set of publicly accepted facts and even of scientifically acceptable expectations which are conditioning our new approach to the problem of establishing a path leading from the sensation conditioned and intellectually limited world of knowledge of Western man to a transcendent realm not only of consciousness, but of actual experience.

Last century the fascinating possibility of transcending our everyday awareness of reality and contacting the "spirits" of the dead gave form to the Spiritualistic Movement; and H. P. B. and those behind her activities used this fascinating possibility to gain the public attention required for the dissemination of her message. As already stated in the third chapter of this book, one hundred years from the date of the rapid spread of Spiritualistic phenomena across the United States and the formation of groups of people involved in seances of various types, the UFO phenomena began to attract the attention of the media and a large public. The

Spiritualistic Movement is definitely Neptunian in character; the UFO phenomena and the fast spreading "communications" claimed to originate in "Space people" have far more a Plutonian significance, for they deal with what is supposed to be physical beings living in material conditions in other solar systems or galaxies. The UFO flying saucers may or may not be actual facts related to galactic space or pointing to new dimensions of space-time; but at least they form the substance of a new "myth," by means of which harassed and confused modern man can release some of his subconscious or superconscious longings for some new kind of "beyond." This century that beyond is Plutonian, while one hundred years ago it was the Neptunian beyond of psychic research, astral plane experiences, and communications with "Masters" through sensitives or trance mediums.

The question almost inevitably comes to mind whether the Occult Brotherhoods, if they are indeed trying to establish a new public contact with mankind during the last quarter of this twentieth century, may not be ready to use the UFO myth for their purpose, just as they used—with quite unhappy results, alas—Spiritualistic and psychic phenomena in order to impress a transcendent kind of knowledge upon the collective mentality of our Western world, and through it, of mankind as a whole. I tentatively evoked such a possibility in the above mentioned third chapter; and at this point in our discussion the suggestion may take a slightly more definite form.

At the time I write these pages, I personally have had no experience with flying saucers or balls of fire in the sky; and my mind is open, but not quite ready to fully accept any one of the theories advanced to explain sightings and phenomena, at least a fair number of which are based on unimpeachable evidence. It seems rather probable however, that the Unidentified Flying Objects are physical in a sense that transcends what we know on earth as strictly material. They undoubtedly can and do dematerialize. The belief in the possibility of human beings dematerializing and rematerializing is part not only of theosophical Occultism but also of the Christian tradition; only in the latter case the Christ (or Jesus) alone is considered to have been endowed with this power. Modern scientific minds attempt to explain such a performance in terms of a fourth dimension (which H. P. B. defined as that of "interpenetration") or even of multiple parallel or interpenetrating universes. In *The Mahatma Letters* it is stated that the several "globes" constituting the total reality of any planet, our Earth included, are in "coadunation but not cosubstantiality." This seems to mean that they form one whole, the several globes interpenetrating and perhaps (yet not necessarily) having a common center. This is the basic concept of a holistic and hierarchical universe which is now held by a number of prominent scientists.[6]

The most practical corollary of this concept is the evident fact that in order to reach galactic space a man has not to go to "heaven" or anywhere. Galactic space, as well as solar system space pervades every cell of a human being. He has not to change space *physically* to be *in* galactic space or to be subjected to galactic forces. We live in the galaxy as fishes live in the sea. If we are not aware of this fact it is because our consciousness is earthbound; and if galactic forces are not *noticeably* affecting the behavior, growth, or decay of our bodies and their cells it can only be because the materials of these bodies vibrate at a rate which make them *unresponsive* to the much higher or faster vibrations of galactic energies. Likewise we do not see X-ray vibrations and radar waves or hear ultrasounds. Awareness depends solely on attunement, which may be blocked or altered by external factors, by cultural prejudices or temporary personal disturbances.

If we understand well such now evident facts, the problem of UFOs may take a different character, especially as several cases have been reported of UFO sightings and near-presence which were followed by (and may be said to have "caused") some form of physical healing or change in consciousness in the witnesses.[7] The UFOs may normally operate in galactic space, yet under the direction of the entities who built them may be able to radiate waves causing the witnesses to become temporarily attuned, or to *resonate* in their consciousness and even cellular-atomic rhythms to the higher galactic vibrations somewhat as we control the operations of our satellites and space-probing mechanisms; likewise a Hindu guru can temporarily arouse psychic vision in his chela. It is also conceivable that the reason for the appearance of so many UFOs is to *raise the vibrations* not only of people seeing them, but of the materials of our planet—in other words, *to induce a slow, gradual yet basic mutation* in the matter of the Earth and therefore of our bodies, and perhaps more specifically of man's capacity to consciously respond to the higher galactic forces.

This would mean that the UFOs do not necessarily come from a distant "place" in the universe, star or planet—or from the hollow core of the Earth, as some people have claimed. They are here with and among us, just as Adepts and Masters are with and among us. Their appearance may involve or seem to involve a certain amount of physical displacement, yet this is more likely to mean the mere appearance of displacement in our physical plane. Various testimonies of individuals able to "travel" outside of their physical body indicate that, by merely *thinking* of where they wanted to be, they were there, either immediately, or what to them seemed to be immediately.

Passing from one kind of space to another may involve what, to us at least, is "no-time", but this does NOT mean that each kind of level of space does not have a time of its own. Time may be concentrated into one moment (or "instant," in a philosophical sense), just as infinite space may be concentrated in the mathematical nondimensional point. Yet if there is a *sequence* of moments of concentration and of dimensional expansion, there must inevitably be if not what we today mostly mean when speaking of time ("I have no time for that"), at least what H. P. B. called "infinite Duration."

What I am speaking of here is a conception of time and space which parallels the relationship between potentiality and actuality. Both polarities must be postulated as the Chinese postulated the balanced yet dynamic opposition and interaction of Yin and Yang. In a holistic and hierarchical universe, everything interacts and interpenetrates within cyclically evolving wholes of experience. The greater encompasses the lesser, yet this lesser is an integral *functional* part of the greater which both pervades and sustains it. As the lesser whole develops its power and its awareness of its role in the greater, what unavoidably happens in due time is that its "gears ratio" of organic existence and mental consciousness changes. And we know how a change of gears can produce harsh noises, if the driver's hand is shaking or if his mind is untrained or preoccupied.

The grating noise of mankind's present change of gears is indeed very harsh and frightening. If we could concentrate on *the movement* producing the change, rather than on *the successive positions* which the gear-shifting operation requires, we would be far more likely to effectuate the change in a smooth and easy manner. But the hand and the foot controlling the gear-changing apparatus (mankind has not yet reached the stage of "automatic" change!) are not only unsteady; they are afraid and emotionally attached to the position they have held for a long time. Mankind it seems, is just learning how mentally to drive, and sooner or later the result might be near-catastrophic if man fails to rely on what may well be his "instructor's" guidance.

It would be most unwise here to speculate on what the near-results of the present crisis might be; but at least to my mind the end results should be thought of as positive and exalting, even though we certainly cannot predict the concrete forms they will take. Did Jesus actually know and visualize the slow roasting of Protestants attached to spikes turned over a low burning fire during the wars of religion of the seventeenth century—this being done "in His Name" to save the souls of the unfortunate dissidents?

It is probable that during the stay of Pluto "within the orbit" of Neptune and especially around 1989-91 when a massing of six planets repeatedly occurs in the sign of Capricorn (in Sanskrit, Makara) (which, according to *The Secret Doctrine,* has some connection with the descent of the Kumaras) world-events of major importance will take place; but *the level* at which they may occur cannot be safely determined, in spite of often conflicting psychic predictions. A change in the orientation of the Earth's polar axis does not seem impossible; but no one can definitely say what this would mean or physically produce.

What seems evident is that a repotentialization of man's collective consciousness is already occurring, slow as it evidently is, and harsh and possibly disastrous as the resistance of the holders of social privileges and possessors of wealth (and of the frightened masses) might be to any radical and widespread transformation of our society. Whether the Second Coming of Christ which many yearn for and confidently expect will occur, and if so what form it may take, is not for me to say. Glowing expectations of a millennial all-spiritual Aquarian Age appear naive and unrealistic, unless they be limited to small relatively isolated sections of mankind; and such an isolation would require at first some kind of world-catastrophe and a much smaller world population.

The vision of a seed remnant of human beings who are guided to safety and allowed to re-begin mankind's history in at least relative peace under "divine" inspiration should not be difficult to accept by minds familiar with Biblical tradition; yet it is not at all certain that we have to expect a new Deluge, be it of water or fire and atomic radiations. A relatively smooth transition to a New Age may be a possibility. This possibility, however, would require a repotentialization of the consciousness of at least a large minority of human beings in positions of influence, and a persistent, steady and unalterable willingness by these people to assume collective as well as individual responsibility for the transition, in the clear realization of what this may entail in terms of everyday living and relationship with the masses of mankind. The idea that any revolution is "popular" makes little sense. The masses provide the *necessary conditioning* without which any large-scale collective and social change is impossible; but only a few individuals ever become the focusing agents for the mutation whose time has matured. And maturity here means that the possibility of the transformation has been deeply felt and clearly—even obsessingly—imagined by the self-consecrated few as having reached the momentum required for the actualization of a new quality of mind and feeling, of a new sense of interpersonal and intergroup relationship, and new principles of social organization.

Imaginators with a clear, powerfully visualizing and unprejudiced mind are needed today, but also human beings whose egos have become purified and whose biopsychic emotional drives have been transmuted in the alchemical fires provided by life-experiences unreservedly and uncompromisingly open to the potential of transformation. The keynote is *repotentialization*. Man's attention has to be focused on potentiality rather than actuality. What is possible is today far more important than what now *is*, in depleted, past-worshipping, utterly concrete and sellable actuality. What is has to be known and evaluated, but known and evaluated in the perspective of the advance of new and untried possibilities. To gain such a perspective in clarity of mind and determination of the purified will, this is the task for all seed-men. Upon them rests the avataric responsibility for the future of Man.

References and Notes

1. The only Westerner to see Baha'u'llah in his later years was Edward G. Browne, an orientalist from Cambridge University. Browne had several audiences in 1890 near Haifa and his description of Baha'u'llah's features almost suggests those attributed by some Theosophists to the archetypal Manu of our Fifth Root-Race: "The face of him on whom I gazed I can never forget, though I cannot describe it. Those piercing eyes seemed to read one's very soul; power and authority sat on that ample brow; while the deep lines on the forehead and face implied an age which the jet-black hair and beard flowing down in indistinguishable luxuriance almost to the waist seemed to belie. No need to ask in whose presence I stood, as I bowed myself before One who is the object of a devotion and love which kings might enjoy and emperors sigh for in vain!"

2. *Most interestingly, Baha'u'llah came to realize fully his mission when chained with criminals on the floor of an empty cistern—this floor being reached by three steps downward* (the "three days in hell" after the Christian Crucifixion?). This symbolizes a complete (number 3) descent into the underground, the realm of roots and of decaying humus (the criminals). It was while in this dreadful state that he became fully aware of his mission; the revelation of it coming to his consciousness in the form of a "heavenly maiden" who brought back to him the remembrance of his "true Name."

3. The number nineteen was the sacred number of the movement started with the Bab in 1844, prelude to the Bahai Faith. It is a soli-lunar symbol, for the Moon's Nodes have a nearly nineteen year cycle, and the Nodes represent the potential integration of solar and lunar forces as their axis is the intersection of the planes of the ecliptic and of the Moon's revolution around the Earth.

4. In a second station (or character) he was essentially human and limited by his "mission" which in turn was conditioned by the need of his time. Baha'u'llah writes in the *Kitab-i-Iqan* (the Baha'i Book of the Law): "Each Manifestation of God hath a distinct individuality, a definitely prescribed mission, a predestined Revelation and specially designated limitation. Each one of them is known by a different name . . . Viewed from the standpoint of their oneness and sublime detachment, the attributes of Godhead, Divinity, Supreme Singleness and Inmost Essence have been and are applicable to those Essences of being, in as much as they are above on the throne of divine Revelation and are

established upon the seat of divine Concealment. Through their appearance, the Revelation of God is made manifest and by their countenance the Beauty of God is revealed. Thus it is that the accents of God Himself have been heard, uttered by these Manifestations of the divine Being."

"Viewed in the light of their second station—the station of distinction, differentiation, temporal limitations, characteristics and standards— they manifest absolute servitude, utter destitution and complete self-effacement. Even as He saith: 'I am the servant of God. I am but a man like you.' " (Quoted in S.E. Esslemont's book p. 51-52.) This is a very clear statement of the dual nature of the Avatar.

We may note in this connection the reversal of letters in the words Abha and Baha. In all alphabets the letter A (the First Point, in the Koran; the Greek alpha) represents the divine fecundating principle (the Greek *Logos Spermatikos*); while the letter B refers to the receptive feminine principle. "Abha" is God in His unconditioned eternal realm; "Baha" means His Glory or the Holy Spirit. The basic question, of course, is always, what actually a person means by "God."

5. Astrologers speak of the "great mutation" of the year 1842, when Jupiter and Saturn were conjunct in an "earth" sign. Such mutations, however, occur about every 200 years.

6. Cf. the book *Hierarchical Structure* (Elsevier, N. Y. 1969) edited by L. L. Whyte and Albert and Donna Wilson. The concept of level of organization is also discussed in this book; this was the result of a symposium under the sponsorship of the Douglas Advanced Research Laboratories and the University of California at Irvine which was "to bring together scientists, engineers, designers and others interested in the function of hierarchical structures in nature, concept and design."

7. Cf. the already mentioned article of Jean Vallee in *Psychic* magazine.

14. AT THE THRESHOLD OF OCCULT KNOWLEDGE

The impetus given by a quantitative mathematics has led to the development of a quantitatively minded world; it is an essential task for the future to develop the *qualitative* aspect of mathematics, so that the generations to come may in time achieve a true science of the living, conscious aspect of the world.

Olive Whicher
Emerson College, Sussex, England
Author of *Projective Geometry*, etc.

In this century, the main focus of the transformative process is the mind. It was to "change the mind of the twentieth century" that—as she herself stated—H. P. Blavatsky was sent among the proud and egocentric individualists of our Western society by those who were able to work through her. From 1775 to 1875 the basic change in the physical and social way of life had already begun to occur in its initial germinative developments. But at the mental level these hundred years represent essentially a spiritually negative, because materialistic phase dominated by a narrow and inflated sense of cultural-intellectual and racial superiority. That phase was meant to destroy the foundation of the European Medieval order with its religious dogmatism and obscurantism; but it also fostered a dogmatism of its own. It produced a somewhat fanatical reliance upon the empirical method exclusively concerned with sense-data totally dominated by an Aristotelian rationalism and an intellectual equalitarianism according to which no fact was admissible unless it could be validated by the laboratory experiments of any trained observers whenever and wherever performed.

As matters today stand, the collective mentality of our Western peoples and of all other races which have accepted Western indoctrination (which of course includes also all Communist countries) is still deeply conditioned by the basic concepts and methodology of nineteenth century science. These concepts and methods still determine our present "official" approach to knowledge; they determine not only our education, but also our academic priorities and governmental regulations of many sensitive professions allowed to control basic social and biological processes. Recent discoveries and electronic technology, on the one hand, have given far more power and virulence to the Establishment's ability to control these processes and various aspects of our individual lives; on the other hand, these new discoveries, especially in atomic physics, biology, and psychology, have compelled the most progressive scientists in many fields to at least tentatively develop various "meta-sciences" which are leading to the very threshold of occult knowledge.

It is not the purpose of this book, nor do I feel qualified, to discuss in any detail what has been happening in many fields of scientific research, as well as of philosophical or psychic speculation attempting to explain all the data revolutionizing last century concepts and our "common sense" view of the world. It seems necessary, however, to point to perhaps the most fundamental changes having occurred in Western man's approach to knowledge and the methods for obtaining that knowledge, because it inevitably is in response to these changes and to the possibilities that have opened up that a new influx (or "descent") of occult knowledge will take form, granted that such an influx is to be expected during the next two decades.

It was in response to what the Industrial Revolution and science and technology developed between 1825 and 1875 that H. P. B.'s message was given its particular form, from *Isis Unveiled* to *The Secret Doctrine*. It was in response to what had been achieved by the pioneering and critical minds of the Enlightenment and the Masonic Lodges that the new American nation and the

French Revolution took their respective forms; and the apparent failure of the work of Mesmer and others was conditioned by the narrowness of the official eighteenth century rationalism. We now may think that we have already witnessed a great transformation of Western man's collective mentality, but actually what has occurred even in the most advanced scientific fields is only the prelude to the expectable transformation which will come as an answer to the ineffectual because biased approach to knowledge which has characterized and still officially characterizes our new globally spread Western civilization.

In spite of recent developments the most basic characteristic of our modern scientific approach is still a rigid empiricism which refuses to admit as evidence anything but perceptions based on sense data, augmented now by an immense variety of instruments. Sense data are accepted solely as facts—proving or disproving theories; and these theories are structured along strictly quantitative and rationalistic either/or lines. The analytical and reductionistic mind with its atomistic outlook is still in control of by far the larger body of official thinking, even though a holistic way of thinking (and of feeling or intuiting) concerning man and his relation to the universe has recently spread among progressive scientists. These scientists nevertheless form still a relatively uneasy minority, usually on the defensive. In order gradually to convince the old guard of official thinkers in control of most social and educational processes, and particularly of the distribution of grants for research, they feel obliged to compromise and tone down their direct intuitive realizations by using indirect techniques in order to quantitatively and empirically prove the validity of their hypotheses. References to metaphysical principles unfamiliar to the European tradition are avoided. What this actually means is that the equally undemonstrable postulates on which much of our Western science has been based since Bacon early in the seventeenth century remain unchallenged. They constitute the sacrosanct paradigms of our European type of culture.

The type of knowledge characterizing true Occultism—which I repeat is not to be confused with what popular magazines and many psychics today call occultism—is essentially based upon the realization that a realm of energy undertones, directs, controls, or guides the phenomena, events, and changes which we perceive with our senses and which the Western mind attributes to a physically material world of objective entities. In *The Mahatma Letters* this occult realm is called "the world of force." It is the dynamic world which opens to the consciousness of the individual who either is led into it through Initiation or, of his own accord and at his own risks (and dangerous risks they are!) manages to force his way into it. What we feel and perceive as our ordinary physical world is the concretized and material projection of such an "occult" realm of forces.

The Secret Doctrine asserts that "the Universe is worked and *guided* from *within outwards.*"(*The Secret Doctrine* II, page 274) The intuitive American philosopher, Oliver Reiser, speaks in all his books of "guiding fields" which pervade, sustain, and control every material body and, at the cosmic level, the whole universe itself. Occultists—and the popularizers who often confuse terms and materialize concepts—speak of an "etheric body" permeating and directing the functional activities of all living organisms. In the early days of The Theosophical Society it was often spoken of as the "astral" realm, using the term astral in its original meaning, the world of light and radiations. This is really the more adequate term which can be related to the Sanskrit word, *akasha,* the essence of which is "vibration" or, as Hindu philosophy asserts, SOUND (in its inaudible far more than in its audible form). By developing the concept of field modern physicists actually have begun to think of the universe in astral terms. The atomic physicist hardly thinks of matter any longer, but only of energy and of their equivalence according to the famous Einstein formula, $e = mc2$, where c represents the speed of light which is supposed to be a constant. (Is it necessarily constant in all phases of cosmic evolution if we give to light its broadest meaning?)

The physicist faces various difficulties if he considers energy as an ultimate. Acting through, and in a sense "beyond" (a confusing term), the astral fields of energy is the realm of what the word Mind can only awkwardly suggest. In its ultimate sense, *The Secret Doctrine* speaks of "Cosmic Ideation" (also in Sanskrit, *Mahat*) and states that "the whole Kosmos is guided, controlled and animated by almost endless series of Hierarchies, each having a mission to perform . . . (as) the agents of karmic and Cosmic Laws." What this means is that we are confronted in the universe, as in man, with three fundamental levels of being: *mind, life-energy* in all its modes of operation (*prana,* now spoken of in scientific research as bioenergy), and *molecular substance* (matter).

The atoms of modern science probably are only condensations of astral energy according to laws of formation which follow universal principles of harmonic relationship resulting in specific wave-patterns. Where the waves interfere (nodes) matter appears and takes geometric shapes. What we call atoms may thus belong to the world of forces and have correlations with transcendent or semitranscendent sound formations, or chords of energy. A scientist, Donald Hatch Andrews in his book *The Symphony of Life,* said that the universe is not made of matter, but of music—linking modern thought to the periodically revived ideas of Pythagoras, some twenty-five centuries ago.[1]

When one speaks of Mind one should refer to a *universal principle of formation.* Wherever we witness form, there Mind is at work. Many progressive scientists today insist that what science ultimately deals with is form rather than matter or even energy-matter. The German physicist Schrodinger, in his well-known little book *What is Life?*, pointed out that in modern physics the stuff of what is observed tends to vanish, the only essential factor being its structure (or *gestalt*), and he ends by evoking a universe that is Mind rather than matter. Other physicists with holistic leanings have stressed the overwhelming importance of the concept of form;[2] and form implies relatedness. It is by the intermediary of form that potentiality becomes actuality. There can be no actual existence without some kind of form. Out of form consciousness arises, because consciousness at any level is the product of relationship, the relationship between what we call spirit and matter, or what the Chinese call Yang and Yin, being the ultimate cosmic relationship.

Because *the process of actualization of potentiality necessitates forms, the quality of this process depends upon the adequacy, purity, and perfection of the forms it uses.* It is this fact which gives its true significance to the concept of "the Beautiful," in the purest and universal sense of the word; because whatever perfectly serves the purpose of actualizing a new potentiality is by this very fact beautiful. If the mathematician speaks of the "elegant solution" of a problem, and the German philosopher Count Keyserling stresses that the value and impact of an idea depends essentially upon its formulation, it is because form is first of all a product of the activity of the Mind. However, what is meant here by Mind is the creative Mind, mind in its *involutionary* aspect. It must be differentiated from the classifying, interpreting, generalizing cogitative mind which operates in response to the forces active in terms of the *evolutionary* development of living organisms.

Unfortunately the word form in the past has most often referred to the external shape of an object; and modern writers on esoteric matters still use it in that sense while they should speak of "particular shapes," the shape of a body. A mathematical equation has form. The

shape of a living organism is a projection and concretization of a form by a creative Mind. At planetary or
cosmic levels, forms in what we call the Divine Mind may
be spoken of as "archetypes."

The paradigms and symbolic images of any culture
reflect these archetypes. They are projections upon the
collective consciousness of a human collectivity of archetypal forms which, by "defining " the release of biopsychic energies determine the character of the culture.
Likewise, it is the material end result—or the concretization and actualization—of this *defining* process
at the level of the life-force which biologists see at work
in the "genetic code" impressed at the core of all the
cells of a living organism. In all cases, we are dealing
with a process of "information," to use a currently
fashionable term. The involutionary creative Mind gives
form to currents of energy; the evolutionary organic
mind "informs" every component part of an organism
with its function in the whole.

The great images, forms, and paradigms of a culture
succumb to the entropy operating in whatever becomes
involved in the frictions and clashes experienced by
material bodies. They lose the sharpness of the defining
outlines; the original information becomes blurred by
loss of magnetic tension between the material units
which carry this information (as we see in magnetic
recording tapes) or perverted and confused by external
interferences and statics. Cultural decadence sets in;
and, in individual bodies, organic decay. Fascism or
Neo-classicism in a culture corresponds to sclerosis in a
living organism and sclerosis is the desperate attempt to
counteract the gradual loss of the cell's ability to
adequately respond to the genetic "information" and to
substitute rigidity (congestive processes and impairment
in the circulation of the *prana* and blood) for flexible
response and the capacity for self-recuperation through
the free absorption of biopsychic energy.

Once we truly think in terms of formative principles in

mental activity and of information processes, we have to accept a holistic approach to existence, thus to man, to the universe, and to the relationship between them. This does not mean that there is no longer any place for analysis and an atomistic approach to objective material entities, which, being material, are, according to the definition of the word, matter, almost infinitely divisible. It means that "the new image of man" has to include more than that which can be divided, analyzed in its operation, and dealt with as an isolated entity. It means that in the case of ill-health no organ of the human body can be significantly treated except in terms of its functional relationship to the whole organism and no disease should be seen as an entity in itself, for it involves the whole man and not merely local symptoms.

Man is not merely *material substance* within an organized system of functional activities, but also the *activity* itself (and the energy making it possible), and whatever *organizes* the system: the formative-creative Mind. What has definitely to be overcome and eradicated from the scientific mind is the "reductionism" which has dominated many basic concepts in our Western society. Baconian empiricism and the abstract equalitarianism of the eighteenth century political theorists and leaders are products of the same reductionist trend according to which everything must be reduced to what can be seen and touched; thought could be explained only in terms of "secretions" (now electric currents) from the brain and no concept could be valid unless its rationally logical corollaries could be proved by facts revealing laboratory experiments. The same type of attitude made us proclaim at the political level that all human beings are equal, because somehow they have a similar bodily form and similar bodily functions that can be seen, touched, analyzed, and reduced to abstract voting units—mere numbers in statistics.

Both the Baconian methodology and political equalitarianism have an uncontrovertible validity and practical usefulness; nevertheless they are materializations or intellectualizations of what is true, but true *only* at a holistic or spiritual level. It is evidently true that theories should be justified by relevant facts; but not only *one kind* of facts artificially produced and analyzed in laboratories and purified by the Aristotelian logic of a sense-built three dimensional universe postulated to be "nothing but" matter, as we know matter to be in our earth-bound human experience. It is also true that spiritually all men are equal and brothers, in the sense in which all the cells of a living organism contain at the core of their nuclei *the same* genetic code *because they had their origin in only one fecundated ovum.* But every cell (or at least group of cells) has a different function, and these functions are not of equal importance in the development, maintenance, expansion, and multiplication (or self-transcendence) of the organism-as-a-whole.

Scientists know that the cells of a human body all originated in the subdivision of the one original cell, yet they so fanatically believe in the exclusive materiality of the universe—a materiality now modified by the realization that matter and energy may be interchangeable according to Einstein's equation—that of course the universe must have begun in an explosive release of this energy-matter at terrific heat. If modern scientists thought along the lines of a cosmic vitalism regarding the whole cosmos as an immense, but finite, organism (or we might say today energy field) they might rather picture the birth of the universe in the form of a *cosmic egg* emerging from an infinite ocean of potential energy. What would follow is the expansion of this egg or force-field with its primordial cosmic substance differentiating into galaxies and various star systems, each with its own potential of functional activity according to a pattern defined by a metacosmic Mind, a "Logos," to use the term so strongly featured in Greek influenced Gnosticism.

Here we have two cosmic theories, or let us say hypotheses, and there is absolutely no absolute or logical reason for the first to be superior to the second. Yet most Western scientists have postulated that the "vitalistic" theory is absurd, and that life can only be the result of the chance confluence and coactivity of chemical molecules having cooled down. Actually there is no proof for the validity of such a postulate because man with his brief life-span has no way of experiencing the "heart beats" of the sun. (H. P. B. relates the 11-year sun-spots cycle to a cosmic, or rather *heliocosmic*, rhythm which may be analogical and relatively as rapid as man's heart-beats.) How can man with his short period of observation perceive any significant indication of the function of a galaxy in the cosmos; or rather, how could he possibly know it has no function and the cosmos is not a living organism? Must terrestial forms of life be the only conceivable life-forms and life *as we know it in our biosphere* the only manifestaion of what can be called in a broader sense Life? We have just discovered that the matter of our ancestors believed to be so dense, solid, and essentially indestructible in its molecular or even atomic form can be dematerialized into energy. Why can we not at least imagine that life too may be a condensation of some cosmic element which might simply be in its ultimate essense pure, eternal motion? Can we not metaphysically conceive of this motion as the whirling of Yin and Yang within the forever contracting and expanding circle of Tao—Tao that at the limit could be conceived as both infinite Space and mathematical point, yet never is *either one* of the two, neither being nor not-being, but the cyclically active rhythm of their interplay?

In saying this I had no intention of introducing a system of metaphysics—indeed a very ancient system. I wanted only to state that by *ruling out* the possibility of such a world-picture, which is based on our experience of life processes rather than on our premise that nothing but matter-energy exists, the science that was born in Europe some five hundred years ago is the result of *only one* of various possibilities of approach to knowledge. To speak of it as SCIENCE is as much the sign of a culture-bound European mentality and intellectual blindness as to regard Renaissance art as the one and only manifestation of true ART.

Once we sufficiently free ourselves from this mental illusion and cultural provincialism and accept the implications of being at the threshold of a global civilization, two main possibilities nevertheless arise: either we can try so to extend the field of investigation of the present-day scientific mind that it will burst out of its five-century-old self-imposed (and also at first Church-imposed) limitations and lead us to a new realm of un-dismissable facts, or else we could try to start from postulates which we accept as basic metaphysical and even metacosmic Principles which older civilizations have considered to be self-evident and upon which their greatness was founded. Then by synthesizing essentials and forgetting superficialities, we could deductively and in-tuitively build up the kind of methodology which would lead us not only to the direct experience of superphysical facts, but also to experiencing in a new light already known physical facts.

The first alternative is being pursued by many progressive and dedicated scientists who are working in groups along the lines of parapsychology and metapsy-chiatry as well as in the field where atomic physics slides into metaphysics and mathematics into mysticism. The second alternative brings us to the threshold of an-cient Occultism by way of a study of concepts and sym-bols hidden under the chaotic, distorted, and often bewildering remains of ancient religious, alchemical, and metaphysical traditions. It is the way which was in-corporated in *The Secret Doctrine* nearly one hundred years ago.

This incorporation, considering the condition of the

society to which it was addressed, could be only partially successful. Yet, at the core of its often confusing complexity and lack of over-all philosophical clarity, definite foundations for the development of a new type of non-Western, or trans-Western, knowledge are apparent. A way of knowledge is outlined that directly and unequivocally challenged and still challenges our Euro-American mentality.

The essential characteristic of a way or path is that one has to walk and proceed along the course it reveals. It is something to go through, not to dwell in. But "going through" means to keep one's perceptions clear, one's mind alert to the possibility of taking apparently similar by-ways which actually represent branchings-out and lead to long detours if not disaster. He who treads the occult way, even in its earliest stages, has to keep his sense of direction steady; and perhaps to carefully study a map he has been given for the journey. Singleness of purpose and an essential ineradicable self-dedication and undeviating will are needed. Yet, at this time of human history, also required is the ability to *understand* the character of the way and the nature of the goal to which it is to lead. A new light of understanding should now be shed on this occult path to knowledge and, above all on the *one source* of that knowledge. It is an integrated and indeed organic kind of knowledge, and all that can be called organic had its origin in one germinating wholeness of being. Failing to understand this fact is to court eventual disaster as one proceeds on the trans-physical as well as transpersonal way.

Knowledge is of the mind. Occult knowledge belongs to an archetypal realm where ideas are like cells of a vast organism of mind. Whoever enters that realm can directly contact, experience or "see" ideas as functional parts of an integrated whole. There, the knower is the seer, and the light with which he sees is the basically one, yet functionally multicolored, radiance of a primordial revelation. It is a re-velation inasmuch as it covers and differentiates the spiritual unity of the original divine Impulse, the Creative Word, by means of multicolored veils that are as many "principles of formation."

These principles can be known, but such a knowledge is inevitably dangerous in that it deals with the early manifestation of the one central Power from which a multitude of structured currents of energies have flown, passing through ever more differentiated forms, each representing a specific mode of release of power. Each of these modes has its functional place and purpose within the whole, somewhat as every life-form in the Earth's biosphere has its *temporary* function in the cyclically transformed ecology of the whole as representative of a particular type of vegetable, animal, human, and superhuman or extrahuman mode of activity and consciousness.

It is because man's mind has the latent possibility to *reflect and respond to* all these modes of activity and consciousness, at least within the total organism of one planet, Earth, that it is dangerous for him to ascend *consciously* to a realm that is close to the one source of all powers released in all the Earth's spheres (lithosphere, biosphere, noosphere, pneumosphere). If he could operate wilfully in that realm he would be able to act upon currents of energy which would affect an immense variety of lower and far more differentiated modes of power release. Whoever pollutes the source of a river can destroy all lives that, in the plains, drink of its water. To put it differently: because cosmic processes are hierarchical, the closer to the summit of the pyramidal structure of "idea-forces" that control these processes, the greater the possibility, either constantly to adjust and readjust the dynamic manifestations of essential cosmic Harmony and Equilibrium, or to introduce discord and conflict. This means the possibility of being godlike, or a devil.

We should nevertheless understand that the introduction of widely destructive possibilities in any field of planetary or cosmic activity implies that the time is soon coming when the cyclic pattern according to which such a field operates has become saturated with waste products and its original and functional purpose on this Earth is no longer able to vitalize and inspire the new generations. Whatever it was possible to accomplish in this particular type of field has become by then self-defeating even if it can be considered a great intellectual and social achievement. Too many opportunities have been missed, too many wrong turns taken because of pride, greed, or insecurity. And this is where mankind in general, and especially our Western society, stands today. Our civilization seems to be fast reaching a point of no-return. Darkness has fallen and it is no longer possible to retrace our collective steps, because in the dark we could not find the old way and we would die of exhaustion and spiritual cold.

As we follow the first above-mentioned alternative—as science extends further its field of investigation until it bursts out of its limitations—the new discoveries *unavoidably* are being used by power-greedy men in control of the basic mechanisms of our society in such a way that the process of destruction of that society is accelerated. Should we deplore such an acceleration? Let us rather realize that this accelerated process also unavoidably polarizes a new Avataric descent. This realization may be the only thing that can save the sensitive and perceptive individual from a sense of futility if not despair.

The great problem nevertheless is: what will mankind do with what this new Avataric focusing of power—this new revelation—will bring?

What any individual or group of individuals will do with it largely depends on *how they understand its character and its source.* The quality of this understanding will condition mankind's over-all responses to what is being revealed and thus, spectacularly or not, brought out into the collective field of human consciousness.

The quality of our understanding: this is the decisive, indeed the crucial, factor in the impending world-situation. Transformative forces are at work. Cathartic events have come; more intense ones may be ahead. But the essential issue is, and during this last quarter of the century will remain, the quality of our mental understanding and our emotional response to them. Love and Knowledge: how we relate to other beings, and on what basis or knowledge our understanding of what changing, freer, more open modes of relating and cooperating in a vital awareness of the meaning of togetherness *mean* and are meant to accomplish.

Everything depends on meaning and understanding. Tomorrow we may meet a divine personage and never realize it or, if we dimly sense his power, fall worshipful at his feet. The meaning of such a meeting would be that we, individually or collectively, have reached the threshold of a new world of reality, and that the opportunity finally has come for us to walk, erect and strong, through that threshold as a link between what was—our past and mankind's past in us—and what must and will be. Always, everywhere and at any level, the one essential question is: How much of the new potentiality whose time for manifestation has come, can we actualize, and what will be the quality and scope of our actualization?

The basic character of the occult way and of truly transpersonal living is that it brings us in contact at an accelerated pace with the potentiality of periodically renewing our consciousness, our feeling responses, and our capacity for action by resonating to new potentialities latent in the planetary (and eventually galactic) archetype, Man. It is indeed a question of "resonance" and the future science will come to learn that power can and should be released by resonating to various modalities of cosmic power, rather than by destroying matter. Destruction inevitably leaves toxic waste products, but he whose whole being has become attuned, and therefore can resonate, to the great rhythms of universal Motion (only an aspect of which we know as life) he alone can act as a focusing agent for the Creative word. At whatever level he operates, he is an Avataric being; and it is the togetherness of all such seed men that factually *is* the living Presence of the Avatar.

This Presence is active, here and now, in this era of transition toward a New Age. It is around us, above us, deep within us if we let it operate. We need not prostrate ourselves to worship it; it needs no worshippers. It needs only powerful, clear, understanding minds, feelings free from self and possessiveness, and the capacity to stand, erect and tall. Then its power *radiating from behind us* will be able to *pass through* our being, and move our hands, our tongue, the whole of us, in blessings to emergent tomorrows.

References and Notes

1. This type of thinking in terms of principles of harmony and form is often found expressed in many articles in the excellent and highly respected magazine *Main Currents in Modern Thought* founded by F. L. Kunz and now directed by Dr. Henry Margenau, a prominent physicist and "philosopher of science" who taught at Yale University.

2. Cf. Lancelot L. Whyte's book *Accent on Form*, p. 28 (Harper: N. Y. 1954). "The normal states of physical systems display definite spatial patterns, such as the linear arrays of atoms and molecules in a crystal, the chain of atoms in fibers and the still obscure but highly significant arrangements in genes, viruses and all working parts of organisms. Here it is the pattern or arrangement which counts for most purposes. The individual particles are indistinguishable and may come and go at random. Indeed apparently the only function of the particles is to build up the patterns, for it is the latter which we actually observe . . . *The "form", in the new sense of underlying structural pattern, is more important than its material components, which lack individuality.*" Also "structure is a name for the effective pattern of relationship in any situation . . . . This idea, structure . . . is *the* creation of this century as far as human understanding is concerned."

THE THEOSOPHICAL PUBLISHING HOUSE

Wheaton, Ill., U.S.A.

Madras, India   London, England

Publishers of a wide range of titles on many
subjects including:

Mysticism

Yoga

Meditation

Extrasensory Perception

Religions of the World

Asian Classics

Reincarnation

The Human Situation

Theosophy

Distributors for the Adyar Library Series
of Sanskrit Texts, Translations and Studies

The Theosophical Publishing House, Wheaton,
Illinois, is also the publisher of

QUEST BOOKS

Many titles from our regular clothbound list in
attractive paperbound editions

For a complete list of all Quest Books write to:

QUEST BOOKS
P.O. Box 270, Wheaton, Ill. 60187